WITHDRAWN

COUNSELING ADDICTED
W O M E N

COUNSELING ADDICTED
W O M E N

A PRACTICAL GUIDE

Monique Cohen

Sage Publications, Inc.
International Educational and Professional Publisher
Thousand Oaks ■ London ■ New Delhi

For information:

Sage Publications, Inc.
2455 Teller Road
Thousand Oaks, California 91320
E-mail: order@sagepub.com

Sage Publications Ltd.
6 Bonhill Street
London EC2A 4PU
United Kingdom

Sage Publications India Pvt. Ltd.
M-32 Market
Greater Kailash I
New Delhi 110 048 India

Printed in the United States of America

Library of Congress Cataloging-in-Publication Data

Cohen, Monique.
    Counseling addicted women: A practical guide / by Monique Cohen.
        p.   cm.
Includes bibliographical references and index.
    ISBN 0-7619-0910-9 (alk. paper)
    1. Women—Substance use—Prevention. 2. Alcoholism counseling. 3.
Drug abuse counseling. I. Title.
    HV4999.W65 C64 2000
    362.29′18′082—dc21
                                                                    99-050415

This book is printed on acid-free paper.

00 01 02 03 04 05 06 7 6 5 4 3 2 1

Acquisition Editor:	Jim Nageotte
Editorial Assistant:	Heidi Van Middlesworth
Production Editor:	Wendy Westgate
Editorial Assistant:	Victoria Cheng
Typesetter:	Christina M. Hill
Indexer:	Cristina Haley
Cover Designer:	Candice Harman

Contents

Conclusion

Preface

We dedicate this book to you, the addiction counselor, along with your staff and your women's programs. We want to inform, inspire, and help you to train your staff to provide the best possible counseling to your female clients.

Our book is based on more than 25 years of the collective experience and firsthand knowledge of our counselors at the CASPAR Outpatient Clinic in Cambridge, Massachusetts. The focus of every chapter, every staff activity, and every client worksheet is compassion—seeing ourselves in the eyes of the women we treat so that we can counsel them effectively and truly meet their specific needs. Whether you are male or female, this book will give you important insight into how to make sure that your women clients get the best treatment.

We have designed a book specifically for women because biologically, culturally, and socially, their modern experience is different from that of men. Women have suffered from alcoholism and drug abuse for centuries—just as long as men have—although formal treatment assistance for women has been recognized as important in the United States only during the past few decades. It has only been since the 1990s that women's health has received adequate attention in the national research agenda.[1] Until recently, research on women's alcoholism in particular has relied far too much on general societal beliefs about women rather than on scientific findings.[2]

The nature and underlying reasons for women's alcohol and drug abuse differ from men's behavior in many ways. It is finally being understood that research on men will not simply translate into effective solutions for women as well. For example, research has shown that due to different socialization patterns, women lack the assertiveness skills of men and need supportive networks to help them remain drug free.[3]

Staff Training Activities are provided at the end of each chapter to help you and your staff put ideas into action. We encourage you to explore both facts and feelings about women and chemical dependency. These activities offer you, the counselor, the opportunity to compare your personal experiences and perceptions of alcohol to society's perceptions of female alcoholics. Throughout the book, we compare the stereotypes of chemically dependent women to their actual diversity and learn how stereotypes can influence our counseling behavior.

Client Training Activities, also at the end of most chapters, allow you to work through similar issues with your clients. Through these training activities, we encourage you to put yourselves in the place of an alcoholic woman and compare her attitudes, feelings, and fears to yours.

You also will find brief summaries of the latest studies and findings about women and alcohol and drug addiction placed throughout each chapter, putting a current perspective on each issue. In addition, we provide a list of national organizations and Web resources to help you find more information on the issues discussed in each chapter.

The book is divided into three parts. Part I examines the social and cultural nature of drinking and drug abuse in our society and how women, in particular, react and respond to that culture. Chapters 1 and 2 explore the societal image and stereotypes of a woman who drinks or uses drugs. How women are socialized in American society has a major impact on how they become chemically dependent and on how quickly they recover.

We consider the relationship expectations of women (e.g., mother, daughter, spouse/partner, lover, caretaker, employee). Each role brings up pressures and issues that can affect a female client's recovery. Chapter 3 introduces the most recent trends in drug and alcohol abuse, summarizing the most important health risks and consequences of abuse for women. We provide a chart of the most commonly abused drugs along with detailed information about the problems women have with each drug.

Part II contains specific information about how to deal with other common issues that come up in conjunction with helping a female client to recover from chemical addiction. Some of the variables that complicate her recovery might include relapses as she approaches each stage of recovery, protecting her fetus if she is pregnant, treating major health problems such as HIV and AIDS, and coordinating additional services if she is dually diagnosed. Chapters 4 to 8 focus on each major issue: treatment strategies, designing effective programs, pregnancy, HIV and AIDS, and dual diagnosis.

Part III deals with the many issues that can arise in working with women across different populations. Chapters 9 to 15 focus on learning how young women, women of color, lesbian and bisexual women, disabled women, homeless women, elderly women, and women in the workplace all have specific issues and considerations that we must acknowledge and incorporate into the counseling experience. Racism, homophobia, and stigmas about disability traditionally have limited the number of available agencies sensitized to the issue. These chapters provide you and your staff with an overview of the types of issues your clients might face and tips on organizing your programs so that you can reach all of your clients effectively.

Our key theme for this book is that a woman who suffers from alcoholism or drug abuse is first and foremost a woman. Wellness for women includes the development of a broad context of relational ties that include family, friends, counselors, and spiritual affiliations. This goes hand in hand with her comfort with her feelings, her inner life, and her sense of self. An ongoing recognition of women's socialization and relationship needs is essential for a full recovery from alcoholism and other drug abuse and to foster a healthy restoration of life.

We wish you the best of luck and hope that the tools provided in this book make it easier for you and your staff to design caring, effective programs for helping women to recover from substance abuse.

References

1. S. J. Blumenthal, "Women and Substance Abuse: A New National Focus," in C. Wetherington and A. B. Roman, eds., *Drug Addiction Research and the Health of Women,* NIH Publication No. 98-4290 (Rockville, MD: National Institute on Drug Abuse, 1998), 13-32.

2. S. B. Blume, "Women and Alcohol: Issues in Social Policy," in R. W. Wilsnack and S. C. Wilsnack, eds., *Gender and Alcohol: Individual and Social Perspectives* (New Brunswick, NJ: Rutgers Center of Alcohol Studies, 1997), 462-89.

3. S. Colletti, "Service Providers and Treatment Access Issues," in C. Wetherington and A. B. Roman, eds., *Drug Addiction Research and the Health of Women,* NIH Publication No. 98-4290 (Rockville, MD: National Institute on Drug Abuse, 1998), 337-44.

Acknowledgments

This book is an updated version of *Getting Sober, Getting Well: A Treatment Guide for Caregivers Who Work With Women,* a practical and popular resource for training counselors in the care and treatment of substance-abusing women. When the previous edition of this book was written during the 1970s and early 1980s, very little substance abuse research involved females. The authors of the early book brought together what research was available at the time as well as a wealth of information from their direct experience with female clients at CASPAR Inc. (Cambridge and Somerville Program for Alcoholism and Drug Abuse Rehabilitation) in Cambridge, Massachusetts. Their book has been widely used by providers across the country as an educational and skill-building tool to increase counselors' understanding of the issues that women substance abusers face as they struggle to recover from the disease of addiction. The book served as a guide for us at the CASPAR Outpatient Clinic as we undertook the process of producing an updated tool that will help counselors to increase their understanding of the disease of addiction and offer them a practical approach to implementing theory into practice.

We express our sincere gratitude to the original authors—Norma Finkelstein, Sally Duncan, Janet Smeltz, and Laura Derman—who continue to do pioneering work in the field of women's substance abuse treatment. Without their commitment to their clients and to the field of social work, this edition would not have been possible.

In addition, we offer our thanks to the many students who worked on this project including Linda Rosen, Angela Brenner, Melissa Godwin, and Judith Bauman. We also thank Hope Steele and Renée Piernot for their brilliant research and developmental editing work. Finally, without the support of Jim Nageotte at Sage Publications, it would not have been possible to bring this book to the attention of the public.

PART I

Putting Women's Substance Abuse in Social and Cultural Context

1

Perspectives on the Socialization of Women

Alcohol is the most widely used psychoactive drug in the United States.[1] More than half of the entire population drinks, and consequently, a large number of drinkers have at one time or another experienced light to extreme alcohol-induced impairment.[2] We live in a drinking society where even if one does not drink, he or she has been exposed to alcohol at an early age through family, friends, and the media. Approximately 43% of the U.S. adult population has been exposed to alcoholism in the family.[3] Our early personal experience with alcohol becomes a major factor in how we view our own and others' drinking.

Prior to counseling and treating women, it is important for counselors to identify their own personal attitudes toward alcohol, the reasons why people drink in our society, and how drinking and drunkenness are perceived. Reflecting on personal drinking experiences—in ourselves and others—is a good starting point for understanding the complexity of issues involved with alcoholism and drug abuse. This chapter is intended to provide you with an opportunity for personal reflection on backgrounds, attitudes, and feelings about alcohol. Only after personal feelings about alcohol have been explored can you begin a healthy relationship with a female client. By understanding and accepting your own personal attitudes and values, you can become more objective and more empathetic as you uncover the circumstances and history of alcohol use of the women you see in treatment.

You might feel uncomfortable discussing alcohol, drinking, and alcoholism with your women clients because it could raise painful personal issues in your own life. However, until you address your own issues, these concerns can stand in the way of openly and comfortably raising issues of alcohol and alcoholism with clients who might desperately need help with their drinking. Many counselors who have had difficulty discussing alcohol with clients have found it helpful to attend an alcoholism education workshop and to talk with alcoholism professionals. The Staff Training Activities at the end of this chapter provide several exercises that can help you to think about your own concerns with these issues.

Exploring Personal
Attitudes Toward
Drinking and
Drunkenness

Treatment counselors vary widely in their
effectiveness. The main personal characteristics that
influence treatment outcomes are interpersonal
communication (including therapist's empathy),
genuineness, and respect for patients.[4]

In the same way as people may hold culturally determined stereotypes about
race, there also are strongly embedded attitudes and prejudices toward alcoholism. It was barely a decade ago when counselors, including physicians,
could complete many years of health and mental health training without ever
addressing alcoholism as a disease. Some of the reasons for this were pessi-
mism about the successful treatment of alcoholics, the view of alcoholism as a
moral issue or a psychological symptom, and the image of the alcoholic as a
"skid row bum." For some counselors, lack of education not only contributes
to a failure to recognize and diagnose alcoholism but also causes them to avoid
dealing directly with clients about alcoholism once it has been diagnosed.

It is not unusual for people to continue to have reservations and personal problems about accepting alcoholism as a disease. In staff training activities, the leader should encourage people in the group to express their opinions
and feelings and let them know that most people need time and education to
develop an understanding and acceptance of alcoholism as something beyond
the individual's control. You also should be familiar with the standard definition of alcoholism as classified in the fourth edition of the *Diagnostic and Sta-
tistical Manual of Mental Disorders* (DSM-IV).[5] As explained by the National
Institutes of Health's *Ninth Special Report to the U.S. Congress on Alcohol and
Health*, the DSM-IV defines alcohol dependence as

> a cluster of cognitive, behavioral, and physiological symptoms which in-
> dicate that a person continues to drink despite significant alcohol-related
> problems. Alcohol abuse generally is characterized as repetitive patterns
> of drinking in harmful situations with adverse consequences including
> impaired ability to fulfill responsibilities or negative effects on social/
> interpersonal functioning and health. The term "alcohol-related conse-
> quences" refers not to a specific diagnostic category but [rather] to a
> wide range of alcohol-related problems that includes difficulties with
> family members and friends, work problems, legal troubles, accidents
> and casualties, and health consequences. It is important to note that
> alcohol-related problems do not necessarily involve heavy drinking pat-
> terns.[6]

This definition has evolved many times over the past several decades
and, no doubt, will continue to be revised as our knowledge of alcoholism
grows. Researchers in many fields, from anthropologists and sociologists to
physicians and pharmacologists, have contributed to the study of the causes
of, and the best methods of treatment for, alcoholism and drug abuse.

Individual differences in drinking behavior cannot be accounted for by genetic and biological factors alone. Psychologists have identified basic cognitive processes that influence drinking behavior and have shown how those processes might temper the effects of biological factors. Social scientists have determined how family, peer, and social context can influence drinking attitudes and behaviors, and anthropologists have investigated the role that culture plays when determining who drinks, when they drink, and how much they drink. Thus, the risk for alcoholism is determined by a complex interplay of genetic, psychological, and environmental factors.[7]

Your initial task in working with women on issues of alcohol and alcoholism is to introduce a common language and convey basic education about alcoholism as a disease including signs and symptoms. A woman in the early stages of treatment combines personal denial with honest misconceptions about the nature of alcoholism. By helping the client to understand a simple definition of alcoholism and helping her to look at the signs and symptoms, you send the message that alcoholism can become part of a dialogue based on common understanding. The more you can share cognitive information about alcoholism as a disease in a nonjudgmental way, the safer the woman in treatment feels in revealing her experiences and concerns.

Societal Attitudes Toward Women Alcoholics

The most widely acknowledged issue for alcoholic women is the double stigma they face as both women and alcoholics. When people feel free to express their honest feelings about alcoholic women, responses range from disgust and impatience to a deep caring and respect, depending on the person's understanding of both women's issues and alcoholism. Society has tended to accept excessive drinking by men and to encourage it through various social patterns and customs. Drunkenness in women never has been acceptable. It always has been linked with promiscuity, immorality, and "unfeminine" behavior. Women traditionally have occupied a strategic place within the family and society. They have been expected to be responsible for the maintenance of moral and social values. Despite changing social norms, a woman still is expected to live up to a higher standard of moral and social behavior than is a man, especially when she is in the role of a mother. Without education and personal awareness, you might unwittingly demonstrate some of these negative attitudes toward alcoholic women who come into treatment.

Alcoholic women live in a world of prejudice and misunderstanding. Educated and understanding counselors can help a woman to overcome her feeling of being a social outcast. For a woman to "come out of the closet" concerning her drinking requires a lot of courage in a society where alcoholic women are considered weak and immoral. Accepting and nonjudgmental attitudes of counselors can play a key role in bringing women into treatment. Counselors need to appreciate the individuality of every woman's life and the special issues such as relationships, mothering, and economic stress that can play important roles in preventing a woman from taking the first step toward recovery.

In working with the alcoholic woman in treatment, it is important to explore her general feelings about alcoholic women. Often, a woman has internalized the prejudices and misconceptions about alcoholic women that she hears and secretly believes these to be true of herself. Counselors need to explore the particular circumstances of a woman's life to help her identify the sources of her guilt and shame. It is important to validate with alcoholic women their feelings of being stigmatized. These feelings are real and important to overcome if a woman is to enter treatment.

Columbia University's National Center on Addiction and Substance Abuse notes in its 1996 report, *Substance Abuse and the American Woman*, that doctors are three times more likely to miss diagnosing alcohol problems in their female patients. Women frequently disguise their alcohol and drug problem by seeking care for symptoms such as depression, digestive trouble, and insomnia without mentioning drug and alcohol use. As a result, doctors often treat the symptoms by prescribing psychoactive drugs instead of referring women to treatment for alcoholism.[8] The National Institute on Alcohol Abuse and Alcoholism has made available a free physician's guide to aid and encourage doctors in screening for alcohol problems. The basic intervention consists of four steps:

1. Ask about alcohol use.
2. Assess for alcohol-related problems.
3. Advise appropriate action (i.e., set a drinking goal, abstain, or obtain alcohol treatment).
4. Monitor patient progress.[9]

Recognizing the Client's and Counselor's Feelings

When working with substance-abusing clients, you must remember to pay constant attention to the intense feelings and emotions that can be stirred up for a myriad of reasons and circumstances for both you and the client. A successful therapeutic relationship requires that both of you understand the various dynamics that affect your view of any given situation. These factors may include a past history of trauma, a past history of responding to various developmental or life tasks either successfully or unsuccessfully, a view of the therapeutic relationship, and any current stressful life events in either person's life.

Outer and Inner Worlds of the Substance-Abusing Client

Working with women in alcoholism treatment and recovery demands a sensitivity and awareness to both the circumstances and feelings that a woman brings into treatment. It is not enough to look only at a woman's use of alcohol and drugs. There is an overarching need for a holistic approach that takes into account the entire fabric of a woman's life. The recognition of the importance of relationships for women leads to an understanding of how intertwined women's lives are in the physical and emotional lives of others.

A woman often is faced with multiple roles as worker, parent, partner, and (sometimes) caretaker of her own parents. The demands of these roles can lead to intense stress, anger, depression, and exhaustion that can exacerbate alcoholism and drug abuse. Women are socialized to put the needs of others before their own and often are labeled selfish or uncaring if they take the time to seek help. Women might have to go against many years of social conditioning to reach out for counseling and alcoholism treatment for themselves. Counselors need to give women the practical help and moral support to take what might feel like an emotionally dangerous step and overcome their resistance to taking action for themselves.

A glaring reality in the lives of women who become alcoholics is that spouses and partners will leave many of them to care for themselves and be single parents. The burden of responsibility for children can be a major issue in women's minds before coming into treatment. Family support systems for alcoholic women often are absent or dysfunctional. A high proportion of alcoholic women come from alcoholic families themselves and have no economic, social, or emotional network of support.

Taking Drug, Family, and Sexual Histories

The first step in working with a woman in alcoholism counseling is obtaining a family history in relation to alcohol, drinking, and alcoholism. This might take more than one session with the client, depending on the extent of alcoholism in a woman's family. Establishing family drinking patterns gives a baseline to help a woman look at her own drinking. The next issue is to help a woman identify her own drinking patterns and the reasons why she either drinks or does not want to drink. Understanding the familial and cultural drinking patterns of a woman can help you to put the client's drinking behavior in a broader perspective. It also can help the client to see her drinking as partly a learned behavior influenced by the family and friends in her life.

Alcoholic women often have the burden of multiple addictions to alcohol and prescription drugs. It is traditional for doctors to view a woman's stresses and problems as psychosomatic and as symptoms of underlying emotional instability. Alcoholic women often find themselves in psychiatric treatment, where they are misdiagnosed and prescribed medications. Not only is this a misdiagnosis of alcoholism, it also is an unwillingness to uncover the reasons behind the social and emotional stressors in a woman's life.

Many women use and abuse mood-altering prescription drugs that they obtain legally through physicians or psychiatrists. Concern about women's use of controlled substances often obscures the real-

> One risk factor that clearly predicts a greater likelihood of problem drinking among both women and men is a family history of problem drinking.[10]

ity that the majority of drug abuse in women takes place within the health care system as part of medical and psychiatric treatment.

It is important to examine the social context in which women are prescribed legal drugs to understand why such drugs have become so readily accessible to alcoholic women already at risk. First, the United States is a society that encourages the consumption of mood-altering substances through advertising and health care promotion both as a way in which to deal with pain and as a way in which to enhance well-being. These include "medicines," alcohol, cigarettes, and even caffeine.

Women traditionally have had a powerless role in the health care system both as consumers and as providers. Policymakers have developed a system around the needs of physicians, hospitals, and the medical industry that often is unresponsive to change. Women participate in the belief that "the doctor knows best," accepting treatment with unexamined trust.

The politics of health care teaches women at an early age not to challenge or question physicians and to passively accept diagnoses and treatment. For alcoholic women, denial of their drinking and the need for addictive drugs make them exploit the physicians' misconceptions of women and prevailing drug-oriented therapies to acquire potentially dangerous drugs for themselves.

In treating a woman, it is critical to obtain a prescription drug history as well as a medical and psychiatric treatment history to begin to challenge and change the client's attitudes toward and behaviors around prescription drugs. Part of treatment might be helping the woman to establish an honest relationship with a physician knowledgeable about alcoholism and prescription drug abuse. You can work with the client on the unexamined beliefs that she might have about taking prescription drugs and medicine without questioning motives and the effects.

Over-the-Counter Drug Abuse

Women also are particularly susceptible to the abuse of over-the-counter nonprescription drugs that may or may not be recommended by physicians but are widely advertised for the treatment of all forms of pain and discomfort. Even if not recommended by one's own physician, slogans such as "four out of five doctors recommend..." might be taken as a sanction for unlimited use. Women who are actively drinking might have difficulty in reading and following dosage instructions, thereby making drugs (including aspirin and Tylenol™) potentially abusive substances. Codeine-based cough medicines, sleeping medications containing alcohol, and diet pills and appetite suppressants containing large amounts of caffeine frequently are abused. You should obtain a detailed history of both over-the-counter and prescription drug use to understand what might be potentially dangerous to the client's life and sobriety.

Taking a Woman's Sexual History: Addressing Feelings of Guilt and Shame

Closely connected to the outer realities of a woman's life are the inner burdens of guilt, shame, and low self-esteem. Counselors who work with both male and female alcoholics report that men tend to find it easier to forgive themselves for their drinking and to accept the illness concept of alcoholism more readily. Women, socialized for many years to assume greater personal guilt and responsibility, view themselves as society does—with shame. This is particularly true around the two areas of sexuality and children. For many women, the roles of wife/partner, mother, and lover are the most important sources of self-esteem and respectability. Low self-esteem is an issue for many women who have been brought up trained to be passive and dependent (especially on men). Research has shown that a poor self-concept and low self-esteem are the most predictable identifiable traits among alcoholic women. Addressing this low self-esteem often is a key to recovery.

It is only during the past two decades that the effects of alcohol and alcoholism on women have been specifically addressed through research and in treatment settings. Prior to 1975, research on alcoholism focused on males, and the results were generalized to women. Even during the 1990s, much of the research has focused on men, although this is slowly changing. Crucial areas specifically related to alcohol use and abuse among women have been overlooked such as alcohol-related health problems in women, women's drinking patterns, the physiological effects of alcohol on women, and premenstrual distress and alcohol use. These topics are just beginning to be researched. Sexual dysfunction related to alcohol abuse in women, sexual stereotyping of women who drink, and sexual issues affecting alcoholic women's recoveries all are areas of concern often overlooked by research and treatment.

It is important to explore some of these concerns with the intent of establishing a basis of factual data about alcohol and women. The Staff Training Activities at the end of this chapter review some facts and myths in these areas.

Learning about alcohol's effects on women and the sexual dysfunction that commonly accompanies alcohol abuse in women is part of becoming comfortable with raising physical and sexual issues. If you encourage women to ask questions about their bodies and sexuality, and if you provide recovering alcoholic women with practical information and realistic expectations of sexuality after sobriety, then you will be providing valuable information and support in an area that often is avoided or ignored.

Talking about your client's health and sexual history is a good way of opening up the wide range of issues related to women's health, sexuality, and alcoholism. The focus at this stage of treatment is to help the woman in treatment make an association between health problems and alcoholism. Alcoholic women might have avoided routine health care for many years. Here is an opportunity to introduce concepts of proactive preventative health care. A sexual history taken in the context of an overall health history allows sexuality to be openly approached. You then can begin to address a woman's fears and concerns about sexual function, dysfunction, and alcoholism.

> In women, the frequency of menstrual disturbances, spontaneous abortions, and miscarriages increases with the level of drinking, and alcohol abuse has adverse effects on fertility and sexual function.[11]

References

1. National Council on Alcoholism and Drug Dependence, *Alcoholism and Alcohol-Related Problems: A Sobering Look*. Available: http://www.ncadd. org/problems.html (retrieved 7 December 1998).

2. U.S. Department of Health and Human Services, *Ninth Special Report to the U.S. Congress on Alcohol and Health,* NIH Publication No. 97-4017 (Washington, DC: Government Printing Office, 1997).

3. National Association for Children of Alcoholics, *Alcohol and Alcohol-Related Problems: A Sobering Look* (Bethesda, MD: National Center for Health Statistics, 1991). Available: http://www.health.org/links.htm

4. U.S. Department of Health and Human Services, *Ninth Special Report.*

5. American Psychiatric Association, *Diagnostic and Statistic Manual of Mental Disorders,* 4th ed. (Washington, DC: APA, 1994).

6. U.S. Department of Health and Human Services, *Ninth Special Report.*

7. Ibid.

8. National Center on Addiction and Substance Abuse, *Combatting the Problem: Substance Abuse and the American Woman* (New York: Columbia University, CASA). Available: http://www.casacolumbia.org/pubs/jun96/womchap5.htm

9. National Institutes of Health, *The Physician's Guide to Helping Patients with Alcohol Problems,* NIH Publication No. 95-3769 (Rockville, MD: NIH, 1995).

10. National Institute on Alcohol Abuse and Alcoholism, *Women and Alcohol: Issues for Prevention Research,* NIH Publication No. 96-3817 (Rockville, MD: NIAAA, 1996).

11. U.S. Department of Health and Human Services, *Ninth Special Report.*

Staff Training Activities:
Perspectives on the Socialization of Women

Activity 1:   First Drink/First Time Drunk

Recall the first time, if ever, you had a drink of alcohol and the first time, if ever, you became drunk, and describe your current drinking pattern. In a group, starting with the leader, each person in turn recalls the story and feelings associated with each event. Some people might never have drunk alcohol or experienced drunkenness. Questions to think about are as follows:

■ How old were you?

■ How did you feel about drinking (getting drunk)?

■ What messages did you get from others about drinking and drunkenness?

■ How were those messages different for you as a female (as a male)?

Activity 2:   Definition of a Drink

Language makes it more difficult to discuss drinking, drunkenness, and alcoholism with others because of the tendency to use euphemisms that contain the word *drink* to discuss *drunk* or *alcoholism*. This usually is done because of people's discomfort with the discussion of alcohol use at all. Some of the ways in which we cover up uncomfortable meanings with nicer sounding expressions are as follows. "Last night we drank and partied" (i.e., got drunk). "Mary drinks too much" (i.e., gets drunk, alcoholic). "Pat is a drinker" (i.e., gets drunk, alcoholic). To talk to women about their drinking, we need to clarify the terms we use.

What is a definition of a drink? To drink means to take in an alcoholic beverage. An alcoholic beverage includes beer or wine, as well as hard liquor, and "take in" means taking as little as a sip or a glass or more. We define one drink in terms of equivalent amounts of alcohol to establish a unit of measurement to use in making responsible decisions about alcohol. There is the same amount of alcohol in 1.5 ounces of hard liquor as in a 5-ounce glass of wine or a 12-ounce can of beer. This might surprise people who feel that beer and wine are safe in any quantity.

Activity 3:   Effect of One Drink

What, besides the strength of alcohol, determines the effect of one drink on a person?

a.   Amount of food in stomach

b.   How diluted the drink is

c.   How long it takes to drink it

d.   Body weight (critical for women)

e.   Other drugs, especially depressants

f.   Female metabolism (women metabolize alcohol slower than do men)

g.   Emotional state (tired or depressed)

h.   Time of day and drinking environment

i.   Tolerance (one's own ability to handle alcohol)

Activity 4:   Defining Low-Risk Drinking and Excessive High-Risk Drinking

Low-risk and excessive high-risk drinking mean different things to different people. For example, women and men reared in families and environments where they see people get drunk every time they drink do not see the possibility of drinking and not getting drunk. Also, those reared in families with alcoholism are likely to see people drink, get drunk, and cause pain. For these people, drinking, drunkenness, and alcoholism are synonymous.

On a continuum of drinking behavior, come up with characteristics of the following:

Low-Risk Drinking	High-Risk Drinking
Moderation at all times	Loss of control
Appropriateness of time and place	Drinking to get drunk
Respecting family and community values	Marked change in personality and behavior
Knowing the law	Negative effects on others
Respecting personal limits	

Activity 5: Definitions of Drinking

■ *Abstinence:* A choice not to drink alcoholic beverages

■ *Moderate low-risk drinking:* A slight effect of alcohol without going beyond socially acceptable behavior, for example, increased gaiety and slight feeling of relaxation and well-being; no personality change and no interference with judgment and decision making

■ *Excessive high-risk drinking:* Having faculties impaired by alcohol, especially judgment and decision making; any degree of personality change that significantly alters behavior; in greater excess, marked loss of control over ordinary physical activities, for example, staggering or confused speech, not knowing what is going on, nausea, and passing out

Based on these definitions, people can establish their own personal baselines for using alcohol and understand more clearly the framework from which they evaluate the drinking of others.

Activity 6: Reasons Why People Drink and Reasons Why People Abstain

Make a list of all the reasons why people drink alcohol in our society. Brainstorm in a group:

Healthy/Integrative	Unhealthy/Dysfunctional
Enjoy taste	To escape or forget
To relax or unwind	Peer pressure
Complement a meal	To feel like a different person
Religious use	To get even
To celebrate	Boredom
Social custom	To get drunk
To quench thirst	To be "grown up"
Social lubricant at parties	To unwind

Go over each reason and decide why one would be considered a healthy/integrative reason to drink versus an unhealthy/dysfunctional reason to drink. Are some reasons both healthy and unhealthy? Responding to reasons brings up personal attitudes and values toward alcohol. For some people having a drink to relax is considered a safe use of alcohol from time to time, whereas for others it is unacceptable. One factor that needs to be considered with every reason is where the power of choice lies. Peer pressure, for example, puts the power of choice in the hands of others.

Activity 7: Cultural Differences in Drinking Patterns and Rates of Alcoholism

Many genetic, cultural, social, and environmental variables appear to play key roles in the development of excessive drinking practices and alcoholism. Although social and cultural factors are by no means the only ones that contribute to a woman's alcoholism, they often play a significant role in the development of people's attitudes and behavior toward drinking and are worth examining. Several sociological studies have looked at why alcoholism is widespread in some national, religious, and cultural groups but is rare in others. In general, research has shown that for groups that use alcohol to a significant degree, the lowest incidence of alcoholism is associated with the following habits and attitudes:

1. Children are exposed to alcohol early in life within a strong family or religious group. Whatever the beverage, it is served in very diluted and small quantities.

2. Beverages commonly used are beer and wine.

3. Beverages are considered mainly as food and usually are consumed with meals.

4. Parents present a constant, consistent example of moderate drinking.

5. No moral importance is attached to drinking. It is considered neither a virtue nor a sin.

6. Drinking is not viewed as proof of adulthood or virility.

7. Abstinence is socially acceptable. It is no more rude or ungracious to decline a drink than to decline a piece of bread.

8. Excessive drinking or intoxication is not socially acceptable. It is not considered stylish, comic or tolerable.

9. Alcohol use is not the prime focus for an activity.

10. Finally, and perhaps most important, there is wide and usually complete agreement among members of the group on what might be called the "ground rules" of drinking.

We all come from diverse backgrounds with implicit and explicit attitudes and guidelines given about alcohol, and so do the women with whom we work. Understanding the cultural ground rules in our backgrounds and in others helps in communicating questions and concerns about drinking. Understanding cultural background can be invaluable in assessing a woman's concept of her use or abuse of alcohol.

Activity 8:   Definition of Alcoholism

Take a moment to examine the following definition of alcoholism, based on the definitions of E. M. Jellinek, the World Health Organization, and the American Medical Association:

> Alcoholism is a chronic, progressive, treatable disease in which a person has lost control over her or his drinking so that it is interfering with some vital area of the person's life such as family and friends, job, school, or health.

The following questions are intended for group discussion:

■ Which area will be affected first?

Someone does not need to have trouble in all these areas to be diagnosed as an alcoholic. If alcohol is interfering with one or more areas, then alcoholism can be identified. Usually in the early stages of alcoholism, family and friends are affected. Personality changes, emotional withdrawal, mood swings, broken promises, and absences due to drinking affect those close to the alcoholic. For some people with alcoholism, it might be years before alcoholism affects outside activities such as job or school, as demonstrated in the expressions "She was a working drunk" and "She never missed a day of work." Health is not affected for some people until years after other areas of living have been damaged by alcoholic drinking. If you wait for health problems to develop as an "absolute" indicator of alcoholism, then you might waste precious time and opportunities to diagnose and treat the disease.

■ Why do we call alcoholism a disease that is chronic, progressive, and treatable?

The American Medical Association has given formal recognition to the "disease concept" since 1956. Certain assumptions that apply to other chronic accepted diseases, such as diabetes, also apply to alcoholism:

1. Alcoholism is something that can be described and defined.

2. Alcoholism has a predictable progression through early, middle, and late stages with definite warning signs at each stage.

3. The loss of control over alcohol is primary to the disease of alcoholism and not a symptom of an underlying disorder.

4. Alcoholism is permanent. Once someone has lost control over her drinking, she will not regain it.

5. Alcoholism is terminal. Alcohol is directly or indirectly the cause of death for most alcoholics who do not seek treatment.

6. Alcoholism is treatable. Total abstinence from alcohol is the necessary first step in the treatment of alcoholism. For most alcoholics, long-term outside support is essential for a lifetime of recovery.

Understanding the disease concept helps to remove the stigma of alcoholism for the alcoholic and the family.

■ Does "loss of control" mean that someone drinks every day or gets drunk every time she or he drinks?

Drinking patterns vary depending on life circumstances and on the progression of the disease. The key to understanding "loss of control" is the inability of the alcoholic to predict what will happen when she does drink. For some people this might mean controlled social drinking interspersed with episodes of drunkenness, and for others it might mean daily compulsive drinking and getting drunk. It is losing the power of choice over what will happen after taking the first drink that is at the heart of loss of control over alcohol.

■ Why is physical addiction not part of this definition?

Only a small percentage of the total population of alcoholics at any given time (12% to 14%) are physically addicted to alcohol. This definition is based on the consequences of someone's drinking, not on whether someone is physically addicted.

Activity 9:   Issue of Professional Avoidance in Dealing With Alcoholic Clients and Where It Comes From

Break the group into smaller groups of two or three to read and discuss Case Study 1. Ask each group to discuss and list what might have prevented the psychiatrist, the marriage counselor, and the social worker from seeing, identifying, and treating the alcoholism in this family. As a large group, share each small group's ideas and discuss in the following context:

Professional Avoidance Issues for General Discussion

Reasons why counselors avoid confronting alcoholism:

a.   Unresolved personal experiences such as concerns about their own drinking or that of people close to them

b.   Lack of knowledge about alcoholism:

■ Inability to diagnose, particularly in the early stages

■ Confusion with psychiatric problems that might be secondary effects of the alcoholism

■ Belief that alcoholism is a moral issue (if they bring it up, therefore, they are saying that their clients are bad persons)

■ Belief that members of certain groups (e.g., women, youths, professionals) cannot be alcoholic

■ Belief that if they can only help their clients to change their living situations, become less depressed, or feel better about themselves, then the women will stop needing to drink the way they do

■ Not knowing that alcoholism is progressive and fatal if untreated

c.   Politeness and discomfort: Fear of angry response and "What if I'm wrong?"

d.   Identification with the client: "It is so awful to be an alcoholic woman, I do not dare to talk about it"

e.   Feelings of hopelessness and helplessness about recovery: "Why bother?"

f.   Fear of getting too involved with, or "swallowed up" by, the alcoholic

g.   Belief that an alcoholic cannot be helped until she asks for help or hits bottom

h.   Fear of losing client or friend

i.   Feeling that the person has so many problems already: "Why should I take her bottle away from her too?"

j.   Wanting to raise the issue of drinking but not knowing how

It is important to stress that these feelings are common to most counselors who have not had an opportunity to learn about alcoholism as a disease, examine their own attitudes, and practice helping strategies. In this chapter and others, people will be learning information and skills to allow them to treat alcoholic women compassionately and effectively.

1. The counselor and client process the log started in the last session(s) together. The counselor can learn a great deal from observing the client during this activity. There may be nonverbal cues such as the client not making eye contact, speaking inaudibly, and being restless that could indicate how great her concerns are about addressing her drinking.

    a. Encourage the client to discuss her experience of keeping the log. What has she noticed? Some of her comments might reveal the following:

    - Patterns of time, place, and mood

    - Resistance to keeping the log and hostility toward the counselor

    - Bargaining with herself over honest reporting or follow-through

    - Minimization of data

    - Feelings of anger, guilt, or relief

    - Attempts at control, knowing that she would be reporting

    - Loss of control, inability to do the log

    - Blackouts and forgetfulness

    b. Be aware of any denial, minimization, anger, or distress in the woman's affect because it can be an indication of a drinking problem or alcoholism.

    c. Give the client specific content-focused feedback on what you see. This should include the following:

    - Patterns you are wondering about

    - Amounts you are concerned about

    - Correlations among mood, activity, and amount

    - Tolerance as indicated by affect

    d. If the client "forgot" or "didn't finish" the log, then process the meaning of this with her. Could this be a symptom of denial or protection of a drinking problem? Does she experience blackouts or pass out for periods of time?

2. Recontract with the client to continue the log and to bring it back to the subsequent sessions. Let her know that she is providing both of you with important information that will help her to feel better and learn more about herself and the role that alcohol or drugs are playing in her life.

3. Assuming that there are reasons to be concerned about the client's drinking, it is important to provide concrete information about warning signs and symptoms of early and middle stage

alcoholism. Now and in subsequent sessions, you will link this information to the woman's own drinking in a warm, concerned, and direct manner.

a. Using information gained from the client's alcohol history and drinking log, begin to share your concerns about patterns, amounts, and effects of her drinking. Begin to make the connections for her among feelings, job, and relationship problems with her alcohol use and abuse.

b. Using the third person, go over the "Symptoms of Alcoholism" list. Discuss with her that these are common signs and symptoms for people who have the disease of alcoholism, although not everyone experiences all symptoms. Introduce the idea of stages of the disease and that the earlier it is recognized, the easier it is to treat. Encourage her to identify any of these symptoms in her own drinking. Talk about what you see with her at this point without pushing her beyond what she is able to hear.

Symptoms of Alcoholism

These symptoms mark the three stages of alcoholism, but not all symptoms are seen in every individual. These stages are intended only as guidelines given that every individual can experience some or all of these symptoms at different times in his or her alcoholism.

Early Stage	Middle Stage	Late Stage
Sneaking drinks	Drinking more than intended (loss of control)	Alcoholic hepatitis
Gulping drinks	Protecting the supply of alcohol	Cirrhosis (enlargement of the liver)
Preoccupation with drinking		Lowering of personal standards
Personality changes when drinking	Drinking to relieve anger, tension, insomnia, fatigue, depression, and social discomfort	Tremors when sober
Drinking to the point of drunkenness		Lowering of tolerance to alcohol
Guilt feelings about drinking	Increased incidence of infections and colds	Blatant and indiscriminate use of alcohol
Missing responsibilities of work and school due to hangovers	Benders	Choice of work situations that facilitate drinking
Seeking companions who are heavy drinkers	Morning drinking	
Blackouts	Drinking despite strong medical reasons not to	Brain damage
Changing forms of alcohol (e.g., vodka to beer)	Drinking despite strong social reasons not to, such as marital and family disruptions and arrests for drunk driving	Alcoholic seizures
Spouse complaining of drinking		Delirium tremens (DTs)
	Repeated attempts at abstinence	Alcoholic hallucinations
Losing interest in activities directly associated with drinking	Paranoid attitude	Fears of "going crazy"
Job changes as a result of interpersonal problems	Projection, resentments, and denial become more severe	Depression, isolation, and suicidal preoccupation

Case Study 1

June is a 45-year-old, pleasant, attractive, well-to-do suburban housewife. She has a lovely home, a successful husband, and an active life in the community. Two of the couple's three children are away at college, and the third is a junior in high school. He rarely is home.

Just before Christmas, June was picked up for driving while intoxicated with a .20 blood alcohol level. Following her arrest, she was admitted to the psychiatric unit of a general hospital by her husband. He felt that this incident indicated she must be crazy. June agrees with him. Shortly thereafter, she was referred to an alcoholic outpatient unit. During her intake interview, she revealed the following information.

She has been seen on a regular basis for the past 2 years by Dr. McFarlane, a prominent psychiatrist, to deal with her depression and feelings of inadequacy. He diagnosed her as a depressive neurotic suffering from a poor self-image, and he prescribed Valium. Much time was spent dealing with her feelings of inadequacy that he feels stem from her position as the middle child in her family of origin.

Several years ago, June and her husband, Jerry, were engaged in marriage counseling with Tom Lyons. Jerry rarely was home long enough to share any family life, supposedly because of the pressures of his job. Eventually, it surfaced that he was involved in an extramarital affair. Both June and her husband were suffering from midlife crises. Tom saw their problems as resulting from growing apart as Jerry rose in his profession, and June was left behind to deal with the children and everyday household problems.

Jerry suggested that they make a conscious and determined effort to get out alone together, have a few drinks and dinner, and become reacquainted.

For a short time, June also shared a family social worker with her adolescent son when he was involved in a vandalism incident at the local high school. He and two friends drank a case of beer and demolished the chemistry lab. Her husband was unable to participate in the counseling sessions at the time because of a heavy workload. Marie George, their social worker, felt that overpermissiveness and a lack of firm limit setting was the underlying source of the problem. She suggested that June learn to deal with this.

Each of the professionals seeing June over the years made an accurate diagnosis and a professionally sound therapeutic attempt to deal with the problem at hand. Each was correct in his or her assumptions.

No one realized that June drank heavily, that she used alcohol to cope, and that she became more and more dependent. They did not ask about her drinking habits, nor did she make any attempt to reveal the extent of her problem drinking.

Why?

Activity 10: Stereotypes of Alcoholic Women

Ask each group member to recall a statement she or he might have overheard or said about an alcoholic woman in the past. Write these statements on the blackboard. Examples might include the following. "I hate to see a woman drunk; it's disgusting." "She's probably sleeping with half the men in town." "How can she do this to her children?" "Women who drink too much are sicker than men."

1.   What images do these statements portray of alcoholic women?

Slut	Irresponsible	Bad mother
Loose	Weak	Poor
Dirty	Out of control	Stupid

2.   How would you react, as an alcoholic woman, if you were present when someone made one of these statements?

3.   How do statements like these create barriers for alcoholic women entering treatment?

"I Am an Alcoholic Woman" Activity

One of the best ways in which to break down prejudices and misconceptions about alcoholics and drug abusers is for counselors to attend Alcoholics Anonymous or Narcotics Anonymous meetings and meet women in recovery. Some counselors, as they learn about alcoholism, might begin to identify people in their own families whose drinking concerns them. Al-Anon Family Groups are an excellent resource for them.

Look at the list of statements at the end of this activity. Assign one statement to each member of your group with the following instructions:

■ Ask group members to be silent during the reading. Ask each person to read one statement slowly and then wait for a few moments before going on to the next person to read.

■ "Remember as you read, you are representing a person. It may be someone you have met in treatment, someone you know, or yourself. Get in touch with your feelings and the feelings of the women who are represented."

■ This activity in a group can create a strong emotional climate. It is important to pause for a few minutes after everyone has read their statements so that group members have time to collect their thoughts. Then, allow more time to discuss their feelings and reaction to the exercise.

Discussion questions:

■ What did you experience when you were listening? (e.g., sadness, isolation, loneliness)

■ What did you feel as you spoke for your alcoholic woman?

■ Did people hear issues in these statements for alcoholic women that they had not thought about before?

■ What are some of the problems and concerns that alcoholic women have that make them different from each other?

Minority women	Young	Depression
Sexual orientation	Mothers	Adult daughters of alcoholics
Poor	Alone	Abused

■ Do these women fit a single stereotype of an alcoholic woman? Why or why not?

■ Why is it important to look beyond the alcoholism to recognize the special circumstances of each woman's life?

Vignettes to use for "I Am an Alcoholic Woman" activity:

I am a sober alcoholic woman, and my kids always want to taste my drinks to see whether there is booze in them.

I am a sober mother, and my kids are acting up all over the place. I thought that when I stopped drinking, everything would be okay.

I am an alcoholic woman, and I know my drinking hasn't affected my son because he's a straight "A" student, the captain of the football team, and very popular.

I am an alcoholic woman and a working mother. When do I find the time to take care of myself?

I am an alcoholic woman, and chances are very high that my husband will leave me.

I am an alcoholic woman, and when my family visits me in detox, they pretend that I'm there for something else besides alcoholism.

I am an alcoholic woman, and I don't know whether I can relate sexually to a man without a drink.

I am an alcoholic woman, and I am the only woman in a 20-bed detox.

I am an alcoholic woman, and everyone says that I am too young and attractive to be an alcoholic.

I am an alcoholic woman and a lesbian, and everyone assumes that I have two diseases.

I am a sober mother. I cry every Mother's Day remembering the Mother's Day my children brought me breakfast in bed and I was so hung over that I yelled at them.

I am an alcoholic mother, and they tell me I have to put my needs first. How can I do that when I have a baby?

I am a sober alcoholic woman, and my kids resent it when I go to Alcoholics Anonymous meetings.

I am an alcoholic mother, and I don't think I know how to parent my children.

I am an alcoholic mother, and I'm scared to go for treatment because I'm afraid they will take my kids away.

I am an alcoholic woman, and my husband left me. I have three children and no job skills.

I am an alcoholic woman and a lesbian. Is there room in family treatment for my lover with whom I've been involved for 5 years? Or, do I lie and tell the counselor that I'm single?

I am an alcoholic woman, and when the police stop me for drunk driving, they say "Go home to your husband" and let me go.

I am an alcoholic woman and a business executive, and if I leave my job for treatment, there won't be a job for me to return to.

I am a black alcoholic woman, and I look around my Alcoholics Anonymous meetings and wonder where all the other black women are.

I am an alcoholic woman and depressed, and I feel helpless to change anything.

I am an alcoholic woman, and my husband gets jealous when I go to Alcoholics Anonymous meetings.

I am an alcoholic woman, and my therapist keeps giving me Valium.

I am an alcoholic woman and a Latina, and no one speaks my language.

I am an alcoholic woman, and I'm uncomfortable around other women.

I am an alcoholic woman, and I look 10 years older than I am.

I am an alcoholic woman, and my family says that my problem is nerves.

I am an alcoholic woman, and no one will talk to me about my drinking.

I am an alcoholic woman and single. I have to try to take care of my children, stay sober, and work full-time.

I am an alcoholic woman. My husband is alcoholic too, but the school blames me for all of our son's problems.

I am an alcoholic mother, and my counselor told me I need a halfway house. There's no one to leave my kids with, and I don't want to turn them over to the welfare department.

I am an alcoholic woman and 16 years old, but everyone's concerned about my brother's drinking.

I am an alcoholic woman, and I feel so guilty about what I've done to my children.

I am an alcoholic woman and pregnant, and I'm afraid I've damaged my baby.

I am an alcoholic woman and need help, but my family says that I'm being silly.

I am an alcoholic woman, and every time I try to sober up, my husband buys me a bottle.

I am an alcoholic wife and mother. My husband says I am responsible for all the problems in the family.

I am a black alcoholic woman, and everyone assumes that I'm hooked on street drugs.

I am an alcoholic woman, and my kid has no friends. I know it's my fault.

I am an alcoholic mother, and I grew up in an alcoholic home. I'm doing the same thing to my kids that my mother did to me, and I hate myself for it.

I am an alcoholic woman, and I must have a partner to protect and take care of me. Without that, I don't think I can survive.

I am an alcoholic woman and am physically abused by my lover. But isn't that better than being alone?

I am an alcoholic woman. I am just now remembering all the times my father got in bed with me when my mother was at work.

I am a Puerto Rican alcoholic woman. My husband keeps telling me that I am not an alcoholic; I just need to learn the art of drinking.

I am an alcoholic woman who grew up with two alcoholic parents. I was lonely and scared then, and I still feel that way now.

I am an alcoholic woman with good reason to be angry; my stepfather abused me, my mother was too sick to take care of me, and my husband left me. But most of the time I just feel nothing.

I am a pregnant alcoholic woman, and my ex-boyfriend is an addict. Now he tells me that his night sweats and his weight loss were happening because he has AIDS. Suddenly, the future looks terrible for all three of us.

I am a sober alcoholic woman. I cannot imagine being intimate with someone without being high.

Activity 11: Guided Imagery: What an Alcoholic Woman Feels

Using a guided exercise, group members put themselves in the place of the hidden alcoholic woman to help them experience her isolation, her fears of being discovered, her search for help, and her entry into a treatment program. The characteristics of this woman were chosen because the issues she faces in terms of acknowledging and dealing with alcoholism are common among women who come to treatment. The goal of this activity is to build up each group member's understanding of an alcoholic woman from *her* perspective. The instructions are as follows:

- The trainer should facilitate getting the group into a relaxed state. This can be done by having the participants relax in their chairs, feeling their bodies as they touch the chairs. Have the group members close their eyes, and lead them through some focused breathing exercises.

- Set the scene for the imagery by describing the time and place.

- Ask people to take the role of the woman in the imagery and to pretend that they are her.

Guided Imagery

Imagine that you are a woman named Diane who is 32 years old. You have been married to your husband, Bob, for 5 years and have two children, Sally and Cathy. Bob is a salesman, and his work often takes him away from home. You and Bob have drunk socially for years and have had fun with alcohol. A series of events has caused anxiety for you, and you have found yourself turning to alcohol for relief. Two years ago, your father died around the time that Sally, now 4 years old, was hospitalized with a tumor. At that time, you found that drinking at night helped you to sleep. Since then, Sally has been operated on, and no further signs of cancer have been detected; however, your drinking has progressed. You learned that drinking helped to relax you in general. You began to drink not only to help you fall asleep but also before giving a dinner party or going out. It was not too long before you began drinking to deal with most situations. You now are drinking alone at home to keep other people from seeing how much you drink. Presently, your sober days are far outnumbered by your drunk days.

Today is like all the rest. You are home alone. It is 10 a.m., and you are having a conversation in your head about how a glass of wine would help you to face the housework and grocery shopping. You have your own supply in the laundry room, where it is easy to get to without anyone knowing.

You feel nervous and tense, and you know that just one glass would take the edge off those feelings and help you to face all this work. You feel that other people do not understand the pressure you are under and might not realize how much the alcohol is helping you to cope. It is getting harder and harder to get through a day without it.

Holding onto what it feels like to be Diane, I now want you to open your eyes and begin to think about a few discussion questions.

Questions for discussion:

- What does it feel like to be Diane? (e.g., tense, anxious, fearful, guilty)

- Why are you trying to keep your drinking hidden? (e.g., shame, guilt, denial, fear of giving up booze)

- Which events would lead you to go for help? (e.g., crisis, being discovered, comments made by husband or kids or others, feelings of desperation)

- Where would you go for help first? (e.g., therapist, counselor, doctor, psychiatric setting)

- What could happen to get you into alcoholism treatment? (e.g., a therapist who asks you questions about your drinking, a family intervention)

◼ Client Training Activities

Activity 1

Explore the client's stereotypes of alcoholic women through imagery and word association. See Staff Training Activities as a reference.

- Ask the client to share her feelings or images when she hears the words *alcoholic woman*. Ask her to freely say what comes to mind and not to censor herself.

- If she has difficulty in doing this, next ask her to recall statements that she has heard others say about alcoholic women.

- Compile a list of the client's statements.

Activity 2

Does the client know any alcoholic women? Family members? Friends? Are these statements consistent with these women's lifestyles or behaviors?

Activity 3

Explore what it might be like and feel like to be a woman such as that described by the client's statements in Activity 1:

- How would this woman feel about herself?

- Would it be easy or difficult to seek help?

- What would prevent her from telling her family or friends about her problem?

- What would you want to say to her?

Activity 4

Talk with the client about the importance of rethinking stereotypes of alcoholic women as a way in which to look more openly at her own drinking or anyone else's drinking that concerns her.

Activity 5

A one-word feeling does not tell enough. If you say, "I feel overwhelmed," does that mean you are "ready for suicide" or just need "a night's rest"? You must try to describe your feelings in detail so that another person can begin to understand what you feel. For example, you can compare your feelings with the following:

■ A situation that is generally recognized ("I feel embarrassed, like when I was called on in school and didn't know the answer")

■ An experience personal to you ("I feel proud and excited, like the time I first saw our baby at the hospital")

■ A physical experience ("I feel tense; my face is flushed, and my stomach is racing inside")

You can try to describe the intensity of your feelings. Here are some feeling words that help to show the wide range of feelings all of us can have:

Distant	Fearful	Strong
Close	Guilty	Affectionate
Dependent	Enraged	Grateful
Independent	Panicky	Compassionate
Talkative	Grief stricken	Sympathetic
Quiet	Calm	Empathetic
Angry	Uptight	Lonely
Evasive	Tense	Proud
Embarrassed	Inadequate	Humble
Mortified	Lost	Alarmed
Worried	Ecstatic	Pleased
Threatened	Scared	Joyful
Comforted	Powerless	Depressed
Sad	Immobilized	Burdened
Comfortable	Seductive	Tired
Beaten	Jealous	Disgusted
Confident	Envious	Self-assured
Contemptuous	Desperate	Lonely
Strong	Aggressive	Happy
Assertive	Mad	Puzzled
Paralyzed	Hopeful	Excited

Resources

Alcohol Research Information Service (ARIS)
Contact: Robert L. Hammond, Director
Address: 1106 East Oakland Avenue, Lansing, MI 48906
Phone: (517) 485-9900

(ARIS invites walk-in visitors and phone queries from 9 a.m. to 5 p.m.)

National Center on Addiction and Substance Abuse at Columbia University (CASA)
Address: 152 West 57th Street, New York, NY 10019
Phone: (212) 841-5200
Web: http://www.casacolumbia.org

(CASA is an independent nonprofit corporation affiliated with Columbia University. The library will respond to questions from professionals.)

National Women's Resource Center for the Prevention and Treatment of Alcohol, Tobacco, and Other Drug Abuse and Mental Illness
Address: 515 King Street, Suite 410, Alexandria, VA 22314
Phone: (301) 770-0850, (800) 354-8824

(This is a national center that provides information on women's issues, reaches underserved groups of women and their children, and helps to integrate the delivery of substance abuse prevention and treatment services for women.)

2

Substance-Abusing Women in Relationships

Overdependence on unhealthy relationships with men or women as lovers, partners, or spouses is a central issue in the lives of most alcoholic or drug-abusing women. The concept of "learned helplessness" developed by Seligman explains how people, as a result of conditioning and socialization, believe that the outcome of a situation has little to do with their input.[1] Adult women who experience this feeling see themselves as having little or no ability to influence life's events. This feeling of helplessness leads to dependency on others as protectors or problem solvers. Substance-abusing women often turn to lovers to take care of them, to keep them sober, to support them financially, and to make their decisions. A woman might feel so needy that one relationship is not enough and, therefore, could get into several at once. This also might give a woman a sense of power that she does not otherwise feel. Sometimes, self-esteem is so low that a woman will stay in an abusive relationship because being alone is more terrifying. Some alcoholic or drug-abusing women who have become accustomed to years of problems and pain seem to believe that their relationships will fail to grow and will die. They might focus on the "other" in the relationship or live in a state of crisis that could be more comfortable than focusing on themselves. They might try to fulfill a self-perception of being worthless and unlovable. There also are women who react to intimacy by fearing it and isolating themselves. In sobriety, some women are afraid of involvement if, in the past, intimacy always was connected to drinking or abusing drugs. Women might confuse intimacy with sexuality, missing the emotional component of closeness. In the absence of a lover and partner, relationship dependence might be transferred to a therapist or other counselors.

Understanding and Helping Significant Others

As you work with a substance-abusing woman, remember that you always have more than one "client." A woman's drinking and drug abuse have a profound impact on the significant others in her life. The Al-Anon Family Groups pioneered the understanding of the impact of someone's alcoholism on others. According to Al-Anon,

> Alcoholism is a family disease. Compulsive drinking affects the drinker, and it affects the drinker's relationships. Friendships, employment, childhood, parenthood, love affairs, and marriages all suffer from the effects of alcoholism. Those special relationships in which a person is really close to an alcoholic are affected most, and the people who *care* are most caught up in the behavior of another person. They react to an alcoholic's behavior. They see that the drinking is out of hand, and they try to control it. They are ashamed of the public scenes, but in private they try to handle it. It is not long before they feel they are to blame and take on the hurts, the fears, the guilt of an alcoholic. They become sick, too.[2]

Codependency Defined

The impact of alcoholism and drug abuse on others has been characterized as "codependency" by professionals in the alcoholism field. Codependency is separate from, but similar to, alcoholism. The term was developed during the late 1970s to describe the patterns of coping of people who were affected by someone else's drinking or substance abuse.

Codependents are "people whose lives have become unmanageable as a result of living in a committed relationship with an alcoholic."[3] Codependency may begin with another's drinking and drug abuse and then develop a life of its own. Many adults who grew up in alcoholic families suffer the effects of codependency long after they stopped living with alcoholic parents.

Some characteristics of codependency are caretaking, low self-worth, controlling behavior, denial, dependency, lack of trust, problems with anger, mood swings, and inconsistent behavior. All of these conditions develop in people involved with a substance abuser but progress on their own until people recognize them and receive treatment. Codependents need help to see that their destructive behavior is a result of denial, which is similar to that of an alcoholic. Codependents are struggling for survival. Codependency includes self-destructive behaviors that may become habitual and progressive.

Enabling Defined

An enabler is anyone close to a woman who unconsciously helps her to continue to drink or abuse drugs and protects her from the consequences. Codependents, children, friends, and associates take on enabling behavior, which not only is destructive to the alcoholic or drug abuser but is equally destructive to themselves as well. Enablers will deny the alcoholic woman's problem or will minimize or rationalize the drinking behavior. They will blame, criticize, and then take over the responsibilities of the alcoholic or drug-abusing woman.

Most people are not aware of their actions and distorted emotions until they receive outside help. Enabling behaviors include denying, minimizing problems, rescuing, protecting, blaming, nagging, and avoiding conflict through "keeping the peace." The enabler's primary feelings are anger and guilt, which stem from the inability to control the alcoholic. Enablers become enslaved to the irrational behavior of the actively drinking alcoholic woman, reacting and trying to control. Children can be enablers as well, making excuses for their mother, taking over parental responsibilities, and retreating into a fantasy world.

Detachment

Detachment is a recovery tool suggested and used in Al-Anon and in many professional treatment services for families. It means letting go of the obsession with a substance-abusing woman's behavior and focusing on recovery from the destructive effects of living with someone who is an alcoholic. Detachment means not taking responsibility for an alcoholic woman's disease or the recovery from it. It is a way that allows codependents to look objectively at their lives and make responsible decisions for themselves. Helping codependents to detach also means teaching skills to live with the feelings of guilt, fear, responsibility, and anger that surface when they "let go" of enabling the substance abuser. Codependents need help in distinguishing between abandonment and detachment and need to practice identifying and focusing on their own feelings and needs.

Codependents need help outside the circle of relatives, friends, and neighbors as well as separate from help that is offered the alcoholic or drug-abusing woman. You should develop an evaluation and referral process for family members and for the substance-abusing woman. Al-Anon Family Groups and Alateen, as well as self-help groups based on the principles of Alcoholics Anonymous (AA), have worked successfully for many codependent adults and children. Al-Anon is for anyone who is affected by another's drinking or drug use—spouses, lovers, friends, parents, adult children, and counselors who work with alcoholics. Alateen is a program for teenagers who live in substance-abusing households. Preadolescent children from 6 to 12 years of age pose a particular problem because of lack of resources. Those children living with alcoholic or drug-abusing mothers may be at special emotional risk. Counselors need to think about finding resources for this age group of youthful codependents as part of working with alcoholic women and their families.

Substance-Abusing Women as Daughters of Alcoholic Parents

Most studies indicate that alcoholic women are more likely than alcoholic men to have grown up in alcoholic families and that daughters of alcoholics are more likely to become alcoholic than are daughters of nonalcoholic parents. Issues of pain, anger, and sorrow associated with growing up in an alcoholic family remain very much intact long after a person moves out of the alcoholic family home.

The fact that so many alcoholic women also are adult children of alcoholics has significant implications for treatment and recovery. These women must contend with not only their own alcoholism and drug abuse but also

"Many women who use drugs have faced serious challenges to their well-being during their lives. About 70[%] of women who report using drugs also report having been abused sexually before the age of 16 [years], and more than 80[%] had at least one parent addicted to alcohol or one or more illicit drugs."[4]

years of particular patterns of behavior and roles in response to growing up surrounded by alcoholism. This often makes recovery for alcoholic women longer and perhaps more complicated. Frequently, after recovering from acute alcoholism, a woman must begin to examine her "adult daughter issues" if she is to continue to grow and recover —often a painful process.

Many adult daughters appear to be vulnerable to either becoming alcoholics themselves or marrying alcoholics or drug abusers. For alcoholic adult daughters, it is important in early sobriety to keep "first things first" and focus on building sobriety skills. However, at a certain point, the losses common to many children of alcoholics, particularly that of parents who no longer are there for them on a consistent basis, might need to be addressed.

Concerns for adult daughters of alcoholics appear to revolve around five central issues: control, mistrust, ignoring personal needs, denial of feelings, and inability to define and limit responsibility (particularly with regard to the alcoholic parent).[5]

In a similar vein, Black reports from her clinical experience that children from alcoholic families are taught not to talk, trust, or feel. Black believes that this upbringing has many ramifications in adulthood including problems of trust, intimacy, control, and expression of feelings.[6] Woititz stresses the problems that adult children have in knowing what "normal" is as well as a wide range of other psychosocial characteristics.[7]

Women who have maintained sobriety for a year or more can profit from a range of treatment services around parental alcoholism. Al-Anon Family Groups provides these women with support and understanding as well as a Twelve Step program of recovery that is the same as that of AA. Al-Anon has specialized groups for adult children of alcoholics. There also are groups in alcoholism treatment centers and mental health settings for adult children. It is important to develop groups for these women, supporting their needs to address deep problems such as incest and family violence. Most recovering women do not feel safe talking about incest and parental abuse in the company of men. It might be advisable for recovering women with histories of incest and family alcoholism to have women counselors.

Roles and Rules of Children in Alcoholic Families

- To survive, children from alcoholic families, like all children, learn coping behaviors. Their behavior and the types of roles they adopt often are based on their sex, the position of their birth (younger or older), and other family dynamics.
- The oldest girl often assumes the role of the mother and takes care of the house and younger siblings. She also is considered to be at high risk for

incest. When she leaves the home, another girl might take over her role and could become the victim of violence.

■ As in many families, children vacillate among different roles at different times. What children do while living in an alcoholic environment they do because it makes sense at the time. These roles somehow make life feel easier or less painful for them.

■ Children also learn "family rules." Black delineates the rules in an alcoholic family:

– *Don't talk:* This is particularly true about real issues or problems such as parental drinking. "What happens in this house stays in this house."
– *Don't trust:* No one will be there for you, and promises and confidences often are broken. The truth is distorted. "Mommy is sick today."
– *Don't feel:* Feelings are denied, ridiculed, and/or invalidated. "How dare you cry when I am talking to you!"

These rules function as survival techniques and protection for children living in alcoholic families. Most of these children grow into adulthood carrying these rules and behaviors with them. Obviously, such roles and rules can present problems in adulthood.

Substance-abusing women often are hidden and protected or abandoned. Most alcoholic women eventually are abandoned by spouses or lovers (the reverse is true of alcoholic men). This creates an added burden on children who have alcoholic mothers. Many alcoholic or drug-abusing mothers also are single parents, so children might have no other parental support. These children have to deal with the double stigma of problem drinking or drug abuse and marital separation. There also is evidence that those husbands and lovers who do stay in the family with children are heavy drinkers or drug abusers themselves. A child might be living with two substance abusers, not just one.

Treatment Issues for Women Who Are Adult Daughters of Alcoholics

It usually is recommended that alcoholic or drug-abusing women who are adult children maintain a minimum of 1 year of sobriety before they get involved in reconstructive therapy for family alcoholism. The uncovering process can be painful and difficult, and their sobriety needs to be solid. Review the major emotional themes in the lives of adult daughters that relate to parental alcoholism.

Control. Adult daughters have a need to control environment, self, and others at all times. This need may be expressed in eating disorders (e.g., bulimia, anorexia), problems with intimacy, and extreme rigidity of thinking and behavior. The need to control is so all-pervasive that it dominates every other concern in these women's lives.

Mistrust. Adult daughters not only mistrust other people but, more important, mistrust themselves. They do not trust their own perceptions, feelings, and decisions. They often will vacillate and refuse to make decisions because of extreme self-doubt.

Ignoring personal needs. It is common for a daughter growing up in an alcoholic family to have had to deny her own personal needs as a child and as an adolescent to take care of an alcoholic parent or younger siblings. Adult daughters might neglect their health, personal appearance, and needs for sleep and rest. Emotional needs also might be unexamined, devalued, or unexpressed.

Denying feelings. Adult daughters have been raised to repress and ignore their feelings in the service of survival in alcoholic families. They might not know what anger feels like and might have experienced it turned inward as depression. They might feel the need to be "up" and "happy" all the time and might have difficulty in acknowledging pain and sadness. They might need to know whether it is okay to cry.

Being unable to define or limit responsibilities. Women are raised to take responsibility for the needs and wants of others. Living with an alcoholic parent means taking responsibility for someone whose life is out of control. Adult daughters still might be continuing to take care of alcoholic parents, spouses, or children who are unable to set limits or protect themselves.

Treatment Resources for Adult Daughters of Alcoholic Families

There are groups for adult children from alcoholic families available in some alcoholism and mental health treatment settings that are not affiliated with Al-Anon. A few have groups solely for adult daughters. Women's groups are particularly helpful for recovering women dealing with painful issues of incest and family violence. Adult children support groups enable adult children to deal with the psychological and emotional aspects of family alcoholism and to develop a fellowship and sense of belonging.

Individual counseling. Some counselors and therapists have gained knowledge and experience in the area of family alcoholism and can help alcoholic women who are adult daughters to deal with the damage of parental alcoholism. Therapists can help recovering women to slowly talk about incest and family violence in a safe and nonthreatening relationship. It is recommended that an alcoholic or drug-abusing woman be actively involved in AA, Narcotics Anonymous (NA), or group treatment and have some length of sobriety— ideally at least 1 year—before entering therapy to deal with family alcoholism issues.

Adult Daughters of Alcoholics: Breaking Family Rules

Any woman who is seeking help to work on issues related to growing up in an alcoholic home deserves support and recognition just for walking through the door and initiating the process. Remember, by seeing you, she has broken at least two of the cardinal rules in alcoholic families as defined by Black: "don't talk" and "don't trust." By making a commitment to initiate her recovery through Al-Anon, counseling, or support groups, she will continue to break these first two rules and will move on to challenge the third rule, "don't feel."

To recover and to address her adult daughter of alcoholic(s) issues, your client will need the following:

- Education about alcoholism including basic information about the disease process
- Education about family dynamics when alcoholism is present including the roles and rules that family members adopt
- Affirmation and support from a variety of resources to break through the isolation, shame, loyalty, and secret keeping that she adopted as a child to survive

Substance-Abusing Women as Partners

One aspect of a woman's self-esteem and self-worth is connected to her ability to form an intimate relationship with another adult as a lover, a partner, or a spouse. The word *dependency* too often has been used to devalue the importance of relationships in women's lives without making a distinction between unhealthy destructive relationships and healthy interconnections. Heterosexual women and lesbians share similar issues of unhealthy dependency and cultural conditioning that can prevent the development of healthy relationships. A woman often enters treatment with a history of failed and abusive relationships that include violence and abandonment. A woman who is in treatment for alcoholism or drug abuse will need help to examine the impact of her past relationships on her life, and she will need help—as a woman—to develop a new model for healthy, nonaddictive, nondestructive intimacy.

There are a number of personal factors that affect a woman's relationships. One is the experience and sense of relationships handed down to a client from her family of origin. Alcoholism, mental illness, family crisis, and loss can play major roles. A history of family violence, incest, and child abuse can devastate a woman's sense of intimacy. A woman might lack healthy sex role models from the past and in the present. She might carry rigid sex role stereotypes. External supports (e.g., family, friends) and the presence or absence of societal sanctions can affect the capacity for relationships and intimacy, especially in the case of lesbian, multiracial, and other nontraditional couples.

Lesbians sometimes are forced to deny or hide aspects of themselves and to lead "double lives" out of fear of family rejection, lack of legal rights, and potential loss of children through custody battles. These outside pressures put stress on a relationship. Partners struggling with internalized homophobia have internalized negative stereotypes about lesbians and may struggle with guilt, self-hate, and subconscious negative beliefs regarding the potential of the relationship. Therefore, sexual expression and intimacy, so connected to a woman's self-esteem, can be hindered by these unresolved conflicts.

Helping women with relational issues in sobriety involves supporting their newly sober lifestyle and working with them to begin developing comfort in close relationships without alcohol or other drugs as a balm or buffer. These women need help in distinguishing healthy dependency and love from unhealthy addictive codependence. They also need to learn to trust and develop friendships and nonsexual relationships with other women. Developing a network of support is an important part of putting an intimate relationship in a new context. Learning to make decisions and choices and to express their needs enables women to be separate and whole in intimate relationships with lovers or partners.

You have the opportunity to model a healthy relationship with a sober woman by being open, honest, trustworthy, and encouraging. Women need acceptance and reinforcement for their needs and desires for intimacy and connection. Developing new behaviors and attitudes toward partnerships will take time. If a woman already is in a committed relationship, then couples counseling or therapy might be helpful after a woman has achieved some emotional stability in her own sobriety.

Violent Relationships

Violence is an ever-present fear for women living in American society. For many women, there is the reality of having actually been the victims of violence. Family violence, incest, sexual abuse, and battering cut across all racial, class, and ethnic lines. Violence usually occurs in the context of intimate relationships with fathers, brothers, lovers, and husbands and is closely connected to women's dependence on men for identity, security, and power. Until recently, most forms of violence against women were hidden or tacitly accepted. Women felt guilty and responsible, and often they were blamed for encouraging or accepting abuse. Today, the thinking about and attitudes toward violence against women have changed. As the Boston Women's Health Collective puts it,

> Women are not guilty for violence committed by men on our body, mind, and spirit. This violence happens because of men's greater power and their misuse of that power. . . . Thousands of daily acts of violence throughout the country create a climate of fear and powerlessness which limits women's freedom of action and controls many of the movements of our lives.[8]

Statistics Regarding Victims of Violence and Substance Abuse

The statistics regarding violence against women are startling. It is estimated that 25 million children under the age of 11 years live in homes where they are sexually abused, most often by fathers or stepfathers. Incest is defined as inappropriate sexual behavior usually perpetrated by an adult family member with a minor child.[10] Incest occurs in many homes and in all socioeconomic classes.

Although some incest victims are infants and others are in their late teens, most are between 5 and 8 years of age. The incestuous activity usually continues for at least 3 years. The oldest daughter appears to be the most vulnerable to be a victim of incest. When she resists or leaves the home, however, another daughter might become the victim. Many studies confirm that female adult survivors of sexual abuse are likely to be adult drug or alcohol abusers.[11,12] In his book, *Understanding Family Violence,* Vernon E. Wiehe suggests that "the relationship between childhood sexual abuse and later substance abuse problems may occur because drugs and alcohol are used to relieve the painful memories associated with the abuse that reoccur periodically for the survivor."[13]

It is crucial to address both incest and alcohol abuse for the safety and well-being of each family member and to prevent the reoccurrence of these issues in subsequent generations. Some research suggests that there might be an intergenerational transmission of family violence just as there is now a demonstrated intergenerational transmission of alcoholism.[14] Children raised in families with both problems are more likely to become alcoholic or drug-addicted adults and to either marry abusing partners or become abusers themselves.

Similar behaviors and thought processes exist in both alcoholism and family violence. Both alcoholics and abusers deny, rationalize, minimize, and display "Jekyll and Hyde" personality changes. Both are unwilling to accept responsibility for their own behavior and defend their actions with alibis and excuses and by blaming others. Drinking and violence inevitably begin to cause problems in every area of the alcoholic's or abuser's life, increasing feelings of remorse or guilt. Without treatment, there is an ongoing cycle of attempts to regain control and promises to change, creating false hopes for all involved.[15]

Family dynamics also are similar where alcoholism and violence are present. Family members in both situations exhibit their own forms of denial by minimizing the impact of what is happening in the family due to the violence or the alcoholism. Sometimes, the abused child or adult accepts responsibility for "causing" the violence, much as those closest to the alcoholic will feel that they "caused" the drinking. "If only I had been a better [or quieter or more loving] wife, this [the drinking or the beating] would not have happened." These assumptions and mistaken beliefs, founded in low self-esteem and attempts to control or fix the situation, actually perpetuate the progression of the drinking or the escalation of the violence. When alcoholism and violence both are present, the need for denial is multiplied, and the sense of helplessness felt by family members is even more acute.

Treating Substance-Abusing Battered Women

In treating an alcoholic or drug-abusing woman who has experienced incest, sexual abuse, or battering, there might be one or more life histories at work. She might have alcoholic parents and also been physically or sexually abused as a child. She might be in a relationship with an alcoholic or abusive partner.

She might be abusing or neglecting her own children. It is extremely important that violence, incest, and sexual abuse are recognized as a reality in many substance-abusing women's lives and that women are asked about these issues, if only to validate their experiences and acknowledge that they are not different or alone. Many women do not remember or have repressed incest experiences. Often in the first or second year after establishing sobriety, memories and flashbacks will start to occur, similar to a posttraumatic stress disorder. The timing of treatment and intervention will differ depending on a woman's sobriety and on whether the abuse is current or something that occurred years ago. Alcoholic or drug-dependent

> More than half of both prison and jail inmates serving time for violence against intimate partners had been using drugs, alcohol, or both at the times of the incidents for which they were incarcerated. Women between 16 and 24 years of age experience the highest per capita rates of intimate violence.[16]

women, some of whom were abused as children, still might be involved in battering situations, especially if they are in relationships with other substance abusers. Certainly, if you are working with a woman or family where alcoholism or drug abuse is present, you should consider the possibility that there was and is some form of family violence occurring. Recognize that, like alcoholism, denial in the client and/or counselor only contributes further to helplessness, despair, and escalating violence.

In working with women, it is important to let them know that you are aware that violence often can occur in substance-abusing homes. This might make it easier for women to admit that violence has been and is part of their lives. Also, be sure to ask other family members about possible abuse. Due to alcoholic blackouts and denial, alcoholics honestly might not remember abusive behavior. It also is important not to assume that with sobriety family violence will automatically stop. Although alcohol or drug use and abuse might be associated with physical and sexual abuse, this is not always the case. The abuse might have occurred in the family whether or not alcoholism or drug abuse was present. We

> Two thirds of victims who suffered violence by intimate partners (current or former spouses, boyfriends, or girlfriends) reported that alcohol had been a factor.[17]

have no way of knowing whether the abusive dynamics have become a pattern now totally independent of the drinking or drugging behavior.

Partner Violence Among Lesbians

Lesbian relationships also are at risk for experiencing partner violence, and many lesbians have called battered women's services seeking help. Violence between lesbians has been hidden by both denial in the lesbian community and fear of service providers' indifference when the batterer's identity or sex is dis-

closed. Counselors should be sensitive to, and ask questions about, violence and abuse that lesbians might have experienced in their relationships.

If counselors are uncomfortable in handling a situation of incest, sexual abuse, or battering with clients due to personal experiences or attitudes of their own, in many communities there are other professionals to turn to who work specifically with families experiencing domestic violence. In cases of current abuse that is ongoing in a recovering woman's life, the primary concern needs to be helping her and her family protect themselves. This can be done by using community resources, filing a temporary or permanent restraining order or marital separation, or (in the case of an abusing parent) filing a child abuse complaint. The woman and her family need to learn the signs of impending violence and need to physically remove those in danger from the home until it is safe to return. The woman and her family should work out a plan of where to go for safety at any time of the day or night. Shelters and safe houses are available in some communities for families or women experiencing violence. If the alcoholic or drug-dependent mother is herself abusing her children, then this is an important tool to use in requiring treatment as a means of protecting the children from violence. A woman needs to understand that she is accountable for her actions while drinking or drugging, including any abuse of her children, and that she must seek help.

References

1. M. Seligman, *Helplessness: On Depression, Development, and Death* (San Francisco: Freeman, 1975).

2. Al-Anon Family Groups, *Understanding Ourselves and Alcoholism* (New York: Al-Anon Family Groups, 1979).

3. Terence T. Gorski and Merlene Miller, "Co-alcoholic Relapse: Family Factors and Warning Signs," *Journal of Drug and Alcohol Dependency* (1984): 78.

4. National Institute on Drug Abuse, *Women and Drug Abuse,* NIDA Capsule Series (Rockville, MD: NIDA, 1994). Available: http://www.health.org/pubs/caps/index.htm

5. C. Black, *It Will Never Happen to Me: Children of Alcoholics as Youngsters-Adolescents-Adults* (Denver, CO: M.A.C. Publications, 1981).

6. Ibid.

7. J. G. Woititz, *Adult Children of Alcoholics* (Pompano Beach, FL: Health Communications, 1990).

8. Boston Women's Health Book Collective, *The New Our Bodies, Our Selves* (New York: Simon & Schuster, 1984).

9. Adapted from Alcoholism Center for Women and Haven House, *Double Jeopardy Manual* (Los Angeles: Alcoholism Center for Women and Haven House, 1987).

10. Black, *It Will Never Happen,* 141.

11. V. Wiehe, *Understanding Family Violence: Treating and Preventing Partner, Child, Sibling, and Elder Abuse* (Thousand Oaks, CA: Sage, 1998).

12. National Institute on Alcohol Abuse and Alcoholism, *Women and Alcohol: Issues for Prevention Research,* NIH Publication No. 96-3817 (Rockville, MD: NIAAA, 1996).

13. Wiehe, *Understanding Family Violence.*

14. R. Sanchez-Dirks, "Reflections on Family Violence," *Alcohol and Health Research World* 4, no. 1 (1979): 12-16.

15. Black, *It Will Never Happen,* chap. 7.

16. Bureau of Justice Statistics, *Violence by Intimates: Analysis of Data on Crimes by Current or Former Spouses, Boyfriends, and Girlfriends,* No. NCJ-167237 (Washington, DC: U.S. Department of Justice, 1998).

17. L. Greenfield, *Alcohol and Crime: An Analysis of National Data on the Prevalence of Alcohol Involvement in Crime,* Publication No. NCJ 168632 (Washington, DC: U.S. Department of Justice, 1998), v.

Staff Training Activities

Activity 1: Definitions of Violence Against Women
Activity 2: General Recommendations for Helping Personnel in Providing Support Services to Battered Women
Activity 3: Vignettes From the Lives of Codependents
Activity 4: Case Study (Martha)
Activity 5: Treating Incest Survivors
Activity 6: Stages of Recovery for Incest Survivors
Activity 7: Case Study (Jane)

Activity 1:   Definitions of Violence Against Women

- *Domestic violence:* Abuse in the family or household; includes woman or spousal/partner abuse, child abuse, incest, sibling abuse, and elder abuse

- *Battered woman:* The victim of repeated physical and emotional abuse by her husband, ex-husband, lover, or friend (male or female), who is jealous and controlling and who uses threats and verbal abuse as well as beatings

- *Battering or abuse:* The use of physical, emotional, and sexual coercion to control and maintain power over someone including frightening and intimidating someone repeatedly over a period of time

- *Victim/survivor:* Someone who has experienced any form of physical, emotional, verbal, or sexual abuse

- *Physical abuse:* The actual physical act of a person punching, kicking, or using a weapon on a family member

- *Emotional abuse:* Continually criticizing a person in a way that is humiliating in private or public; regularly threatening to leave or telling the person to leave; withholding approval or appreciation as punishment; ever-present threat of physical assaults

- *Verbal abuse:* Name-calling, shouting, or using words as a means of controlling a person; always criticizing the way in which things are done; threatening to hurt a person or a family member

- *Sexual abuse:* When sexual interaction is unpleasant, frightening, or violent, with the woman having nothing to say about her own sexuality; when a person feels demeaned, disrespected, forced, or violated in sexual interactions (by the partner or by others)

- *Child abuse:* The act of inflicting or allowing injury that includes physical abuse or neglect, sexual abuse, or emotional mistreatment

■ *Child neglect:* Failure of a parent or caretaker to provide adequate food, clothing, shelter, medical care, and supervision

■ *Incest:* Inappropriate sexual behavior between any family members including stepparents and live-in partners

■ *Marital rape:* A crime of violence carried out through sexual means between partners in which there is no mutual consent

■ *Date rape:* A crime of violence carried out through sexual means against someone who has consented only to be a social friend

■ *Acquaintance rape:* A crime of violence carried out through sexual means by someone known to the victim in which there is no mutual consent.

SOURCE: Adapted from Alcoholism Center for Women and Haven House, *Double Jeopardy Manual* (Los Angeles: Alcoholism Center for Women and Haven House, 1987).

Activity 2:   General Recommendations for Helping Personnel in Providing Support Services to Battered Women

1. Speak with the woman privately.

2. The environment for the interview should be as quiet and comfortable as possible.

3. Actively express concern for the woman's feelings and well-being.

4. Attempt to develop trust and rapport.

5. Statements should be clear and concrete.

6. Avoid making assumptions and value judgments.

7. Initially, focus questions on gaining information.

8. Do not rush to give advice.

9. Be aware of the effect that verbal and nonverbal responses have on the woman.

10. Some of the feelings the battered woman may be experiencing include guilt, shame, shock, numbness, fear, pain, loss, failure, and anxiety.

11. The woman should not be pressured to file a complaint.

12. The woman should not be expected to want to separate from her spouse.

13. When possible and appropriate, explore the presence of numerous family problems commonly associated with domestic violence.

14. The woman should be made aware of support systems available to her.

SOURCE: Adapted from a handout prepared by the Los Angeles County Commission on the Status of Women.

Activity 3:   Vignettes From the Lives of Codependents

Each vignette describes someone whose life has been affected by an alcoholic woman. Read and discuss each vignette. This activity also may be done in small groups. The following questions can be asked of each vignette:

■ How is this person's life affected by an alcoholic woman?

■ What is this person feeling?

■ What would you say to this person in a counseling situation?

■ How do you think this person appears to others? Upset? Angry? Sad?

> My name is Geri. I'm 32 years old, and I'm a business executive. Both my parents are alcoholics, and they both are in detox now. I spend all my free time helping one or the other out of one problem or another.

> My name is Greg, and I'm 67 years old. My wife, Nancy, is in detox now for the second time in 3 months. I don't know much about alcoholism, and I certainly don't understand the changes in Nancy. I'm retired, but I have many hobbies and friends that could be happily filling my time. But I'm so frightened by the possibility of Nancy's falling and hurting herself or for her falling asleep with a lit cigarette that I don't dare leave the house and leave her alone.

> My name is Maria. I'm 62 years old and the mother of Ann, who is 33 and in detox for the first time. I've been told by a psychiatrist that events in my daughter's childhood have caused her alcoholism, so of course I feel terribly guilty. To cover up my guilt, I've developed a hostile and defensive manner. The only reason I'm attending this group is because of the urging of Ann's detox counselor.

> My name is Sheila. I'm 18 years old and in the last year of high school. I've had to assume more and more of the responsibility for our family because of my mother's drinking. I have to leave school right after my last class to get home in time to care for my younger brothers and sisters. I do all the cooking and cleaning. I have no life of my own, and that makes me so angry that at times I feel ready to explode. But I also feel terribly guilty about being angry with my mother.

> My name is James, and I'm 41 years old. Carol, my wife, is in an alcoholism halfway house. Ever since she's been in that place, she's been talking about leaving me. Why are they trying to break up our marriage? For years, I've taken care of Carol and helped her solve legal, financial, and work problems. I'm hurt and confused that now she wants to leave me.

> My name is Harriet, and I'm 23 years old. My mother is an alcoholic, but she denies that she has any problem with her drinking. She's made two suicide attempts, which landed her in a psychiatric hospital. I'm furious with those doctors because no one there talked to her about her drinking. I'm scared that her next attempt might be successful. I also feel guilty because I don't visit her very often, but the truth is that I don't like to spend time with her.

> My name is Shirley. I'm 41 years old and in detox for the first time. I've been learning a lot about alcoholism in here. I'm starting to think I may be alcoholic, but my husband and psychiatrist say I'm emotionally

upset and that's my problem. I'm confused and ashamed, and I'm afraid to see the counselor with Roy and the kids.

My name is Roy, and I'm 40 years old. I'm not too pleased at having to see this counselor again. I went to Al-Anon since she made such a fuss about it, but it was a waste of my time. There were only women there talking about alcoholism. My wife is plain crazy; she's not alcoholic. She's self-indulgent, and that's why she's in detox. If she'd give up her part-time job and concentrate on things at home, everything would be fine.

I'm Donna. I'm 16 years old, and I've been going to Al-Anon for about a year. Before that, I was doing all the things my mom used to do like taking care of the twins, cooking meals, and cleaning the house. With the help of Alateen, I'm doing that less and less now. I've also been trying to talk with my father and the twins about my mom's alcoholism, but they don't want to hear me.

My name is Joan, and I'm 9 years old. Donna takes me to a kids' group, where we play games and talk about drinking. Yesterday, we saw a movie about a woman alcoholic. She reminded me a lot of my mom.

I'm Jim, and I'm 9 years old. Joan goes to this dumb group. You wouldn't catch me there. Besides, I like it when Joan isn't around, so we stop fighting for a while. My dad says my mom is crazy, and I think he's right. She doesn't do anything the way she used to.

My name is Agnes. I'm 70 years old, too old to be taking care of my daughter's children. I'm so ashamed of her and ashamed to be here in this place, but I do love her and want to do what is best.

My name is Sara, and I'm 45 years old. When Diana and I became lovers 10 years ago, I thought that settling down together would help her change her drinking habits. Ten years later, my patience is exhausted and I've tried everything to get her to stop—money for treatment, no pressure, ultimatums. None of our friends will see us anymore. I feel isolated, alone, and nearly hopeless, but after 10 years I'm not quite ready to let go.

Activity 4   Case Study (Martha)

Martha is a 38-year-old alcoholic woman who has been sober and attending outpatient groups for 7 months. She missed a few group meetings, so the counselor called to see how she was doing. She said that she had started to drink again but had stopped after 3 days and is now sober. She has an appointment today to see her counselor. Martha comes in with bruises on her face and arms.

Martha is feeling very ashamed that she had a slip and very self-conscious about her appearance. Her ex-husband came by when she was drinking and beat up Martha. She never has talked to her counselor about being abused by Ted. She is afraid that the counselor will make her report it to the police, and then Ted would really go after her. Martha feels that she brought this on herself and that if she had not been drinking, then maybe Ted would not have beat her.

The counselor is very upset by Martha's appearance. The counselor wants to discuss what happened to Martha, but the client has not mentioned anything about it during the half hour the two already have been talking together. Martha is acting as if there is nothing unusual about her appearance.

Activity 5:   Treating Incest Survivors

In working with adult alcoholic or drug-dependent women who were physically or sexually abused as children, our recommendation is that major uncovering or therapeutic work in this area should not happen in early sobriety. Women who are incest survivors need acknowledgment of the incest experiences, empathy, and assurance that the experiences never were their fault. However, we believe that further work, such as an incest survivors' group, should be left until a woman has developed substantial sobriety supports (at least 1 year's sobriety, if possible). Sometimes, due to the urgency of the situation or a woman's continual relapses, this is not possible, and then you need to make sure that any incest treatment is done by a practitioner who is familiar with the issues in recovery and fully supports a woman's efforts to establish a safe and sober life.

Activity 6:   Stages of Recovery for Incest Survivors

Recovery for a sober woman who also is an incest survivor is maintaining sobriety, having her memory under voluntary control, being able to reach back and talk about the incest with appropriate affect, and having a sense of mastery and control in her day-to-day life.

Stage 1: Self-Care and Self-Protection

- Getting and staying sober and drug free with self-help groups and/or counseling (usually for at least 1 year)

- Establishing a safe physical living situation

- Taking care of personal hygiene, eating, and sleeping

- Capacity to bring herself into a state of relaxation

- Becoming financially sound and dealing with employment issues

- Being able to hold onto her sense of personal identity and an acceptable level of self-esteem

Activity for Client at This Stage

The client should choose two or three things to do for herself—just for herself—and share the experience with you.

Stage 2: Recovering and Integration of Traumatic Memories

- Short-term incest survivor groups in which she can share her story

- Mourning of losses and grieving of past

- Expression of anger

- Support to recover and make sense of past experience

- Encouragement for woman to express mastery and power over her life

Activity for Client at This Stage

You might wish to take a client through a guided imagery activity to recall a selective memory from the past experiences of incest. It is not necessary to recover everything. One memory can sum up an era.

Stage 3: Coming Up With New Meanings and Moving On

- Longer term therapy groups and support groups around incest survival

- Exploration of who she is now as a recovering woman and an incest survivor

- Expanding her capacity to trust herself and others

- Developing a new agenda for her life with understanding and acceptance of her past

Activity for Client at This Stage

Ask the woman to reflect on the meaning of the past trauma in her life today. Have her explore the strengths and understandings she has gained in the process of recovery.

SOURCE: Model presented by Mary Harvey, director of Victims of Violence Program, Cambridge Hospital, Cambridge, MA, 1988.

Activity 7: Case Study (Jane)

Jane had been coming regularly to outpatient groups and using Alcoholics Anonymous. She was sober for 6 months until she relapsed. She missed several meetings and never responded to the notes that the counselor sent. Jane has come in today for the first time in 2 months. She is visibly upset and shaking but says that she has not been drinking for 2 weeks.

This slip really scared Jane. She thought that she was controlling her drinking. She did okay until one night 2 weeks ago when she was leaving the bar and a strange man followed her home. Jane was walking and defenseless. All that evening, she was flooded with memories of times in which her father would wait for her after school when her mother was working and then would follow her around the house until he had "talked her into" going to bed with him and performing oral sex and intercourse. Jane has been so ashamed and scared that she has not said a word about this to anyone. The memory of it all horrifies her. She has come to see the alcoholism counselor because she trusted the counselor in the past. Jane is ashamed, but she is desperate to talk.

The counselor is pleased to see Jane again, but she is so obviously shaken that the counselor is concerned about her. Jane was very open in the past, but today she is hesitant and withholding. The counselor is uncertain about how to approach her.

▨ Client Training Activities

Activity 1

Bill of Sexual Rights

1. I have a right to own my own body.

2. I have a right to my own feelings, beliefs, opinions, and perceptions.

3. I have a right to trust my own values about sexual contact.

4. I have a right to set my own sexual limits.

5. I have a right to say no.

6. I have a right to say yes.

7. I have a right to experience sexual pleasure.

8. I have a right to be sexually assertive.

9. I have a right to be the initiator in a sexual relationship.

10. I have a right to be in control of my sexual experience.

11. I have a right to have a loving partner.

12. I have a right to my sexual preferences.

13. I have a right to have a partner who respects me, understands me, and is willing to communicate with me.

14. I have a right to talk to my partner about the incest.

15. I have a right to ask questions.

16. I have a right to receive accurate sexual information.

SOURCE: Wendy Maltz and Beverly Holman, *Incest and Sexuality* (Lexington, MA: Lexington Books/D. C. Health, 1987). Reprinted by permission.

Resources

Adult Children of Alcoholics (ACA)
World Service Organization Inc.
Address: P.O. Box 3216, Torrance, CA 90510-3216
Phone: (310) 534-1815
E-mail: info@adultchildren.org
Web: http://www.adultchildren.org

Al-Anon Family Group Headquarters Inc.
Address: 1600 Corporate Landing Parkway, Virginia Beach, VA 23454
Phone: (757) 563-1600
E-mail: wso@al-anon.org
Web: http://www.al-anon.alateen.org

(This is a self-help program for family members and friends of those with alcohol problems)

Children of Alcoholics Foundation Inc.
Contact: Director of Public Information
Address: West 60th Street, 5th Floor, New York, NY 10023
Phone: (800) 359-COAF (359-2623)
Web: http://www.lafn.org/community/aca

National Association for Children of Alcoholics (NACOA)
Address: 1426 Rockville Pike, Suite 100, Rockville, MD 20852
Phone: (301) 468-0985
E-mail: nacoa@erols.com
Web: www.health.org/nacoa

(NACOA provides information, education, advocacy, and community networking on behalf of children and families affected by alcoholism and drug dependencies)

National Association for Native American Children of Alcoholics (NANACOA)
Address: 130 Andover Park East, Suite 230, Seattle, WA 98188
Phone: (206) 248-3539
E-mail: nanacoa@nanacoa.org
Web: http://www.nanacoa.org

(Organized by more than 70 Native Americans from 30 different tribes, NANACOA serves as a source of information, training, and support for Native American communities around the needs of children of alcoholics.)

National Clearinghouse on Family Violence (Canada)
Address: 1918C2, Floor-18, Jeanne Mance Building, Tunney's Pasture, Ottawa, Ontario, Canada K1A 1B4
Phone: (800) 267-1291, (613) 957-2938, (800) 561-5643 (TTY)
Web: http://www.hc-sc.gc.ca./nc-cn

(This is a national resource center for information and solutions to violence in the family, providing information to frontline workers, researchers, and community groups as well as responding to queries from individuals.)

National Coalition Against Domestic Violence
Address: P.O. Box 18749, Denver, CO 80218-0749
Phone: (303) 839-1852

(This is a national membership organization that promotes the development of many programs that meet the special needs of battered women of all social, racial, ethnic, religious, and economic groups; ages; and lifestyles.)

Trauma Foundation
Address: 1001 Potrero Avenue, Building One, Room 300, San Francisco General Hospital, San Francisco, CA 94110
Phone: (415) 821-8209, ext. 26
Web: http://www.traumafdn.org

(This is the home office for the San Francisco Injury Center and the Pacific Center for Violence Prevention, with a special library on injury and violence prevention including a large range of alcohol and drug information.)

3

Types of Drug Abuse and Counseling Strategies

Social and cultural changes during the past three decades have had a profound impact on illicit drug use and women. Beginning in the 1970s, the changing roles of women have since removed some of the traditional barriers toward nonconformity, allowing women to experiment with illicit drugs more openly and in larger numbers. Illicit drug use affects a broad cross section of the female population. Today, more than 4.4 million women use illicit drugs, and this is roughly 37% of the illicit drug-using population in the United States.[1]

Although women still use significantly fewer illicit drugs than do men, women's use of heroin, cocaine, marijuana, and other psychoactive drugs has been increasing. Most female illicit drug users are introduced to and obtain drugs in the same way. Women are most likely to be introduced to and supplied with illicit drugs by men as part of intimate or sexual relationships. The subculture of illicit drugs has been dominated by men who frequently have succeeded in making women dependent and subservient. Women often will start using illicit drugs in the context of relationships with male partners as "protectors." Illegal drug use, which may start in a connected relationship, ends by destroying a woman's capacity for a relationship, her health, and her life. One drug abuse program describes its female clients as follows:

> Many women with drug and alcohol problems experience chaotic and abusive lives and find themselves disconnected from relationships. They experience a profound sense of despair with "failed" attachments and find that drugs and alcohol relieve the pain of their perceived knowledge that they are on the outside of relationships. Early trauma and feelings of alienation operate as antecedents to addiction. For many women, addiction is closely allied with feeling unlovable, unwanted, and incompetent and is accompanied by intense feelings of low self-esteem.[2]

Risks and Consequences for Women Drug Abusers

An alcoholic woman who uses illicit drugs might be doing so to mask her alcoholism, to manage it, to substitute for alcohol, or because she is dually addicted. For many addicted women, alcohol and illicit drugs are used in a variety of patterns. Doweicko explains that "the chemical(s) a person uses at any point in time is frequently influenced by its availability and price."[3] A woman may drink to "dull" the edginess caused by cocaine. She may smoke marijuana when alcohol is unavailable. She may drink alcohol or smoke marijuana when cocaine is too expensive or otherwise undesirable. She may use different drugs at different times—cocaine and stimulants to feel "up," and alcohol and marijuana to mellow out and relax. A woman may quickly develop cross-tolerance and cross-dependence so that even if she never drank alcoholically while she was using opiates, for example, if she ceased the use of opiates and turned to alcohol, she would develop a dependency and tolerance for alcohol.

Deception is a fact of life in the illicit drug marketplace. An ever-present danger in the use of illicit street drugs is the unknown substances with which they often are cut. These can be deadly, especially if a woman drinks and experiences a multiplied reaction not only from the illicit drugs and alcohol but also from unknown substances in the illegal street drug.

Women who abuse illicit drugs have certain shared characteristics that result from the cycle of addiction and the danger and uncertainty of the illegal drug world. Some observers suggest that behaviors common to the middle stages of alcoholism are present virtually from the beginning of illicit drug abuse because

Cross-tolerance: Instantaneous ability to withstand the effects of drugs pharmacologically and chemically, similar to alcohol, such as tranquilizers, sedatives, and all other central nervous system depressants. (Example: An alcoholic might need to have an increased dosage of prescription pills to get the desired effect, the same way as she needs to increase the dose of alcohol to get the desired effect, which can have dangerous repercussions.)

Cross-addiction: Dependence on more than one drug, which can occur in alcoholic women when tranquilizers and prescribed drugs are used, knowingly or unknowingly, to mask the effects of alcohol withdrawal; also known as cross-dependence or polydrug abuse. (Example: Alcohol might be used in conjunction with cocaine to mitigate or ease the intense "high" that is experienced.)

Synergy: Dangerous multiplication of effects that occurs when alcohol is combined with other drugs that depress the central nervous system such as tranquilizers, sedative-hypnotics, barbiturates, and anti-anxiety agents. (Example: Alcohol potentiates the effects of these drugs such that even small combinations of alcohol with low doses of medication cause a chemical interaction that can lead to serious and even fatal outcomes.)

the substances are not legally available. These include the need for secretiveness, concern for the supply, and feelings of guilt and apprehension.

Treatment Issues for Multiple Drug Addiction

Alcoholic women who abuse illicit drugs often do not fit into clear diagnostic categories of alcoholism or drug abuse. Women with both alcohol and illicit drug abuse problems often are overlooked and misdiagnosed. Many alcoholism treatment programs will not admit women who use intravenous drugs even if they have acknowledged alcohol problems. Drug abuse treatment programs might not accept an alcoholic woman who is using illegal drugs because they feel she belongs in an alcoholism treatment system.

Women in young and mid-adulthood entering alcohol and drug treatment programs frequently have histories of multiple substance abuse that includes alcohol and one or more illicit drugs—often marijuana, cocaine, and/or opiates. Women also may have obtained prescription drugs illegally or on the street, in which case they become "illicit" substances. Multiple substance abuse is defined broadly as the simultaneous abuse of different mood-altering drugs including alcohol, illicit drugs, and prescription drugs.[4] In a study of chemically dependent women in treatment, it was found that many women under 35 years of age were more likely to have a multiple substance abuse problem including abuse of illicit substances. Older women (35 years or above) tended to abuse alcohol and prescription drugs.[5]

Commonly Abused Drugs

Heroin

Heroin addiction has long been considered one of the most dangerous of opiate addictions and is one that affects the lives of women. Heroin addiction is an increasing cause of death among drug-addicted women. The health risks to a heroin-addicted woman and her children involve not only the drugs themselves but also the lifestyle and dangers of the drug subculture in which heroin exists.

Women who are addicted to heroin often feel like the "lowest of the low." They see themselves as more socially deviant than their male counterparts and have extremely low self-images and low self-esteem. Women report using drugs as a conscious attempt to relieve emotional problems and to cope rather than for pleasure. Women often are forced to trade sex for heroin or for the money to purchase it. A woman's physical appearance might deteriorate over time when she is using heroin. She frequently is the victim of physical and sexual abuse from male partners. These women feel like outcasts from mainstream society, alienated from family and friends and frequently separated from children or unable to adequately care for them.[6]

Health problems often are acute among heroin-addicted women. Neglect of normal hygiene and lack of routine health care, combined with the physical problems associated with street life and prostitution, increase the risk

Heroin is an illegal, highly addictive drug. It is both the most abused and most rapidly acting of the opiates. Heroin is processed from morphine, a naturally occurring substance extracted from the seed pod of certain varieties of poppy plants. It typically is sold as a white or brownish powder or as the black sticky substance known on the streets as "black tar heroin." Although purer heroin is becoming more common, most street heroin is "cut" with other drugs or with substances such as sugar, starch, powdered milk, and quinine. Street heroin also can be cut with strychnine or other poisons. Because heroin abusers do not know the actual strength of the drug or its true contents, they are at risk of overdose or death. Heroin also poses special problems because of the transmission of HIV and other diseases that can occur from sharing needles or other injection equipment.[7]

of chronic infections and sexually transmitted diseases, especially AIDS and other serious gynecological disorders.

The lifestyle of heroin-addicted women puts them and their children in grave social, emotional, and physical jeopardy.

Heroin-addicted women are coming into treatment in greater numbers than in the past. As the separation of women in treatment programs by drug of choice becomes less important, alcoholic women who also are heroin addicts are being treated in alcoholism and drug abuse inpatient and residential settings. More women than men seek treatment for health problems resulting from their addictions because their health frequently is so compromised. They often go into treatment in the face of opposition from actively using partners. Women who are heroin addicted do well in intensive treatment settings that provide them with social support and life skills education. As one researcher describes,

Addicted women, who frequently lack social/emotional supports, often find the programs highly supportive, not only in terms of staff and services provided but also stemming from the interactions with other female addicts. The treatment setting may become a rich social world (many women bring their small children with them to treatment) of friendship, camaraderie, sharing, and understanding, with new clients being taken under the wings of veterans. An extension of these relationships is provided in the increasing number of women's groups being organized in treatment programs. These programs offer education in such vital areas of particular relevance to addicted females as prenatal care (attendance in such groups may be mandatory in the case of pregnant addicts), nutrition, hygiene, and parenting techniques. Furthermore, they help women learn to get along in strong relationships with other women, providing a sense of supportive sisterhood, raising their self-esteem, and diminishing their belief in the inevitability of victimization. Since in some cases peer pressure led to addiction, peer pressure may help them get their lives together.[9]

Heroin abuse is associated with serious health conditions including fatal overdose, spontaneous abortion, collapsed veins, and infectious diseases including HIV/AIDS and hepatitis.

Heroin-addicted women might enter treatment distrustful of the institution, authority figures, and counselors because of past problems with the legal system due to prostitution, petty theft, and/or drug-related arrests. They might be distrustful of other women and initially prefer male counselors and the company of men. Women's treatment groups and residential settings help to break down a woman's fear of other women and foster interdependence.

There are a number of approaches used in treating a heroin-addicted woman. Some programs provide long-term maintenance on methadone, a synthetic substitute for heroin, with minimal counseling and support. Others provide short-term methadone maintenance (1 year or less) with supportive counseling and transition to a drug-free life. Heroin-addicted women are being successfully treated in chemical dependency programs that provide detoxification along with counseling and support to become free from all mind-altering substances. The focus of treatment usually is to help women become part of a Twelve Step program, either Alcoholics Anonymous (AA) or Narcotics Anonymous (NA). NA has provided a setting of support and recovery for heroin-addicted men and women who make the choice to become drug free. Most women who choose to become sober and drug free from heroin are facing a long struggle to recovery. Female heroin addicts often are stigmatized as prostitutes and "amoral" long after they become drug free. They usually have to rebuild lives that have been shattered by a dangerous lifestyle. Long-term counseling, women's groups, NA, and AA all are important parts of a woman's recovery. Relapse often is part of the recovery process during the first year of treatment. Full recovery is a process taking many years and requiring much support from both self-help and professional programs.

Cocaine and Crack

Cocaine has been called the "recreational drug" of the 1980s. During the 1970s, cocaine use spread into a broad segment of American society as attitudes toward recreational drugs became liberalized due to the widespread acceptance of marijuana. The addictive nature of cocaine was unknown, and because of its high cost, it became associated with an affluent upper class subculture. It was considered chic, exclusive, daring, and nonaddicting. The popularity of cocaine, which is a stimulant drug in the same classification

Science has taught us that when medication treatment is integrated with other supportive services, patients often are able to stop heroin (or other opiate) use and return to more stable and productive lives.[10]

as amphetamines, also was increased when manufactured amphetamines became more difficult to obtain during the mid-1970s because their prescribed abuse had become widespread.[11]

Women appear to be using cocaine at an earlier age and in as great or greater quantities than are men. One treatment center reported women spending twice as much money as men for cocaine in a given week. As with

Cocaine is a powerfully addictive drug of abuse. Once having tried cocaine, an individual cannot predict or control the extent to which he or she will continue to use the drug.

Physical effects of cocaine use include constricted peripheral blood vessels; dilated pupils; and increased temperature, heart rate, and blood pressure. The duration of cocaine's immediate euphoric effects, which include hyperstimulation, reduced fatigue, and mental clarity, depends on the route of administration. The faster the absorption, the more intense the high. On the other hand, the faster the absorption, the shorter the duration of action. The high from snorting may last 15 to 30 minutes, whereas that from smoking may last 5 to 10 minutes. Increased use can reduce the period of stimulation.

Some users of cocaine report feelings of restlessness, irritability, and anxiety. An appreciable tolerance to the high may be developed, and many addicts report that they seek but fail to achieve as much pleasure as they did from their first exposure. Scientific evidence suggests that the powerful neuropsychological reinforcing property of cocaine is responsible for an individual's continued use despite harmful physical and social consequences. In rare instances, sudden death can occur on the first use of cocaine or unexpectedly thereafter. However, there is no way in which to determine who is prone to sudden death.

High doses of cocaine and/or prolonged use can trigger paranoia. Smoking crack cocaine can produce a particularly aggressive paranoid behavior in users. When addicted individuals stop using cocaine, they often become depressed. This also may lead to further cocaine use to alleviate depression. Prolonged cocaine snorting can result in ulceration of the mucous membrane of the nose and can damage the nasal septum enough to cause it to collapse. Cocaine-related deaths often are a result of cardiac arrest or seizures followed by respiratory arrest.[12]

other illicit drugs, women usually are introduced to cocaine by men. Just as many women turn to prostitution to support their heroin addiction, the same is true when cocaine becomes an addiction.

The vulnerability for cocaine abuse might be associated with growing up in alcoholic families. In two treatment centers that treat cocaine addiction, 80% of the patients came from alcoholic families.[13]

Few women who are cocaine abusers use only cocaine. Insomnia, depression, paranoia, agitation, and irritability resulting from cocaine usually are the downside of the cocaine high. Most women use large amounts of alcohol, tranquilizers, or barbiturates to deal with the side effects of cocaine and to self-medicate. For an alcoholic woman, cocaine abuse makes it that much more difficult to stop drinking because alcohol is part of the upper-downer syndrome of cocaine addiction. For women who abuse cocaine without previous alcohol histories, they may readily develop a secondary dependence on alcohol. Women are coming into alcohol and drug treatment centers with combined alcoholism and cocaine dependence. Unless the treatment center is well informed about the treatment of cocaine abuse, women might receive inadequate information. Alcoholism-trained staff also might have ambivalent or negative attitudes toward the treatment of simultaneous cocaine abuse and alcoholism. Moreover, cocaine-abusing women might be abusing not only alcohol but also heroin or prescription opiates. Some intravenous drug-using women might do "speedballs," that is, injecting combinations of heroin and cocaine—a potentially fatal mix. Dual physical dependence, as well as triple physical dependence on alcohol, cocaine, and heroin, presents a serious threat due to complications and severity of withdrawal.

The definition of addiction most helpful in addressing cocaine is *a compulsion to use a drug, loss of control over the amount used, and continued use in spite of adverse consequences.* Using this definition, cocaine is considered a drug with high addiction potential. One treatment program describes the process of cocaine abuse:

When people mix cocaine and alcohol consumption, they are compounding the danger that each drug poses and unknowingly forming a complex chemical experiment within their bodies. National Institute on Drug Abuse-funded researchers have found that the human liver combines cocaine and alcohol and manufactures a third substance, cocaethylene, that intensifies cocaine's euphoric effects while possibly increasing the risk of sudden death.[14]

The cocaine patients we have treated used cocaine compulsively, and their use was limited only by cocaine availability or legal, medical, or psychiatric complications. They continued to use despite loss of their personal or business financial resources, the negative impact on their marriages and families, and deterioration of their work capacity or employment. Even within the structure of an outpatient recovery program, many cocaine abusers have great difficulty remaining cocaine free.[15]

Cocaine-abusing women are a heterogeneous group in terms of the severity of their cocaine abuse and their treatment needs. Women may be taking cocaine intranasally, injecting cocaine intravenously (a high risk for AIDS transmission), or (most dangerous) smoking cocaine freebase in the form of crack.

Some women are occasional users. Most alcoholic women who start as occasional users increase the frequency and quantity of their use. One survey of people calling a cocaine hotline revealed that 70% had binged on cocaine, using it continuously for 24 hours or more.[16] Crack, a powdered form of cocaine that comes in smokeable "rocks," is particularly dangerous because of its easy availability, low cost, and highly addictive potential. The intensity of the crack high is extreme, but the effect wears off quickly.

Women who have developed cocaine or crack addictions need intensive treatment and support. The recidivism rate, especially for crack, might be

Crack is the street name given to cocaine that has been processed from cocaine hydrochloride to a freebase for smoking. Rather than requiring the more volatile method of processing cocaine using ether, crack cocaine is processed with ammonia or sodium bicarbonate (baking soda) and water and is heated to remove the hydrochloride, thus producing a form of cocaine that can be smoked. The term crack refers to the crackling sound heard when the mixture is smoked (heated), presumably from the sodium bicarbonate.

There is great risk, regardless of whether cocaine is ingested by inhalation (snorting), injection, or smoking. It appears that compulsive cocaine use may develop even more rapidly if the substance is smoked rather than snorted. Smoking allows extremely high doses of cocaine to reach the brain very quickly and brings an intense and immediate high. The injecting drug user is at risk for transmitting or acquiring HIV infection/AIDS if needles or other injection equipment are shared.[17]

high in the beginning. Women might need to go through a treatment program more than once if they are multiply addicted. Many women might resist giving up both cocaine and alcohol because they do not see themselves as dually dependent. According to cocaine treatment professionals, it is important to stress the importance of total abstinence for a number of reasons.

The clinician must emphasize that complete abstinence offers the widest margin of safety, evidenced by the following considerations. First, while staying away from cocaine, one often is more likely to switch to other substances for substitute highs even in the absence of previous problems with these substances. Second, substances that have been used in conjunction with cocaine, such as alcohol and marijuana, acquire the capacity through associative conditioning to trigger intense urges and cravings for cocaine. Third, even a single glass of wine or beer or a single marijuana cigarette may reduce one's ability to resist temptation for cocaine due to the "disinhibiting" effects of these substances. Finally, a thorough evaluation of the patient's present and past use of various mood-altering substances often reveals more significant abuse patterns than were previously recognized; that is, because alcohol and other drugs often are used to self-medicate cocaine side effects rather than to get high, the user often is unaware of having acquired a simultaneous dependency on other substances.[18]

Depression is a common experience for women who are getting sober and clean. It often is drug related and will subside in the first year of abstinence. Severe sexual dysfunction also might persist in early abstinence, although this condition can improve as a woman gains time away from cocaine. For cocaine-addicted women, the layers of guilt, grief, and fear in relation to sex and cocaine are numerous. Relapse prevention work can help women to explore guilt about drug-related sexual behavior as well as feelings of loss about a drug that many women experience as initially enhancing and empowering during sex.

A combination of individual and group therapy provided in an outpatient setting has been found to be successful with multiply addicted women after an initial detoxification in an inpatient setting of 3 to 4 weeks. Additional emphasis should be placed on helping the cocaine addict to structure her time and include an exercise regimen. Research shows that regular aerobic exercise affects the areas of the brain that induce drug cravings, lowering the urges to use drugs. Craving for cocaine is experienced intensely for most cocaine-abusing women and can last for many months. Groups of recovering cocaine abusers can help each other in their efforts to deal with cocaine craving. In some communities, Cocaine Anonymous, a program similar to NA and AA, is a valuable resource for women who have been cocaine addicted. All three self-help groups are supportive to women who need to address both cocaine and alcohol.

Marijuana

The liberalization of attitudes toward recreational drug use is directly related to the wider acceptance of marijuana during the 1970s. In 1980, two thirds of young adults had smoked marijuana, compared to 5% during the mid-1960s. Although marijuana is an illegal substance, its use is not considered an illegal behavior by many Americans. Marijuana remains the most commonly used illicit drug in the United States.[20] There were an estimated 2.4 million people who started using marijuana in 1995. According to data from the 1996 National Household Survey on Drug Abuse, more than 68.6 million Americans (32%) 12 years of age or older had tried marijuana at least once in their lifetimes, and nearly 18.4 million (8.6%) had used marijuana during the preceding year.[21]

Marijuana is a green or gray mixture of dried, shredded flowers and leaves of the hemp plant *Cannabis sativa*. There are more than 200 slang terms for marijuana including pot, herb, weed, boom, Mary Jane, gangster, and chronic. It usually is smoked as a cigarette (called a joint or a nail) or in a pipe or bong. In recent years, it has appeared in blunts, that is, cigars that have been emptied of tobacco and refilled with marijuana, often in combination with another drug such as crack. Some users also mix marijuana into foods or use it to brew tea.

The main active chemical in marijuana is THC (delta-9-tetrahydrocannabinol). In 1988, it was discovered that the membranes of certain nerve cells contain protein receptors that bind THC. Once securely in place, THC kicks off a series of cellular reactions that ultimately lead to the high that users experience when they smoke marijuana. The short-term effects of marijuana use include problems with memory and learning, distorted perception, difficulty in thinking and problem solving, loss of coordination, increased heart rate, anxiety, and panic attacks.[19]

Marijuana may be a substitute or secondary drug of abuse and is not usually described as the "drug of choice." The effects of marijuana often are less dramatic than those of other drugs but can have serious consequences nevertheless. The psychoactive ingredient in marijuana, THC, affects every organ of the body, dissolving in fatty tissues and staying in the body for a month or more. Marijuana abuse is known to irritate the lungs, depress the immune system, interfere with cognitive functioning, and increase heart rate. Young adult women who are regular users endanger reproduction and pregnancy. THC causes irregular ovulation and menstrual cycles and travels through the placenta, causing complications in pregnancy. Marijuana is addictive, producing symptoms of withdrawal including sleeplessness, irritability, appetite change, and a drug craving that can persist weeks after a woman has stopped using it. The dangers of addiction to marijuana recently have been associated with its increased strength. Marijuana in some parts of the country is 10 times stronger than it was 10 years ago.

Women coming into treatment for alcoholism and/or illicit drug abuse might fail to report their use of marijuana unless explicitly asked. A woman might not consider marijuana an addictive drug or might not be willing to disclose smoking it because she wants to continue its use. She needs to be informed about the dangers of marijuana use and its potential threat to her sobriety. Continuing to use marijuana will undermine her resolve to stay sober and drug free. It will reduce her energy, confuse her thinking, and set up a craving that usually can be satisfied only by picking up another drink or drug. Many professionals and recovering people agree that a woman is not truly sober if she continues to smoke marijuana after she stops drinking or using other drugs. Marijuana withdrawal may be a factor in early sobriety if a woman has been a heavy user. Several weeks after alcohol is out of the system, a woman might experience flu-like symptoms of marijuana withdrawal. She will need to understand the long-term physical withdrawal involved in marijuana abuse and will need reassurance that in time the symptoms will subside.

Other Illicit Drugs

Widespread nonmedical use of prescription drugs, such as minor tranquilizers, barbiturates, antidepressants, amphetamines, and narcotic analgesics, constitutes a form of illicit drug abuse. Current prevalence rates for women are more than double those for men, with sedatives (including minor tranquilizers) and stimulants accounting for most of the difference. Poor and less educated women were found to be more likely to abuse these drugs than middle income women. When prescription drugs are obtained "on the street" or illegally, they might put a woman in the same dangerous subculture as that of other illicit drugs.

Hallucinogens and Psychedelics

Hallucinogens include LSD, mescaline, and psilocybin. LSD is manufactured from lysergic acid and is sold on the street in tablets, capsules, or (occasionally) liquid form. Mescaline, which comes from the peyote cactus, usually is smoked or swallowed in the form of capsules or tablets. The effects of hallucinogens are highly unpredictable and can be frightening. The long-term effects of hallucinogens persist in the form of flashbacks. A woman who has used psychedelics heavily might continue to have mental and emotional problems resulting from the use of these drugs well into her sobriety.

Methamphetamine is commonly known as speed, meth, or chalk. In its smoked form, it often is referred to as ice, crystal, crank, or glass. It is a white, odorless, bitter-tasting crystalline powder that easily dissolves in water or alcohol. The drug was developed early in this century from its parent drug, amphetamine, and originally was used in nasal decongestants and bronchial inhalers. Methamphetamine's chemical structure is similar to that of amphetamine, but it has more pronounced effects on the central nervous system. Like amphetamine, it causes increased activity, decreased appetite, and a general sense of well-being. The effects of methamphetamine can last 6 to 8 hours. After the initial rush, there typically is a state of high agitation that can lead to violent behavior in some individuals.[22]

Methamphetamine or "Crystal"

Methamphetamine is a powerfully addictive stimulant that dramatically affects the central nervous system. The drug is easily made in clandestine laboratories with relatively inexpensive over-the-counter ingredients. These factors combine to make methamphetamine a drug with high potential for widespread abuse.

Methamphetamine is a potent form of speed that is easily produced from legal ingredients in "labs" throughout the country. This drug may be taken intranasally, dissolved in water, or shot intravenously. More than one third of crystal abusers who come to emergency rooms are women, as are one fourth of those who die as a result of its use. Crystal, like cocaine, quickly escalates in use. In some cities, the number of intravenous crystal abusers is similar to that of heroin users. Women who become addicted can suffer immobilizing depression after using the drug, often prompting the simultaneous use of tranquilizers and barbiturates. Crystal addiction can lead to extreme weight loss, personality change, and psychosis. Withdrawal from crystal produces anxiety, intellectual confusion, and sleepless nights for up to 6 months after it has been stopped. A woman who has been abusing crystal will need a great deal of support on a 24-hour basis for many months to deal with acute withdrawal symptoms.[23]

Prescription Drugs Most Frequently Abused

Minor Tranquilizers: Valium, Librium, Serax, Equanil, Miltown, Xanax

These drugs are called "minor" tranquilizers to distinguish them from "major" tranquilizers given for psychosis. They usually are given to relieve anxiety and tension and as muscle relaxants. Valium is one of the most commonly prescribed drugs in the country, especially for women. It also is found in many emergency room cases associated with drug overdoses. Alcoholic women frequently are given these drugs by physicians for the "emotional" problems they experience while drinking. These drugs also are mistakenly sought by women who are attempting to stay away from alcohol and use these drugs as substitutes. These drugs have an extended half-life in the system and can produce a painful and protracted withdrawal. For alcoholic women, the availability and access to mood-altering legal drugs can lead to serious and life-threatening situations.

Minor tranquilizers such as Librium, Valium, and Xanax have pharmacologies similar to that of alcohol. Combining these prescribed drugs with alcohol can produce cross-addiction as well as cross-tolerance. Cross-addiction is a physical and psychological dependence on alcohol and another drug with similar pharmacology, and cross-tolerance is an increasing need for either or both substances to maintain the same effect. The similar effects of alcohol and minor tranquilizers permit women to use prescription drugs as a substitute for alcohol, thereby abstaining from alcohol but using powerful prescription drugs to do so. This sometimes is referred to by professionals as "chewing" one's alcohol. The availability of prescription drugs to alcoholic women becomes life threatening because of intentional and unintentional drug overdoses while drinking. Suicide attempts are frequent among women who have access to bottles of prescribed drugs. Combining alcohol and certain mood-altering drugs, such as tranquilizers and barbiturates, creates an additive or synergistic effect that increases addiction and withdrawal and can increase the possibility of accidental overdose as well. Synergy, an additive action, means that an equation is not one drug plus one drug equals two drugs; rather, the combination is much greater than the two parts combined. Also, women who go into treatment may experience long and difficult withdrawals if they are abusing prescription drugs as well as alcohol. Seen as "medicine," prescription drugs, as well as over-the-counter drugs, often are overlooked in intake assessments and drug histories taken only on illicit substances.

> *Potential interaction with alcohol:* Excessive sedation; decreased alertness and judgment; increased likelihood of auto, home, and workplace accidents

Barbiturates: Amytal, Butisol, Nembutal, Seconal

These depressant drugs are given mainly to women by physicians to treat insomnia and anxiety. They have a high potential for addiction in themselves and can be life threatening in combination with alcohol dependence and misuse. Barbiturate withdrawal requires medical supervision, as does alcohol withdrawal, and the combination can require an extended hospitalization.

> *Potential interaction with alcohol:* Increased sedation, increased depression of autonomic (involuntary) nervous system to the point of being life threatening or fatal

Sedative-Hypnotics (nonbarbiturate): Quaalude, Dalmane, Doriden, Nodular

These drugs are given to induce sleep. They have many of the same risks as barbiturates for addiction potential. When they are given to alcoholic women, they may create life-threatening situations from overdose. Sedative-hypnotics also may be stored in a woman's fatty tissue, and she may feel their effects long after she has ceased taking them.

> *Potential interaction with alcohol:* Excessive sedation, major interference with autonomic and central nervous systems, respiratory arrest; can be fatal

Antidepressants: Sinequan, Tofranil, Elavil, Norpramine, Pertofrane, Aventyl

These drugs are called tricyclic antidepressants. They are considered effective in some types of depression. Although not physically addictive, they do have side effects and may produce nausea and vomiting if stopped abruptly. It is important to obtain competent professional evaluation with a depressed client before either prescribing or discontinuing antidepressant medication.

> *Potential interaction with alcohol:* Confusion, delirium, increased intoxication, reduction in central nervous system functioning, hypertension (elevated blood pressure); possible life-threatening crisis when taken with red wines

Amphetamines: Benzedrine, Dexedrine, Preludin, Ritalin

These stimulant drugs continue to be prescribed as appetite suppressants primarily to women. The Food and Drug Administration disapproved their use for weight loss in 1978, and they have been banned in some states. These drugs produce physical tolerance within a few weeks of use, requiring increasing dosages, and have a high potential for abuse and dependence. For alcoholic women, these drugs produce a serious hazard, both while drinking and while abstinent, and should be avoided for their addiction potential and the physical hazards of excessive use.

> *Potential interaction with alcohol:* Excessive rise in blood pressure with alcoholic beverages containing tyramine (Chianti, Vermouth, pasteurized beer)

Over-the-Counter Drugs Most Frequently Abused

Cough, Cold, and Sleeping Medications: Nyquil, Robitussin, Sominex

Some of these contain alcohol and can produce the same physical and psychological dependence and withdrawal as can any other alcohol-containing beverage. Others contain antihistamines that can become psychologically addictive. Women who are staying sober should abstain from these drugs entirely. These have high addiction potential for alcoholic women. Other non-alcohol-based cold medications and non-codeine-based cough medicines can be used instead.

Stimulants and Diet Pills (containing caffeine): No-Doz, Vivarin, Dexatrim

These medications contain from 100 to 200 milligrams of caffeine, and with extended use, they can produce insomnia, anxiety, and depression. Not only do these medications not work over time, but they can produce withdrawal symptoms such as headaches, irritability, and fatigue. Actively drinking, alcoholic women may use these to counter the effects of excessive drinking and often will abuse them.

Pain Relievers: Aspirin, Tylenol, Excedrin, Dristan, Anacin

In moderation, these drugs might have beneficial effects to relieve pain. However, actively drinking alcoholic women can abuse and overdose on even these relatively benign drugs because of their inability to remember or follow proper dosage. Women in sobriety might need help to learn how to take pain relievers as directed. It also might be important to help these women to explore nondrug alternatives to relieving pain.

Mouthwashes

Some mouthwashes contain alcohol and should be avoided by recovering women. Although not ordinarily ingested, some people fight the temptation to do so when they are newly sober. For those who are particularly sensitive to alcohol, the alcohol in mouthwashes might stimulate a physical craving for more and lower defenses against picking up a drink.

The Importance of a Psychopharmacologist in Planning Treatment

This chapter has touched on only the types of drugs commonly abused in an effort to provide you with a basic background knowledge of the types of problems your clients face with each drug of abuse. After you have taken a thorough drug history, including prescription and over-the-counter drug use, you should seek the advice of a pharmacologist in planning the most appropriate treatment method for your client. For further drug reference, look for a chart from the National Institute on Drug Abuse listing commonly abused drugs in the Staff Training Activities at the end of this chapter. Also, look at the Client Training Activities for basic facts just about alcohol that you can use with your client. Finally, resources are listed at the end of the chapter that provide much more comprehensive and detailed drug information than could be included here.

Intervention and Counseling Strategies

Women who abuse illicit substances are more likely to cite health problems as a main reason for seeking treatment. An important first priority in treating multiply addicted women is physical health care and assessment. They also enter treatment with a multiplicity of stressful life situations that include financial problems, child-rearing issues, family crises, and difficulty with partners. Multiply addicted women also might be under pressure from the criminal justice system and children's protective services. They might suffer from loneliness and isolation but desire connection. Usually, they have no experience seeking help for emotional and interpersonal problems.[24]

Women who are illicit substance abusers need supportive counseling and might require a number of years in treatment. Some of the roles you might play in the course of treatment are limit setter, advocate, treatment coordinator, educator, and therapist. Women who have been involved in an illicit subculture of drug abuse initially might be distrustful and manipulative and could have frequent setbacks. Their progress in the beginning could be slow, and you might become disappointed and frustrated. You will need to understand your feelings and expectations and to set realistic goals for you and your clients. By being flexible and moving into different roles as the need arises, you can meet the challenge of helping a woman with multiple addictions start to live a sober and drug-free life.[25]

References

1. A. Leshner, "Filling the Gender Gap in Drug Abuse Research," *NIDA Notes* 10, no. 1 (1995): 3, 7, as cited in K. Sanders-Phillips, "Factors Influencing Health Behaviors and Drug Abuse among Low-Income Black and Latino Women," in C. Wetherington and A. B. Roman, eds., *Drug Addiction Research and the Health of Women*, NIH Publication No. 98-4290 (Rockville, MD: National Institute on Drug Abuse, 1998).

2. Emanuel Peluso and Lucy Silvay Peluso, *Women and Drugs: Getting Hooked, Getting Clean* (Minneapolis, MN: CompCare, 1988), 109-10.

3. H. Doweicko, *Concepts of Chemical Dependency*, 3rd ed. (Pacific Grove, CA: Brooks/Cole, 1996), 3.

4. Peluso and Peluso, *Women and Drugs*, 4.

5. P. A. Harrison, "Women in Treatment: Changing over Time," *International Journal of the Addictions* 24, no. 7 (1989): 655-73.

6. David N. Nurco, Norma Wegner, and Philip Stephenson, "Female Narcotics Addicts: Changing Profiles," *Focus on Women: Journal of Addictions and Health 3* (Summer 1982): 62-106.

7. National Institute on Drug Abuse. *Heroin: Abuse and Addiction*, NIH Publication No. 97-4165 (Rockville, MD: NIDA, 1997). Available: http://www.nida. nih.gov/researchreports/heroin/heroin2.html#what

8. National Institute on Drug Abuse. *Heroin: 012*. Available: http://www.nida.nih. gov/infofax/heroin.html (retrieved 25 May 1999)

9. Nurco, Wegner, and Stephenson, "Female Narcotics Addicts," 82.

10. National Institute on Drug Abuse. *Heroin: 012*.

11. David E. Smith and Donald R. Wesson, *Treating the Cocaine Abuser* (Center City, MN: Hazelden Foundation, 1985), 5-10.

12. National Institute on Drug Abuse, *Crack and Cocaine: 011.* Available: http://www. nida.nih.gov/infofax/cocaine.html (retrieved 25 May 1999)

13. James Lieber, "Coping with Cocaine," *Atlantic Monthly* (January 1986), 41.

14. National Institute on Drug Abuse. *Crack and Cocaine: 011.*

15. Smith and Wesson, *Treating the Cocaine Abuser,* 11-12.

16. Peluso and Peluso, *Women and Drugs,* 121.

17. National Institute on Drug Abuse. *Crack and Cocaine: 011.*

18. Arnold M. Washton, "Cocaine Abuse and Treatment," *Psychiatry Newsletter 3* (September 1985): 52-53.

19. National Institute on Drug Abuse, *Marijuana: 015.* Available: http://www.nida. nih.gov/ infofax/marijuana.html (retrieved 25 May 1999)

20. Ibid.

21. Ibid.

22. National Institute on Drug Abuse, *Methamphetamine Abuse and Addiction,* NIH Publication No. 98-4210 (Rockville, MD: NIDA, 1998). Available: http://www. nida.nih.gov/research-reports/methamph/methamph2.html#what

23. Peluso and Peluso, *Women and Drugs,* 151-54.

24. Paddy Cook, Christopher D'Amanda, and Elaine Benciavengo, *Intake and Diagnosis of Drug-Dependent Women,* Treatment Services for Drug-Dependent Women, DHHS Publication No. (ADM) 87-1177 (Rockville, MD: National Institute on Drug Abuse, 1981), 78-79.

25. Landry Wildwood and Susan Samson, *The Process of Counseling Drug-Dependent Women,* Treatment Services for Drug-Dependent Women, DHHS Publication No. (ADM) 87-1177 (Rockville, MD: National Institute on Drug Abuse, 1981), 109-12.

TABLE 3.1 Commonly Abused Drugs: Street Names for Drugs of Abuse

Substance	Examples of Proprietary and Street Names	Medical Uses	Route of Administration	Drug Enforcement Agency Schedule[a]	Period of Detection
Stimulants					
Amphetamine	Biphetamine, Dexedrine; black beauties, crosses, hearts	Attention deficit hyperactivity disorder, obesity, narcolepsy	Injected, oral, smoked, sniffed	II	1-2 days
Cocaine	Coke, crack, flake, rocks, snow	Local anesthetic, vasoconstrictor	Injected, smoked, sniffed	II	1-4 days
Methamphetamine	Desoxyn; crank, crystal, glass, ice, speed	Attention deficit hyperactivity disorder, obesity, narcolepsy	Injected, oral, smoked, sniffed	II	1-2 days
Methylphenidate	Ritalin	Attention deficit hyperactivity disorder, narcolepsy	Injected, oral	II	1-2 days
Nicotine	Habitrol patch, Nicorette gum, Nicotrol spray, Prostep patch; cigars, cigarettes, smokeless tobacco, snuff, spit tobacco	Treatment for nicotine dependence	Smoked, sniffed, oral, transdermal	Not scheduled	1-2 days

Hallucinogens and Other Compounds

LSD	Acid, microdot	None	Oral	I	8 hours
Mescaline	Buttons, cactus, mesc, peyote	None	Oral	I	2-3 days
Phencyclidine and analogs	PCP; angel dust, boat, hog, love boat	Anesthetic (veterinary)	Injected, oral, smoked	I, II	2-8 days
Psilocybin	Magic mushroom, purple passion, shrooms	None	Oral	I	8 hours
Amphetamine variants	DOB, DOM, MDA, MDMA; Adam, ecstasy, STP, XTC	None	Oral	I	1-2 days
Marijuana	Blunt, grass, herb, pot, reefer, sinsemilla, smoke, weed	None	Oral, smoked	I	1 day to 5 weeks

Hashish	*Hash*	None	Oral, smoked	I	1 day to 5 weeks
Tetrahydrocannabinol	Marinol, THC	Antiemetic	Oral, smoked	I, II	1 day to 5 weeks
Anabolic steroids	Testosterone (T/E ratio), Stanazolol, Nandrolene	Hormone replacement therapy	Oral, injected	III	Oral: up to 3 weeks (for testosterone and others); injected: up to 3 months (Nandrolene up to 9 months)

Opioids and Morphine Derivatives

Codeine	Tylenol with codeine, Robitussin A-C, Empirin with codeine, Fiorinal with codeine	Analgesic, antitussive	Injected, oral	II, III, IV	1-2 days
Heroin	Diacetylmorphine; *horse, smack*	None	Injected, smoked, sniffed	I	1-2 days
Methadone	Amidone, Dolophine, Methadose	Analgesic, treatment for opiate dependence	Injected, oral	II	1 day to 1 week
Morphine	Roxanol, Duramorph	Analgesic	Injected, oral, smoked	II, III	1-2 days
Opium	Laudanum, Paregoric; *Dover's powder*	Analgesic, antidiarrheal	Oral, smoked	II, III, V	1-2 days

Depressants

Alcohol	Beer, wine, liquor	Antidote for methanol poisoning	Oral	Not scheduled	6-10 hours
Barbiturates	Amytal, Nembutal, Seconal, Phenobarbital; *barbs*	Anesthetic, anticonvulsant, hypnotic, sedative	Injected, oral	II, III, IV	2-10 days
Benzodiazepines	Activan, Halcion, Librium, Rohypnol, Valium; *roofies, tranks, xanax*	Antianxiety, anticonvulsant, hypnotic, sedative	Injected, oral	IV	1-6 weeks
Methaqualone	Quaalude, *ludes*	None	Oral	I	2 weeks

SOURCE: National Institute on Drug Abuse. Available: http://www.nida.nih.gov.

NOTE: Street names are in italics.

a. Drug Enforcement Administration Schedule I and II drugs have a high potential for abuse. They require greater storage security and have a quota on manufacture, among other restrictions. Schedule I drugs are available for research only and have no approved medical use. Schedule II drugs are available only through prescription, cannot have refills, and require a form for ordering. Schedule III and IV drugs are available through prescription, may have up to five refills in 6 months, and may be ordered orally. Most Schedule V drugs are available over the counter.

Staff Training Activities

Activity 1: Questions to Ask a Woman With an Illicit Drug Addiction
Activity 2: Common Definition of Multiple Substance Abuse
Activity 3: Most Commonly Recognized Illicit Drugs
Activity 4: Definition of a Controlled Substance
Activity 5: Facts and Myths About Marijuana

Activity 1:   Questions to Ask a Woman With an Illicit Drug Addiction

The program of Narcotics Anonymous has developed a comprehensive series of questions to ask a woman about her illicit drug abuse. Review the "Am I an Addict?" questionnaire. Go over each question as a group. Which questions are drug specific and which apply to all drug abuse?

Am I an Addict?

Only you can answer this question.

This may not be an easy thing to do. All through our usage, we told ourselves, "I can handle it." Even if this was true in the beginning, it is not so now. The drugs handled us. We lived to use and used to live. Very simply, an addict is a person whose life is controlled by drugs.

Perhaps you admit you have a problem with drugs, but you don't consider yourself an addict. All of us have preconceived ideas about what an addict is. There is nothing shameful about being an addict once you begin to take positive action. If you can identify with our problems, you may be able to identify with our solution. The following questions were written by recovering addicts in Narcotics Anonymous. If you have doubts about whether or not you're an addict, take a few moments to read the questions below and answer them as honestly as you can.

1. Do you ever use alone?

2. Have you ever substituted one drug for another, thinking that one particular drug was the problem?

3. Have you ever manipulated or lied to a doctor to obtain prescription drugs?

4. Have you ever stolen drugs or stolen to obtain drugs?

5. Do you regularly use a drug when you wake up or when you go to bed?

6. Have you ever taken one drug to overcome the effects of another?

7. Do you avoid people or places that do not approve of you using drugs?

8. Have you ever used a drug without knowing what it was or what it would do to you?

9. Has your job or school performance ever suffered from the effects of your drug use?

10. Have you ever been arrested as a result of using drugs?

11. Have you ever lied about what or how much you use?

12. Do you put the purchase of drugs ahead of your financial responsibilities?

13. Have you ever tried to stop or control your using?

14. Have you ever been in a jail, hospital, or drug rehabilitation center because of your using?

15. Does using interfere with your sleeping or eating?

16. Does the thought of running out of drugs terrify you?

17. Do you feel it is impossible for you to live without drugs?

18. Do you ever question your own sanity?

19. Is your drug use making life at home unhappy?

20. Have you ever thought you couldn't fit in or have a good time without drugs?

21. Have you ever felt defensive, guilty, or ashamed about your using?

22. Do you think a lot about drugs?

23. Have you had irrational or indefinable fears?

24. Has using affected your sexual relationships?

25. Have you ever taken drugs you didn't prefer?

26. Have you ever used drugs because of emotional pain or stress?

27. Have you ever overdosed on any drugs?

28. Do you continue to use despite negative consequences?

29. Do you think you might have a drug problem?

"Am I an addict?" This is a question only you can answer. We found that we all answered different numbers of these questions "Yes." The actual number of "Yes" responses wasn't as important as how we felt inside and how addiction had affected our lives.

Some of these questions don't even mention drugs. This is because addiction is an insidious disease that affects all areas of our lives—even those areas which seem at first to have little to do with drugs. The different drugs we used were not as important as why we used them and what they did to us.

When we first read these questions, it was frightening for us to think we might be addicts. Some of us tried to dismiss these thoughts by saying: "Oh, those questions don't make sense. " Or, "I'm different. I know I take drugs, but I'm not an addict. I have real emotional/family/job problems." Or, "I'm just having a tough time getting it together right now. " Or, "I'll be able to stop when I find the right person/get the right job, etc. "

If you are an addict, you must first admit that you have a problem with drugs before any progress can be made toward recovery. These questions, when honestly approached, may help to show you how using drugs has made your life unmanageable. Addiction is a disease which, without recovery, ends in jails, institutions, and death. Many of us came to Narcotics Anonymous because drugs had stopped doing what we needed them to do. Addiction takes our pride, self-esteem, family, loved ones, and ever our desire to live. If you have not reached this point in your addiction, you don't have to. We have found that our own private hell was within us. If you want help, you can find it in the Fellowship of Narcotics Anonymous.

"We were searching for an answer when we reached out and found Narcotics Anonymous. We came to our first NA meeting in defeat and didn't know what to expect. After sitting in a meeting, or several meetings, we began to feel that people cared and were willing to help. Although our minds told us we would never make it, the people in the fellowship gave us hope by insisting that we could recover. Surrounded by fellow addicts, we realized that we were not alone anymore. Recovery is what happens in our meetings. Our lives are at stake. We found that by putting recovery first, the program works. We faced three disturbing realizations:

1. We are powerless over addiction and our lives are unmanageable;

2   Although we are not responsible for our disease, we are responsible for our recovery;

3   We can no longer blame people, places, and things for our addiction. We must face our problems and our feelings.

The ultimate weapon for recovery is the recovering addict."[1]

SOURCE: Copyright © 1986 by NA World Services, Inc. Reprinted by permission.
NOTE: [1]*Narcotics Anonymous*, 5th ed. (Van Nuys, CA: Narcotics Anonymous World Services, Inc., 1988), p. 15.

Activity 2:   Common Definition of Multiple Substance Abuse

Ask the group to brainstorm a definition of multiple substance abuse. Give the following definition and discuss it:

> Multiple substance abuse is defined as the use and abuse of different mood-altering drugs. This may involve the use and abuse of more than one drug, either at the same time or over a period of time, including alcohol, marijuana, other illegal drugs, prescription drugs, or psychoactive over-the-counter drugs. Multiple substance abuse is dangerous because different substances interact with each other to produce unexpected effects and dangers. Dangers include cross-tolerance, cross-dependence, overdose, health problems, accidents, and multiple social and interpersonal problems.

Discussion points:

■ "Street drugs" contain additional substances that can be life threatening, especially because they are unknown.

■ Drugs and alcohol can work against each other to cover up each other's effects. A woman can feel less impaired than she actually is.

■ Once a woman begins to rely on one illegal drug such as marijuana, abuse of other drugs becomes more likely.

■ Alcoholic women who abuse an illegal drug are at high risk for developing dependence and tolerance quickly.

■ Women might use an illegal drug to balance or enhance the effects of alcohol, control their mood, or enjoy the "thrill" of an illegal substance.

■ Alcohol is especially dangerous with the following substances: opiates, cocaine, marijuana, amphetamines, barbiturates, and tranquilizers.

Activity 3: Most Commonly Recognized Illicit Drugs

TABLE 3.2 Controlled Substances

Classification of Drug	Popular Names of Major Drugs	Medical Uses and Possible Effects
Narcotics (opiates)	Heroin Morphine Opium Codeine Paregoric Methadone Darvon Demerol Dilaudid	These drugs are used medically to relieve pain, cough, and diarrhea as well as to induce sleep. They may cause euphoria, drowsiness, respiratory depression, constricted pupils, and nausea. Overdose causes slow shallow breathing, clammy skin, convulsions, coma, and possible death. Potential of physical and psychological dependence is high. Withdrawal lasts from 4 hours to 7 days and usually requires medical intervention.
Depressants	Barbiturates Phenobarbitol Librium Valium Seconal Xanax Equanil Miltown	Sedatives are primarily used as sedative-tranquilizers or sleeping hypnotics pills. The medical use of depressants ranges from calming people down to promoting sleep. Possible effects are slurred speech, disorientation, and drunken behavior without odor or alcohol. Overdose causes shallow respiration, cold and clammy skin, dilated pupils, weak and rapid pulse, coma, and possible death. Potential of physical and psychological dependence is high. Withdrawal symptoms are anxiety, insomnia, tremors, delirium, convulsions, and possible death. These drugs are particularly dangerous in combination with alcohol. Depressants are common drugs of abuse.
Hallucinogens	LSD Mescaline Psilocybin DMT PCP ("angel dust")	There are no medical uses for these drugs (other than PCP, which was developed as a veterinary anesthetic). These drugs produce hallucinations and altered perceptions of time and space. They have no known physical dependence; PCP produces strong psychological dependence. Effects of use are unpredictable. Large amounts can produce drowsiness, convulsions, and coma. Sensations and feelings can be frightening and cause panic, psychosis, and long-term emotional problems. PCP use can produce violent, bizarre behavior as well as death from reported convulsions, heart and lung failure, or ruptured blood vessels in the brain.
Cannabis	Marijuana ("pot") Hashish ("hash") THC	Cannabis has limited medical use. THC can be used with glaucoma and cancer patients. Possible effects of these drugs are euphoria, relaxed inhibitions, increased appetite, and disoriented behavior. These drugs have demonstrated psychological dependence after long-term use. Effects of overdose are fatigue, paranoia, and possible psychosis. A motivational syndrome (burnout) can occur for marijuana smokers after prolonged use, producing apathy and isolation. Withdrawal symptoms include insomnia, hyperactivity, and decreased appetite in some people.
Stimulants	Amphetamines Benzadrine Dexedrine Ritalin Biphetamine Cocaine Crack	Stimulants have limited medical use. Amphetamines are prescribed for short-term treatment of obesity, narcolepsy, and hyperactivity in children. Cocaine is illegal except when used by a physician as a local anesthetic. Effects of these drugs include increased alertness, excitation, euphoria, dilated pupils, increased pulse rate and blood pressure, insomnia, and loss of appetite. The potential for psychological dependence is high. Data regarding physical dependence is inconclusive. Overdose causes agitation, increases in the body temperature, hallucinations, convulsions, and possible death. Withdrawal symptoms are apathy, long periods of sleep, irritability, depression, and disorientation.

SOURCE: This information was excerpted from Drug Enforcement Administration, *Drugs of Abuse,* vol. 6, no. 2, and adapted for use by the CASPAR Alcohol Education Program in Learning About Drugs, a K-6 drug curriculum.

Activity 4:   Definition of a Controlled Substance

Controlled substances are drugs that have the potential to produce substantial and detrimental effects on the health and welfare of people who use them. Many of these drugs have legitimate medical uses but are liable to cause psychological and physical dependence. Others affect the central nervous system so that they might render the user dangerous to himself or herself or to others. All pose recognizable social and behavioral problems.

Drugs of abuse, together with certain of their immediate precursors, are specifically cited in Title II of the Comprehensive Drug Abuse Prevention and Control Act of 1970, commonly known as the Controlled Substances Act. The Drug Enforcement Administration is the federal agency directly responsible for enforcing the provisions of this act.

■ Major control mechanisms impose restrictions on the manufacturing, purchasing, and distributing of substances listed under this act. Drugs are divided into schedules, ranging from Schedule I (drugs with a high potential for abuse and no accepted medical use) to Schedule V (drugs with a low potential for abuse and current accepted medical use). In making decisions about the level of control to place on a drug, the following factors are considered:

a. The drug's actual or relative potential for abuse

b. Scientific evidence of its pharmacological effects (if known)

c. The state of current scientific knowledge regarding the drug or other substances

d. Its history and current pattern of abuse

e. The scope, duration, and significance of abuse

f. What, if any, risk there is to the public health

g. Its psychological or physiological dependence liability

h. Whether the substance is an immediate precursor of a substance already controlled under this title

Activity 5:   Facts and Myths About Marijuana

Marijuana often is not considered a dangerous illicit drug by women. Many women will not admit to marijuana use because of misinformation and denial. Review the myths and facts about marijuana.

Myth: Only a few hippies, radicals, and artists smoke pot.

Fact: Marijuana is the most commonly used illicit drug in the United States.

Myth: Marijuana is a safe drug.

Fact: The daily use of one to three marijuana joints can produce the same lung damage and potential cancer risk as smoking five times as many cigarettes. Smoking marijuana and using cocaine simultaneously can overtax the cardiovascular system and cause severe heart rate and blood pressure increases. Marijuana can impair critical skills related to learning, attention, and memory even 24 hours after stopping use.

Myth: Marijuana is not addictive.

Fact: People can become psychologically dependent on pot and have physical withdrawal symptoms after stopping heavy use.

Myth: Marijuana makes people more creative and social.

Fact: A series of studies showed that marijuana often is used to avoid dealing with difficulties. Although marijuana users believed that the drug helped them to understand themselves, the studies indicated that the drug actually serves as a barrier against self-awareness.

Myth: Marijuana does not have long-term effects as do other drugs.

Fact: Long-term marijuana use produces changes in the brain similar to those seen after long-term use of drugs such as cocaine, heroin, and alcohol. These changes may make a person more vulnerable to addiction to other drugs by "priming" the brain to be more easily changed by drugs in the future.

Client Training Activities

Activity 1

See "Am I an Addict?" questionnaire in Staff Training Activities.

Activity 2

Regarding the effects of alcohol, the following is reprinted from *Criminal Conduct and Substance Abuse Treatment:*

Session 7: Basic Knowledge About Drugs

1. Objectives of session:

   - Give your view of addiction

   - Learn some basic facts about alcohol and other drugs

   - Learn how alcohol affects the body

2. For thought and discussion: What is and what causes alcohol and drug addiction?

3. Here are some basic things about drugs that people who have developed [alcohol or drug] problems need to know so as to make changes in their [alcohol or drug] use:

a. About drugs

1. Definition of *drug:* A drug is a substance that changes or alters the way in which a person feels, thinks, or acts.

2. Drugs work because they have an effect on both the person's nervous system by changing the flow of electricity and the release of the body's natural nerve chemicals called *neurochemicals.*

3. There are two types of drugs: drugs that slow down the nervous system and drugs that speed up the working of the nerves.

    ■ Drugs that slow down the nervous system are called *suppressors,* sedatives, or downers (e.g., alcohol, barbiturates, tranquilizers, opioids).

    ■ Drugs that speed up, excite, or pick up the nervous system are called *enhancers,* stimulants, or uppers. Some of these drugs speed up the body and mind (e.g., speed, cocaine). Some of these drugs speed up only the mind (e.g., acid, PCP).

4. Drugs have a direct and an indirect effect on people:

    ■ The direct effect (during use effect) is what happens when you are on the drug. It may be physical (e.g., alcohol causes sleepiness) or psychological (alcohol makes you feel good).

    ■ The indirect effect is what happens after the drug no longer is in the body. The body reacts to its absence. This is the abstinence reaction. *Indirect effect of alcohol:* unable to sleep. *Direct effect of cocaine:* unable to sleep.

5. Different types of drugs will have different direct effects and different indirect (withdrawal) effects:

    ■ Direct effects of a drug will be different and usually the opposite of indirect effects of a drug. When alcohol is in the blood, it slows down the nervous system (go to sleep). When it is gone, the nervous system speeds up, and you might shake or be unable to sleep. When cocaine is in the body, the nerves speed up. When cocaine leaves the body, the nervous system slows down.

    ■ Both the direct and indirect effects of a drug can cause problems.

    ■ Table 3.3 provides the direct and indirect effects from the two different types or classes of drugs.

6. When drugs are taken, they make the body toxic.

    ■ Drugs toxify or poison the body. When the drug (*drug* also includes alcohol) has been in the body for a time, the body has to detoxify when the drug leaves the body. This can cause a shock to the body. We call this the *abstinence reaction* or *withdrawal.* Sometimes this reaction is only mental; often, it is a direct physical response of the body. It can be dangerous. The reaction can be so strong that the nervous system can have a very strong shock even to the point where it will result in an epileptic seizure.

7. Your tolerance for drugs can increase, and you can become physically and psychologically dependent on drugs.

TABLE 3.3 Two Classes of Drugs With Their Direct and Indirect Effects

	System Enhancers (stimulants)	
System Suppressors or Depressants	Mental Enhancers	Mental-Physical
Alcohol	Cannabis	Amphetamines
Sedatives (barbiturates)	Hallucinogens (speed)	Cocaine
Inhalants (small amounts)	Phencyclidine (PCP)	Caffeine
Opioids (heroin)	MDMA (ecstasy)	
Tranquilizers		

Direct effects
- Drowsiness
- Slurred speech
- Lack of motor coordination
- Confusion
- Aggressive actions
- Poor work performance
- Auto accident
- Driving while intoxicated
- Decreased social and interpersonal involvement
- Depression

Indirect effects
- Hyper and excited
- Stimulation
- Agitation and irritability
- Hallucinations/delusions
- Anxiety, fear, panic
- Shakes and tremors
- Unable to sleep (insomnia)
- Interpersonal impairment
- Work impairment
- Decreased responsibility to others

Direct effects
- Insomnia
- Weight loss
- Tremors
- Hyperactivity
- Panic
- Poor work performance
- Hallucinations/delusions
- Aggressive actions
- Inappropriate social and interpersonal behavior
- Stimulation

Indirect effects
- Sedation and slowness
- Depression
- Fatigue
- Guilt
- Indifference, lethargy
- Body slows down
- Sleeping too much
- Interpersonal impairment
- Work impairment
- Decreased responsibility to others

As you use a certain drug, you might need more and more of the drug to get the same reaction, or you might find that the same amount of drug will give you less of what you expect from the drug. This is what we call *tolerance*. It varies from drug to drug. Where two drinks might have brought on a "buzz" or feeling of relaxation, after some time of using alcohol, you might find that you need three drinks to get the same buzz or to feel the same amount of relaxation. A daily quart of vodka might be required to get the same effect as a half pint of vodka once did. You might need as much as 10 times the amount of some narcotics (e.g., heroin) to get the same effect. This is one reason why people get dependent on drugs.

8. Mixing two drugs in the body at the same time may increase the strength of one or both drugs. We call this *drug interaction*.

A drug may get stronger because another drug is in the body. This can be very dangerous. The presence of alcohol and a barbiturate in the body at the same time lowers the fatal dose of the barbiturate by 50%.

b. About alcohol

Because alcohol is one of the most commonly used drugs, we look at some specific facts about alcohol:

1. Alcohol is a sedative-hypnotic drug; it puts you to sleep. It is a system suppressor— a downer.

2. Alcohol per drink: One drink equals about one half ounce (12 grams) of pure alcohol. Each of the following is considered one drink:

    a. One 12-ounce can of beer

    b. One 4-ounce glass of wine

    c. One mixed drink: 1 ounce of 80 proof (40% pure alcohol) or one half ounce of pure alcohol

3. Alcohol in the body is measured through the *blood alcohol concentration* (BAC). BAC is the percentage of alcohol in the body. A BAC of .10 means that you have one tenth of 1% of alcohol in your body. That does not sound like much, but consider the following.

4. Our response to different BAC levels:

    a. 02-.03: feel relaxed and decreased judgment

    b. 05: not walk normally; decreased judgment; perform poorly; in Colorado, legally impaired

    c. .08: definite driving impaired; legally drunk in some states

    d. .10: clearly not able to function normally; lack of muscle control; poor coordination; poor judgment; decreased emotional control; legally drunk

    e. .15: more severe impairment than .10; 25 times more likely to have fatal accident

    f. .20: all of the preceding including amnesia, blackouts; 100 times more likely to have fatal accident

    g. .30: most will lose consciousness or pass out

    h. .40: almost all will lose consciousness

    i. .45-.60: fatal for most people

5. The level of BAC depends on the weight of the person, the number of drinks, and the length of time over which these drinks are taken. Table 3.4 provides the approximate information for number of drinks within three time periods that will result in either a .05 or a .09 BAC. This table is generalized to men and women. Table 3.5 provides information regarding approximate number of hours from the first drink to a zero BAC based on varying numbers of drinks for both men and women.

6. Alcohol dissolves in water. About 98% is broken down in the digestive system, and 2% leaves the body through the breath and urine.

TABLE 3.4 BAC Levels by Body Weight, Hours Over Which the Person Drinks, and Number of Drinks

Number of Hours of Drinking	120 Pounds		140 Pounds		160 Pounds		180 Pounds	
	.05 BAC	.09 BAC	.05 BAC	.09 BAC	.05 BAC	.09 BAC	.05 BAC	.09 BAC
1 hour	2	4	2	4	3	5	3	5
2 hours	3	5	3	5	4	6	4	6
3 hours	4	6	4	6	5	7	5	7

NOTE: BAC = blood alcohol concentration. BAC based on number of drinks and body weight. Men and women will vary. Figures in table refer to numbers of drinks for the given time periods.

TABLE 3.5 Approximate Hours From First Drink to Zero Blood Alcohol Concentration Levels

Number of Drinks	120 Pounds	140 Pounds	160 Pounds	180 Pounds	200 Pounds	220 Pounds	240 Pounds	260 Pounds
Men								
1	2.0	2.0	2.0	1.5	1.0	1.0	1.0	1.0
2	4.0	3.5	3.0	3.0	2.5	2.0	2.0	2.0
3	8.0	5.0	4.5	4.0	3.5	3.5	3.0	3.0
4	8.0	7.0	6.0	5.5	5.0	4.5	4.0	3.5
5	10.0	8.5	7.5	8.5	6.0	5.5	5.0	4.5
Women								
1	3.0	2.5	2.0	2.0	2.0	1.5	1.5	1.0
2	6.0	5.0	4.0	4.0	3.5	3.0	3.0	2.5
3	9.0	7.5	6.5	5.5	5.0	4.5	4.0	4.0
4	12.0	9.5	8.5	7.5	6.5	6.0	5.5	5.0
5	15.0	12.0	10.5	9.5	8.0	7.5	7.0	6.0

NOTE: Figures in table refer to numbers of hours before reaching a blood alcohol concentration of zero.

7. An average drink of one half ounce pure alcohol has about 80 to 90 calories. Four drinks make up 325 calories based on pure alcohol. One beer, one glass of wine, or one mixed drink can give the body about 200 calories.

8. Drinkers often are classified based on the amount of alcohol used on one occasion:

   a. Light drinker: one drink

   b. Moderate drinker: two to three drinks

   c. Heavy drinker: four to five drinks

   d. Excessive drinker: six or more drinks

9. The frequency of drinking often is classified as follows:

   a. Infrequent: less than one time a month

   b. Occasional: less than one time a week

   c. Frequent: one to three times a week

   d. Consistent: four or five times a week

   e. Daily/sustained: six or seven times a week

10. What type of drinker have you been? Find this out by putting together how often you drank with the amount you drank. For example, if you drank two or three drinks one to three times a week, then you would be classified as a frequent-moderate drinker.

11. You will get more drunk and have less control over alcohol if you weigh less, are female have no food in the body, have little sleep, drink over a longer period of time, and are relaxed. A person who has been drinking for several years and who has had six or seven drinks might not look drunk or intoxicated but could have a BAC of .10. This is due to what we call *behavioral tolerance.*

12. Impact on the body:

    Liver: The liver can become diseased when there is a buildup of fatty tissue in the liver. Fatty tissue separates the cells. Fatty tissue builds up when you drink a lot or even moderate amounts a day. When fatty tissue separates the cells, less blood gets to the cells. The cells die. This leads to what we call *cirrhosis.* This is the replacing of dead liver cells with scar tissue. Drinking more than six drinks a day will increase the risk of liver disease and cirrhosis.

    Your stomach and digestive organs: Alcohol irritates the stomach lining, and this can lead to development of ulcers. This can occur in moderate to heavy drinkers, depending on how vulnerable the person is to stomach ulcers. This risk increases if alcohol is used with other stomach irritants such as aspirin.

    Your heart and blood system: Heavy to excessive amounts of alcohol, particularly associated with smoking, can increase risk of heart problems and can increase blood pressure. One or two drinks a day will most likely not increase risk of heart problems or high blood pressure.

    Our brain and nerves: Heavy to excessive amounts of alcohol can hurt the brain and our body nerves. The brain has a way of blocking alcohol from getting to it if the alcohol amount is small. This is the blood-brain barrier. But several drinks can break this barrier. When this barrier is broken, the brain cells might be hurt or damaged by the alcohol. Excessive drinking can damage nerve cells in all parts of the body. Excessive drinking can damage the nerve cells in the hands, feet, and other body extremities noted by the tingling of the fingers and feet.

13. Breaking down the alcohol:

    The body breaks down the alcohol. We call this the *metabolism* of alcohol. The breakdown of alcohol depends on gender and body fat. A person with a lot of body fat will break down alcohol at a slower rate. That person might actually end up with a higher BAC. Table 3.5 shows that if a heavier person drinks the same as a lighter person, the heavier person might have a lower percentage of alcohol in his or her blood. But if the heavier person has more body fat, then the heavier person might end up with a higher BAC level. The person with high body fat also might have a greater risk of alcohol damaging or harming the body. Because women have a higher percentage of body fat, they may be at more risk for developing physical problems from drinking.

14. The frequent-heavy to frequent-excessive drinker has a much higher risk of alcohol harming the body.

SOURCE: Kenneth W. Wanberg and Harvey B. Milkman, *Criminal Conduct and Substance Abuse Treatment: Strategies for Self-Improvement and Change—The Participant's Workbook* (Thousand Oaks, CA: Sage, 1998), 45-50.

Activity 3

Take a thorough drug history using the Drug Use History inventory and the prescription and over-the-counter use survey handout. This might take more than one session and could require additions as the client's memory becomes clearer. Familiarize yourself with names of drugs in each category because clients more often recognize individual names. For example, a client might not recognize that PCP (angel dust) is a hallucinogen or that Percodan and Dilaudid are narcotics.

Drug Use History

Frequency	How Taken	Severity
0—No use during past month	1—Oral	0—Not a problem
1—Once per month	2—Smoking	1—Slight
2—Once per week	3—Inhalation	2—Moderate
3—Two to three times per week	4—Intramuscular	3—Severe
4—More than three times per week	5—Intravenous	
5—Once daily	6—Two to three times daily	
	7—More than three times daily	

Past History	Current Use (during 1 month prior to treatment)	
Year of First Use Frequency of Use	Age of First Use Usual Dose	Current Use (yes = regular use) How Taken

Drugs used

Heroin

Nonprescribed methadone

Other narcotics (opiates) or synthetics (specify)

Alcohol

Barbiturates

Amphetamines

Valium

Other sedatives or sedative-hypnotics

Cocaine

Marijuana/hashish

Hallucinogens

Inhalants

Over-the-counter drugs

Tranquilizers

Other(s) (specify)

| Current drugs of preference | Primary: | Secondary: |

Activity 4

Clients can benefit greatly from frank discussion and help with working through the intense cravings or urges for drugs. Have the client identify five cues or "triggers" that bring on the desire to use cocaine such as the following:

- Certain songs

- A salt shaker

- Sexual attractions

- Times of the day or days of the week

- Seeing a small hand mirror

- A certain restaurant

Each week, add others to the list. Go over the "Weekly Self-Monitoring of Craving" form to help the client learn triggers and coping skills. Collect on a weekly basis and spend time identifying patterns and encouraging the positive actions the client has taken.

Weekly Self-Monitoring of Craving

Week of _____ First name _____

Date	Time of Day	Describe Situation Before Craving (e.g., what you were doing, who you were doing it with, body state, mood)	Identify substance craved (alcohol or other drug)	Rate severity of craving (1 = low, 10 = severe)	Length of Craving	Effectiveness of Your Action Taken to Deal With Craving	Activities in Dealing With Craving

Circle the number that indicates the usual degree of craving you experienced during the past week:

0	1	2	3	4	5	6	7	8	9	10
None		Low			Moderate			Severe		

Activity 5

Due to the damaging effects of drug use, it is vital to attend to health care and to involve recovering women in taking responsibility for their own health. Dental care and a physical examination with a gynecological workup probably will be necessary. Counselors should be prepared to follow up with detailed information about birth control and preventing sexually transmitted diseases in language that is appropriate and culturally relevant to the client. Frankness with health care providers about drug use is advised because certain routes of administering drugs put women at risk for various illnesses.

Activity 6

Clients who have injected drugs should be provided with information about preventing transmission of HIV and AIDS. Discouraging the sharing of "injecting drug works" (i.e., syringes, needles, cotton) and instructing clients in how to use bleach to clean needles and the importance and details of safer sex are critical parts of this information. Even if clients currently are drug free, they might have partners and friends with whom they can share the information. Having education and practicing new behaviors might prove vital if a client should relapse.

Activity 7

Encourage clients to begin to make lifestyle changes. Because many of these probably will feel overwhelming to the client, be prepared to listen, offer support, and encourage change even in the smallest of increments:

- Throw out all drugs and paraphernalia
- Avoid drug-using friends, partners, former dealers, and drug-using environments
- Plan leisure time and include exercise, although nothing strenuous until the client has a physical examination
- Seek positive involvement with other recovering people to end boredom and make client feel useful by attending Narcotics Anonymous, Alcoholics Anonymous, and informal support groups
- Assess and begin to address old debts, outstanding warrants, and legal problems

Activity 8

Client education and structured sessions or groups should address the following:

- Symptoms of withdrawal
- Substitution of other drugs
- Alcohol use (women might deny alcohol dependence but, in fact, have multiple addictions)
- Life skills (e.g., job counseling, referral to training or school programs, reentry skills for work world, parenting skills, budgeting, nutrition)
- Identity issues as a non-drug user ("Who am I now that I do not use drugs?")

Resources

American Council for Drug Education (ACDE)
Address: 164 West 74th Street, New York, NY 10023
Phone: (800) 488-3784
E-mail: mgagne@phoenixhouse.org
Web: http://www.acde.org

(ACDE provides information on health hazards related to using tobacco, alcohol, marijuana, cocaine, crack, and other drugs.)

Canadian Centre on Substance Abuse (CCSA)
Address: 75 Albert Street, Suite 300, Ottawa, Ontario, Canada K1P 5E7
Phone: (613) 235-4048
E-mail: webmaster@ccsa.ca
Web: http://www.ccsa.ca

(CCSA is a national agency that disseminates information on the nature and consequences of substance abuse and also supports and assists organizations involved in substance abuse treatment, prevention, and educational programming.)

National Clearinghouse for Alcohol and Drug Information (NCADI)
Address: P.O. Box 2345, Rockville, MD 20847-2345
Phone: (800) 729-6686, (301) 468-2600
E-mail: info@health.org
Web: http://www.health.org

(As the information service of the Substance Abuse and Mental Health Services Administration of the U.S. Department of Health and Human Services, NCADI distributes bibliographies and publications, posters, videotapes, and prevention curricula and also maintains an extensive full-service library.)

National Cocaine Hotline
Phone: (800) COCAINE (262-2463)

National Institute on Alcohol Abuse and Alcoholism (NIAAA)
Address: 6000 Executive Boulevard, MSC 7003, Rockville, MD 20892-7003
Phone: (301) 443-3885
Web: http://www.niaaa.nih.gov

(NIAAA conducts research and provides health information on preventing alcohol abuse and treating alcoholism.)

National Institute on Drug Abuse (NIDA)
Address: Parklawn Building, 5600 Fishers Lane, Rockville, MD 20857
Phone: (301) 443-6480
Web: http://www.nida.nih.gov

(NIDA conducts research and provides health information on the prevention and treatment of drug abuse.)

New Jersey Alcohol/Drug Resource Center
Address: Center of Alcohol Studies, Smithers Hall-Busch Campus, Rutgers University, 607 Allison Road, Piscataway, NJ 08854-8001
Phone: (732) 445-5528

(This agency serves institutions of higher education, state agencies, communities, and school districts throughout the state and responds to information requests from the general public in New Jersey and beyond with subject bibliographies, fact sheets resource guides, videos on loan, copies of articles, prepared handouts, and more.)

PART II

Special Issues in Enhancing Women's Treatment

4 Guidelines for Counseling

One of the most rewarding experiences for counselors is to see health and confidence return to a woman client after she stops drinking or using drugs. A sober woman in recovery begins to be able to take control of her life once again and, in many ways, for the first time. Counselors who stay involved with sober clients have the opportunity and privilege to observe an exciting process begin to unfold—the reawakening and strengthening of human beings. But the timing in dealing with issues that are appropriate to each stage of women's recovery is of utmost importance.

First Stage: Physical Sobriety

The essential first step for every alcoholic or drug-abusing woman is to obtain and maintain physical sobriety. Stopping drinking or using drugs is the primary requisite for change and growth in every other area of the client's life. Before a client stops drinking or using drugs, she might be very resistant. You might need to work with an actively drinking or drugging woman for many sessions to help her through her denial and become involved in treatment. This often can be a difficult and frustrating period of time for both you and the client. Once a woman has become physically sober, the client and counselor are involved in a different and more gratifying new relationship involving patience, acceptance, and gradual change.

The early or first phase of sobriety for an alcoholic woman lasts from her first day sober up to 2 years, although the process, emerging feelings, and quality of the experience vary greatly between the first month and the 24th month. Your role during this first stage is to support and help a woman stay sober and establish a firm foundation of sober daily living. This is a critical time in a woman's recovery, and she can be easily overwhelmed by the circumstances of her life. Research supports the theory that the relationship between the treatment provider and woman client is a key factor in keeping the client in treatment. It also is suggested that in the recovery process, the woman client first connects with the treatment process and then with herself by learning to meet her own needs.[1]

If you are working with a woman at this stage of sobriety and recovery, you can encourage and support her involvement in Alcoholics Anonymous

(AA) and Narcotics Anonymous (NA), with other sober women, and in alcoholism and drug treatment services. A recovering woman needs to know and feel that she is not alone. She needs to talk to and listen to the experiences of successfully sober women who can provide role models of recovery. You might want to suggest that she find a female sponsor in AA/NA and attending women's groups in AA/NA or in treatment services. It also is helpful if you are able to talk openly about relapse with the client and to let her know that she should continue going to meetings and stay involved in treatment. Relapse back to drinking or using drugs happens to some people during the first year, but it is not an indicator that they are incapable of achieving permanent sobriety. Clients need to understand that it might be necessary to put life issues that arouse too much anxiety and stress "on hold" for a period of time. During this first year or 18 months, you can safely focus on practical issues such as finances, jobs, school, parenting, and the logistics of making time to get to meetings regularly (especially if child care is an issue). It is best to advise a client to guard against substituting love relationships for alcohol and drugs during this period and to keep a real focus on staying sober and taking care of herself.

Relapse Prevention Techniques

Relapse prevention during the early stages involves education about the nature of the disease of alcoholism, covering the thinking processes such as denial and rationalization including education as well as alcohol and drug withdrawal. This education is crucial because neurological and physiological effects and discomfort can cause a client to rationalize a return to drinking or using drugs, thinking that "at least I was not this confused or crazy when I drank." Gorski and Miller describe a list of symptoms that they term "post-acute withdrawal syndrome" or the longer term effects of alcohol withdrawal. Symptoms include poor concentration, shortened attention span, sleep impairments, forgetfulness, difficulty conceptualizing or completing thoughts in a logical manner, and emotional overreaction followed by emotional numbness. These symptoms may begin after abstinence of 2 weeks and may peak at 3 to 6 months, depending on the stage to which the woman's alcoholism had progressed prior to abstinence.[2]

The feelings and emotions that surface during the first phase of sobriety can be overwhelming and puzzling for the newly sober woman. A variety of experiences can happen. Women may report feeling "numb" or "dead inside." When emotions surface, they usually are experienced as depression or anger. Mood swings often are reported during the first year, and these emotional ups and downs appear to happen without cause; sadness, panic, and irritability seem to "come out of nowhere." In actuality, many of these states are related to protracted withdrawal from alcohol and other drugs and have a physiological basis, namely, damage to the central nervous system caused by alcohol. There also can be a "pink cloud" elated feeling during the initial phase of sobriety, from which clients can "crash." Counselors can help clients by predicting or describing these conditions and correlating them with the effects of alcohol use and alcohol withdrawal on the body. Extremes can be lessened by cutting back on caffeine and sugar, which further deplete the body, and instituting a rest and relaxation schedule.

During the latter part of this phase, at 12 to 24 months of sobriety, it is a nearly universal experience that a new layer of feelings becomes available to the recovering alcoholic woman. Whereas feelings earlier were experienced mainly as anger or depression with few subtleties in between, a new range of feelings now emerges that women need help in identifying and expressing. At this time, reconstructive therapeutic work may begin.

You can be immensely helpful in working with the sober woman to understand and deal with feelings that might be overwhelming and frightening. This might take many months of sharing and practicing new behaviors and responses.

Second Stage: Psychological Issues

The second phase of recovery, as defined here, begins at roughly the 2-year mark of abstinence. Having learned how to live sober and to recognize and deal with the feelings, sober women are now able to look at some deeper personal issues that may range from traumatic childhood experiences to issues such as success and conflict avoidance. For a substance-abusing woman, achieving and maintaining sobriety is extremely difficult and emotionally draining work, usually requiring an entire reordering of her life. During the first phase of sobriety, a woman is not ready to deal with difficult psychological issues and unconscious material because she does not have adequate coping skills and the necessary support systems in place. If you attempt the "uncovering" process too soon, then you are risking that the client will return to alcohol and drugs, her old standby for dealing with stress and anxiety. Treatment issues such as incest, child abuse, and sexual identity usually require a strong foundation in sobriety to discuss in safety. It might be necessary to support a woman's denial when she says, for example, "At least my kids haven't been affected." During the early stages of treatment, it is important to show her understanding and support for the difficult tasks she is confronting living as a sober person for the first time. This requires patience, perspective, and self-restraint on the part of the counselor. After establishing a foundation in sobriety, women will be able to look at and face the effects of their drinking on their families as well as any psychological problems preceding their alcoholism.

Once both counselor and client understand that recovery from substance abuse and reestablishment of physical, mental, and emotional health will unfold slowly, it is possible to let the recovery process unfold and to deal with a wide range of concerns, each in its own time. Crises and stress always will occur, however, and the best predictor of a successful outcome will be the client's continuing use of her support network. The Twelve Steps of AA provide a framework for continual self-examination and growth, and a strong foundation in AA provides a recovering woman with a structure and philosophy with which to handle changes and challenges. Other self-help groups, NA, and Women for Sobriety also provide support networks for recovery.

The fact that alcoholism is a disease means that there is a possibility for relapse if treatment and self-care do not remain a priority. This is as important for counselors and clients to recognize at 3 months of sobriety as it is at 3 years or even 13 years of sobriety. In a recent study of 182 women and 148 men in outpatient drug abuse programs, women were much likelier than men to have psychological characteristics predisposing them to drug relapse. These characteristics include low self-esteem, depression, anxiety, and suicidal behavior. Fortunately, women who participated frequently in group counseling lessened their risk for relapse.[3]

Symptoms Leading to Relapse and Trauma Work

Once a woman has gone through detoxification (physical withdrawal from any substance) and achieved initial early sobriety, much of the work you will do involves helping her to achieve an increased understanding of herself in two significant areas. First, for the client to increase her length of sobriety, she must learn to recognize those symptoms that personally lead her to relapse. At the end of this section is a list of potential relapse triggers by broad category. For most women, there are signs early on of patterns of relapse that are important for you to help identify and bring into the work with a client. When she understands how to identify her own trigger behaviors, it will help to reduce the likelihood that these behaviors will lead to a full relapse. Although at times the client might not want to look at the way in which these behaviors are reappearing, it is important to demonstrate in the work that their existence points to a significant risk for relapse. Second, to achieve longer term sobriety, it is important to understand the role that traumatic events (past or current) have played in her life. This can be done by exploring how and why certain traumatic events are triggered by various individuals, life situations, feelings, or physical places. By teaching new coping strategies, you can help the client to soothe herself in positive ways when in pain instead of turning to alcohol and/or drugs. It cannot be stressed enough that you approach trauma work carefully with a client by preparing her well in advance for it. This ensures that the content and timing of trauma work does not jeopardize her sobriety.

Summary

Recovery occurs in stages. The first stage is to provide the necessary education and support to an active woman to help her make the decision regarding how and when to abstain from substance abuse. Different themes will emerge during different time periods with each individual client. Timing of the discussions of these themes will depend on the willingness of the client to cope with relevant personal material.

References

1. A. J. Brooks, "Factors Influencing Women's Recovery from Substance Abuse: A Grounded Theory Approach," *Dissertation Abstracts International* 56, no. 10 (1996): 5759B.

2. T. Gorski and M. Miller, *Staying Sober: A Guide to Relapse Prevention* (Independence, MO: Independence Press, 1986).

3. V. Gil-Rivas, R. Fiorentine, and M. D. Anglin, "Sexual Abuse, Physical Abuse, and Posttraumatic Stress Disorder among Women Participating in Outpatient Drug Abuse Treatment," *Journal of Psychoactive Drugs* 28, no. 1 (1996): 95-102.

▓ Staff Training Activities

Here is a set of case studies for counselors to learn more about the impact of relapse. They can be used by counselors either in staff training sessions or directly with clients. The goal is to deepen one's understanding of the ways in which each client is triggered by her own unique set of relapse triggers given her background, set of values and beliefs, personality, and degree of personal insight.

Activity 1: Case Study—Early Sobriety
Activity 2: Case Study—Middle Sobriety
Activity 3: Case Study—Later Sobriety
Activity 4: Stages of Sobriety for Alcoholic Women

Activity 1: Case Study—Early Sobriety

Susan, 32 years old, has been attending outpatient women's discussion groups and Alcoholics Anonymous for the past 7 months. In group, she is generally quiet and shy, and she rarely speaks unless she is spoken to directly. She has as much sobriety as many others in the group but feels that she has little to offer in terms of her experience. In fact, the other women like hearing from her because she has valuable ideas to contribute and expresses herself well.

When Susan began attending groups, she recently had left a halfway house. She describes her stay there as very positive because it helped her start to open up to other women. Until that time, she had kept all her thoughts, fears, and wishes within.

Over the past few months, she has described herself as withdrawing more from people and feeling very scared to try anything new. She wants to look for work but questions her ability to do anything. In talking about her work history, she minimizes what she has done by saying, "Anyone could have worked there. It was easy." She, in fact, has an excellent work history for the years prior to her alcoholic drinking.

Susan sees other women in the group getting into school or starting work, and she wishes it could be her. She is beginning to resent being an alcoholic and questioning whether it is necessary to go to Alcoholics Anonymous and the group.

Discussion and Reactions to the Case

■ Which of the following issues apply to this client?

a. Questioning her own alcoholism ("Why me?" "Maybe I'm overreacting, and I'm not really an alcoholic")

b. Resenting not being able to drink

c. Mood swings

d. Anxiety, anger, confusion, and grief reaction to giving up alcohol

    e.   Lack of self-confidence

    f.   Transference with counselor

    g.   Lack of sober support network (not active in Alcoholics Anonymous, no sponsor, no group)

    h.   Guilt and shame over past and over drinking or using drugs

    i.   Denial on the part of friends and family

    j.   Physical problems (lack of sleep due to withdrawal, lack of good health care)

■ How would you help her?

Activity 2: Case Study—Middle Sobriety

Dorrie is a 31-year-old woman who has been sober for 18 months. She is a twin who always felt second best to her sister, who is very outgoing and bright. For years, Dorrie tried to compete and then decided to give up.

At this point, Dorrie is using Alcoholics Anonymous and an outpatient group. In the group, she has acknowledged that her anger was what got her into trouble when she was drinking. What she fails to see is the effects of her anger now that she is sober. In the group, she spent the first year depressed and not speaking, even when addressed directly. Now when she does talk, her answers are abrupt and pointed. For example, when asked by the leader how she was doing last week, Dorrie snapped, "What difference does it make to you? You're just doing your job." Her presence causes so much tension in the group that people have chosen to ignore her. She is feeling isolated and does not know how to reach out to people.

Discussion and Reactions to the Case

■ Examine the following issues of anger as they apply to this client:

    a.   Depression usually is the result of repressed anger.

    b.   A woman might be getting rid of a lifetime of buried resentments in angry outbursts.

    c.   A woman needs permission to acknowledge and understand her anger.

    d.   Anger can isolate and alienate a woman from others.

    e.   Women need help to express anger in constructive ways.

    f.   Sober anger can be a tool for identifying other real life concerns and problems.

■ What would you do to help her?

Activity 3: Later Sobriety

Donna is a 41-year-old recovering alcoholic with 3 years of sobriety achieved with the support of Alcoholics Anonymous. She called her clinic for an appointment because she has been having difficulty sleeping. She has been waking during the night feeling extreme anxiety and guilt, which lessens during the day but still is present. Much of her middle of the night fears focus on her children.

Donna's partner of 5 years, Jess, also is a recovering alcoholic who is $1\frac{1}{2}$ years sober. They live with Donna's two children, Eddie (14 years old) and Lisa (17 years old). Lisa has begun to experiment with alcohol and drugs. Several nights during the past few weeks, she came home late smelling of alcohol and acting belligerent. Donna thought that she had worked through a lot of her guilt about her parenting, but recently she is feeling as bad as she did during early sobriety.

Donna herself is from an alcoholic family. When she was a child, her mother progressed from heavy drinking to alcoholism. Her father is alcoholic as well. Her mother became sober 7 years ago, and her father is still actively drinking.

Donna's sense of well-being at work is in sharp contrast to her feelings of well-being at home. In addition to being upset about Lisa, she is feeling increasing unhappiness in her relationship with Jess. She is not sure why, but she has a vague sense of wanting more than she receives. She feels guilty, anxious, and afraid of the possibility of being alone if she begins to tell Jess what she is unhappy about.

Discussion and Reactions to the Case

- Which of the following issues apply to this client?

    a. Family history of alcoholism

    b. Guilt and confusion over parenting

    c. Lack of involvement in Alcoholics Anonymous, Narcotics Anonymous, Women for Sobriety, and ongoing treatment

    d. Failure orientation

    e. Success avoidance (guilt and tension from success)

    f. Conflict avoidance (conflict not addressed or left to fester)

    g. Extreme approval needs (constant proof she is accepted)

    h. Difficulty in communicating needs openly

- How would you help her?

Activity 4: Stages of Sobriety for Alcoholic Women

You should be aware of the time it takes for a client to work through the process of recovery. Resist the temptation to uncover psychological issues and other problems before a sober and drug-free woman has the resources to deal with them. Any timetable of recovery needs to be flexible, adapting to your client's particular needs.

Issues to address in the first year of sobriety:

■ Denial and shame about alcoholism

■ Multiple addictions, the danger of substituting other drugs for alcohol, and the importance of total abstinence from mood-altering substances

■ How to become actively involved in Alcoholics Anonymous, Narcotics Anonymous, Women for Sobriety, and women's support groups

■ How to build a sober support network

■ Education about withdrawal from alcohol and postacute withdrawal syndrome symptoms

■ Alcoholism and drug education as well as the emotional and physical nature of the disease of alcoholism

■ Daily coping skills, especially how to stay away from a drink or a drug and strengthen one's defenses

■ Any immediate health, mental health, and basic living issues such as homelessness, major mental illness, eating disorders, active child abuse, or current family violence

■ Nutrition, rest, routine, and structure

Issues to address as sobriety continues but still in the first 2-year period:

■ Low self-esteem

■ Anger and depression

■ Beginning attempts at naming and identifying a range of feelings

■ Vocational/career-related concerns (including school)

■ Parenting and child care

■ Deepening involvement in Alcoholics Anonymous, Narcotics Anonymous, or Women for Sobriety as well as use of sponsor

■ Dependency and abuse problems with spouses/lovers and developing healthy adult relationships

- Recognition of family-of-origin issues

- Sexuality and sexual identity concerns

- Acceptance of identity as an alcoholic in recovery

- Examination of personal life beyond maintaining sobriety ("Who am I now that I don't drink?")

Issues of concern for 2 to 5 years of sobriety and beyond:

- Strength of continuing Alcoholics Anonymous, Narcotics Anonymous, and Women for Sobriety involvement

- In-depth look at family-of-origin issues, especially if your client is an adult child of alcoholic parents

- Past sexual abuse, incest, or family violence

- A closer look at interpersonal behavior, assertiveness skills, and addressing conflict avoidance

- Underlying emotional and psychological conflicts, guilt, and grief (perhaps over time and opportunities lost due to active alcoholism)

- Effects of your client's alcoholism on her children and loved ones

- Your client's codependency and other addictions

Working relapses into the recovery timetable:

- Should your client relapse, your counseling work should return to the issues presented in early sobriety, even if she was 5 years sober at the time of her relapse.

    1. Review symptoms leading to relapse with your client. Make certain that she understands all of the concepts.

    2. If your client has relapsed previously, then ask her to identify what symptoms, if any, were present prior to relapse.

    3. Discuss with your client any awareness she has of how these symptoms currently are present in her life or in her attitude toward sobriety.

    4. Over a specified period of time, have your client keep a log of symptoms she notices in herself. Have her make a list of which symptoms reoccur. Ask her to share these with you, her Alcoholics Anonymous sponsor, and her support system to educate her sober network about possible ways in which to intervene if she were to start building up to taking a drink. This reinforces the theory that the alcoholic's denial often causes her to be the last one to realize she is in trouble.

Resources

Alcoholics Anonymous General Service Office (AA)
Address: Box 459, Grand Central Station, New York, NY 10163
Phone: (212) 870-3400
Web: http://www.alcoholics-anonymous.org

(General Service Office responds to inquiries, keeps lists of the thousands of AA groups around the world, and provides literature and audiovisual materials.)

Cocaine Anonymous World Services Inc. (CA)
Address: 3740 Overland Avenue, Suite G, Culver City, CA 90034
Phone: (310) 559-5833 (administrative office), (800) 347-8998 (24-hour referral line)
E-mail: cawso@co.org
Web: http://www.ca.org

(CA is a fellowship of people who help each other recover from their addiction to cocaine and other mind-altering substances.)

Crystal Meth Anonymous World Services Inc. (CMA)
Address: 2100 North Beachwood Drive, Suite 412, Los Angeles, CA 90068
Phone: (323) 465-5332
Web: http://members.xoom.com/cma

(CMA is a fellowship of recovering addicts meeting regularly to help one another stay clean using a Twelve Step model.)

National Alliance of Methadone Advocates (NAMA)
Address: 435 Second Avenue, New York, NY 10010
Phone: (212) 595-NAMA (595-6262)
E-mail: nama@interport.net
Web: http://www.methadone.org

(NAMA is an organization composed of methadone patients and treatment providers working together for greater public understanding and acceptance of methadone treatment.)

Narcotics Anonymous World Services Inc. (NA)
Address: P.O. Box 9999, Van Nuys, CA 91409
Phone: (818) 773-9999, ext. 131
Web: http://www.na.org

(NA is a Twelve Step program, modeled after Alcoholics Anonymous, for persons for whom drugs have become a problem and who wish to stop using.)

Nicotine Anonymous World Services (NA)
Address: P.O. Box 591777, San Francisco, CA 94159-1777
Phone: (415) 750-0328
Web: http://www.nicotine-anonymous.org

(NA is a self-help program that helps members and others to live without smoking using the Twelve Step self-help program model adapted from Alcoholics Anonymous.)

National Self-Help Clearinghouse
Address: 25 West 43rd Street, Room 620, New York, NY 10036
Phone: (212) 354-8525
E-mail: info@selfhelpweb.org
Web: http://www.selfhelpweb.org

(This agency conducts training for professional and lay people about self-help methods, carries out research activities, maintains an information and referral databank, publishes materials, and addresses professional audiences about policies affecting self-help groups.)

Women for Sobriety
Address: P.O. Box 618, Quakertown, PA 18951
Phone: (800) 333-1606

(This is a nonprofit organization dedicated to helping women to overcome alcoholism and other addictions.)

5

Designing Treatment Programs

Many women who recover from drug or alcohol dependence do so without entering formal treatment programs. A study exploring the reasons why these women avoid treatment centers has identified a variety of barriers to treatment. These include the fear of being stigmatized for entering treatment, ignorance of available treatment options, problems with child care, worries about the time and financial costs of treatment, and fear of harsh treatment by counselors.[1]

A survey done by the Association of Junior Leagues to obtain information on barriers to treatment, needed services, and services provided to women found the following:

> All three samples (authorities, treatment centers, and gatekeepers) named the same three barriers as the most serious to women in need of treatment for alcohol problems: (a) personal denial of alcohol problems by women themselves, (b) responsibility for care of dependent children, and (c) family denial of women's alcohol problems and/or opposition to women's seeking treatment. . . . Authorities, treatment centers, and gatekeepers agreed almost as uniformly about the three most-needed services for women with alcohol problems: (a) treatment facilities offering child care, (b) halfway houses for women, and (c) all-female self-help groups.[2]

Within the past decade, according to an analysis of the National Drug and Alcohol Treatment Unit Survey[3] (NDATUS, a census of public and private treatment programs), there has been a 53% increase in the percentage of programs offering specialized services for women.[4] However, a recent study of women clients' perceptions of treatment effectiveness shows that even though drug treatment programs might advertise special women-only programs, they do not facilitate them in a way that is supportive and positive for women. The women in the study still experienced negative stereotyping and even sexual harassment.[5]

Comprehensive, nonsexist treatment programs for women need to be developed in every community. Even existing women's substance abuse services might need to be modified to adequately treat different female popula-

> More than 4 million women in the United States need treatment for drug abuse.[6]

tions. Alcoholic or drug-abusing women also may be women of color, elderly, mothers, lesbians, incest survivors, or part of another special population. Women's needs often are complex and diverse. The woman who develops a substance abuse problem needs the help of a society that understands that she has an illness and not a moral failing. She needs to be treated for her alcoholism or drug abuse in a system that recognizes that she is different from men and often has needs for different types of services.

Once in treatment, a woman should be offered a range of treatment options including separate space where she can be free of the pressures to interact with men, particularly during the early stages of recovery. She needs a place to develop confidence in herself as a whole, competent person and to learn from the experiences of other recovering sober women who can serve as healthy role models. She needs to see choices in her life, particularly the choice to live without alcohol and drugs. Because the life context in which women develop substance abuse is different in significant ways from that of men, the treatment context and set of issues for women might require separate treatment time and space.

Women enmeshed in many relationships and "systems" are particularly vulnerable to fragmentation of services. These women often must deal with several treatment and service systems at once such as welfare, mental health, child care, and family services. All too often, such women get shuttled between systems instead of getting the services they need from each system. Studies have shown that women substance abusers often do not enter treatment until they have reached a crisis point, and they will not be able to focus on their addiction until critical basic needs have been sufficiently met such as housing, child care, transportation, and medical assistance.[7]

Insensitivity to the psychological needs of alcoholic women often is coupled with apparent indifference to some of their most urgent practical concerns. For example, the typical woman entering an alcoholism treatment program is in serious financial difficulty and in dire need of job training. According to research by the National Center on Addiction and Substance Abuse, up to 80% of drug-addicted women are unemployed. They have transportation and financial problems. Medicaid often is their only source of health support, and it may be turned down by treatment providers.[8] More often than not, the woman is divorced, has custody of her child(ren), and is receiving little or no support from her ex-husband. Her job skills are likely to be minimal, and she probably has been unable to work steadily for some time. Many women are literally prevented from getting any type of alcoholism treatment because they cannot find anyone to take care of their kids.[9]

The practical realities of a woman's life, as much as her denial, might keep her away from treatment. Consequently, it is not enough to wait for women to come forward asking for help or for an alcoholic or drug-abusing woman to walk in the door of a treatment program. She should be approached in the many settings and systems in which she is presently involved. By helping a woman to negotiate the system and access the services she needs, you have a good opportunity to establish trust early on.[10]

Counselors in all areas of our social services need to identify and invite the substance-abusing woman into treatment. The earlier, the better. Research indicates that women are less likely than men to admit that alcohol is their main problem, and they often enter treatment with more severe and progressed alcoholism or psychiatric disorders.[11] By creating strong outreach programs and community education programs designed specifically to reach various populations of women, we can reach women earlier. Everyone working with women needs to know how to recognize alcoholism or drug abuse, confront a woman with an alcohol or drug problem, begin to break down her and her family's denial, and make a referral for help. By educating ourselves, our agencies, other community counselors, women's organizations, and health care personnel about alcoholism and drug abuse in women, we are more likely to reach hidden populations of substance abusers. For counselors working in an agency, training, consultation/supervision groups, and case presentations that focus on general issues of alcoholic women and on individual clients are an ongoing necessity.

Elements of a Comprehensive Women's Substance Abuse Program

At CASPAR Inc., we have developed a comprehensive treatment approach specifically geared to the needs of women substance abusers. Following is a suggested list of program elements to educate and support individual clients, organizations, and communities. When developing a treatment approach, it is important to involve one's client base and community in the process and to acknowledge that the treatment approach will need to be evaluated over time given changes in client needs, staffing patterns, payment structures, and community programs.

A comprehensive approach to women's substance abuse treatment includes certain key components—training, outreach, and consultation to human service counselors working with women; inpatient services for women needing detoxification and medical care including arrangements for child care; outpatient services that include child care and services for families and significant others; residential treatment programs including services for pregnant women and women with children; graduate housing; and services that are inclusive of special needs populations. For most counselors, the work of enhancing women's treatment begins with learning about the dynamics of women's alcoholism and drug abuse as well as how to treat it. The next step might involve changing their agency to make it more responsive to substance-abusing women. Developing resources in the community for women and/or making the existing alcoholism and drug abuse resources responsive to developing separate women's services are worthwhile long-term goals.

It is important to stress that alcoholic or drug-abusing women are an underserved and overlooked population that lacks understanding advocates. Community change begins with individuals and agencies becoming educated and concerned about substance-abusing women. It is this concern that can lead to the first steps in creating a safe, nonsexist treatment system for women with alcoholism and drug abuse problems.

Outreach

- Outreach workers to do substance abuse education and consultation with community agencies and organizations
- Media work including radio, television, and publication of materials on women and substance abuse for newspapers, magazines, and books
- Linkages with local women's organizations and human service agencies for training, consultation, and information sharing
- Training and consultation for substance abuse providers on women's issues

Inpatient Unit

- Women's detox or separate women's wing and warm home-like atmosphere
- Women counselors and women administrators
- Women's discussion groups and individual counseling
- Individual, group, and family counseling
- On-site and community child care services

Residential Programs

Residential programs, which usually last from 3 to 6 months, help to provide the support and structure the woman needs in her life while she begins living sober. The woman who has a long history of substance abuse might especially benefit from a residential program as a model for sober living and a constant source of support during the first few challenging months of sobriety. There are fewer regulations in these programs than in inpatient programs, but there are many more regulations than there would be if she were living on her own.

These programs are particularly helpful if the woman does not yet have an available sober support network, without which she is at much greater risk to resume drinking or using drugs. Residential programs provide the tools for leading a more structured, disciplined, and responsible life, preparing the woman to live independently when she graduates from the program. For example, most halfway houses require that the woman find work within a certain amount of time after beginning the program. Here are the elements of what a good residential program might offer:

1. All-women's house and homey atmosphere
2. Women counselors and women administrators
3. Accommodations for women with their children
4. On-site child care and child treatment

5. A variety of groups including the following:

   a. Narcotics Anonymous/Alcoholics Anonymous (NA/AA) meetings
   b. Substance abuse education
   c. Parenting skills
   d. Mothers' support group
   e. Sexuality
   f. AIDS education
   g. Vocational/educational issues
   h. Health, personal care, and nutritional counseling
   i. Exercise/relaxation group
   j. Aftercare planning

6. Services for families

   a. Films and discussions
   b. Short-term family group treatment
   c. Individual, couple, and family treatment for family members
   d. Joint treatment of mother and children
   e. Individual work for residents on family issues

Outpatient Program

1. Women's groups including the following:

   a. Substance abuse education
   b. Decisions about drinking/drugging groups
   c. Short-term and long-term clean/sober groups
   d. Special groups for special populations such as the following:

      1. Pregnant women
      2. Mothers
      3. Lesbians
      4. Hispanic women
      5. Black women
      6. Elderly women
      7. Young women

2. Short- and long-term groups addressing family issues

   a. Adult daughters
   b. Children
   c. Friends and partners

3. Short- and long-term individual counseling for substance-abusing women and those close to them

   a. AIDS education and support
   b. Child treatment
   c. Child care for all groups

Alternative
Approaches

Alternative approaches to treatment incorporate a growing appreciation of a more holistic understanding of recovery, reflective of the general trend by both providers and consumers in the fields of health and mental health. These approaches are best used in conjunction with counseling and Twelve Step programs or other support programs. There are a number of different alternative approaches available, and it certainly is not the aim of this manual to try to cover all of them. Overall, the aim of the counselor should be to empower the woman to make choices as to the best treatment combination available to her from a wide range of options. Following are some possibilities.

Acupuncture

Acupuncture is increasingly being used in detox settings because it is believed that it helps to block the cravings and anxiety associated with withdrawal. There still is speculation as to the overall effectiveness of acupuncture; however, some women find it helpful even after the process of detoxification as a way of helping to relieve anxiety.

Nutrition and Vitamin Regimes

There are a few theories as to the role of physiology and food in developing an addiction, and these theories generally center on alcoholism rather than drug addiction. For example, there is a belief that cravings for alcohol are heavily influenced by food allergies that the alcoholic might be unaware of such as those to corn and yeast—common components of alcoholic beverages. Thus, treatment would entail abstinence from all foods or other products containing these ingredients as well as a vitamin regimen to restore needed nutrients.

Addictions also are increasingly being connected with the body's difficulty in metabolizing sugar and producing the natural stimulants and relaxants that the body requires. So, a woman turns to addictive substances as a way of artificially producing these biochemicals. A woman who has difficulty in metabolizing sugar is prescribed a diet that is low in sugar and carbohydrates and is high in protein. Alcohol also has been connected to hypoglycemia and diabetes, and a low-carbohydrate/low-sugar diet and vitamin regime can be useful for both of these.

Relaxation Techniques

Techniques such as massage and meditation can be very effective in counteracting the stress that comes with the challenge of living sober. In the past, the substance-abusing woman turned to substances as a way of coping with stress. Now, she might find it useful to learn the ways in which stress manifests itself in the body and the ways in which she can learn to relax.

Stress Reduction Techniques

Exercise and techniques such as bodywork also are very helpful in providing healthy means of coping with stress and tension. It should be noted that methods that involve being touched by others, such as massage and bodywork, are not necessarily recommended for certain women during early recovery, for example, women also in recovery from sexual abuse for whom touch has not been associated with positive things.

References

1. J. Copeland, "Qualitative Study of Barriers to Formal Treatment among Women Who Self-Managed Change in Addictive Behaviours," *Journal of Substance Abuse Treatment* 14, no. 2 (1997): 183-90.

2. Association of Junior Leagues, *Woman to Woman Community Services Survey* (New York: AJL, 1988), 2.

3. NDATUS is now known as UFDS (Uniform Facility Data Set), performed every few years by the Substance Abuse and Mental Health Services Administration.

4. U.S. Department of Health and Human Services, *Ninth Special Report to the U.S. Congress on Alcohol and Health*, NIH Publication No. 97-4017 (Washington, DC: Government Printing Office, 1997), 376.

5. L. Nelson-Zlupko, M. M. Dore, E. Kauffman, and K. Kaltenbach, "Women in Recovery: Their Perceptions of Treatment Effectiveness," *Journal of Substance Abuse Treatment* 13, no. 1 (1996): 51-59.

6. National Institute on Drug Abuse, *Women and Drug Abuse,* NIDA Capsule Series C-94-02 (Rockville, MD: NIDA, 1994). Available: http://www.health.org/pubs/caps/index.htm

7. S. Coletti, "Service Providers and Treatment Access Issues," in C. Wetherington and A. B. Roman, eds., *Drug Addiction Research and the Health of Women*, NIH Publication No. 98-4290 (Rockville, MD: National Institute on Drug Abuse, 1998), 239.

8. National Center on Addiction and Substance Abuse, *Substance Abuse and the American Woman.* Available: http://www.casacolumbia.org/pubs/jun96/womchap5.htm (retrieved 5 October 1998)

9. Marian Sandmaier, *The Invisible Alcoholics: Women and Alcohol Abuse in America* (New York: McGraw-Hill, 1980), 223.

10. Coletti, "Service Providers."

11. U.S. Department of Health and Human Services, *Ninth Special Report,* 382.

Staff Training Activities

Activity 1: Enhancing a Substance-Abusing Woman's Treatment
Activity 2: Changing Your Agency to Make It More Responsive to a Substance-Abusing Woman's Needs
Activity 3: Preparing a Case Presentation for New Nonsober Clients and Newly Recovered Clients
Activity 4: Enhancing a Woman's Treatment on a Community Level

Activity 1:   Enhancing a Substance-Abusing Woman's Treatment

Ask people to spend a few minutes reflecting on their professional activities with women or alcoholics and then develop some personal objectives and tasks to help them work more effectively. Discuss how people who work with women in community settings will need help in learning about alcoholism and drug abuse and in talking about it with their clients. People working in alcoholism and drug abuse programs might know about substance abuse but know very little about its impact on women's lives.

Following are some ideas:

■ Attend open Alcoholics Anonymous or Narcotics Anonymous meetings and talk with sober recovering women

■ Take courses on substance abuse and women's issues

■ Develop a comfort in raising the subject of alcohol and drugs with female clients

■ Have a series of alcohol-related questions to ask new clients

■ Visit and talk with alcoholism and/or women's service providers in the community

■ Find women counselors (if you are a man) who can work with substance-abusing female clients

■ Attend workshops on special issues for alcoholic or drug-abusing women

Have each person share her ideas with the group as a whole and discuss them.

Activity 2:   Changing Your Agency to Make It More Responsive to a
Substance-Abusing Woman's Needs

Break the group into pairs or groups of three. Ask each group to develop guidelines and recommendations for its agencies to make them more responsive to the needs of alcoholic or drug-abusing women. Again, the focus for caregivers outside of the alcoholism and drug abuse field will be on substance abuse, whereas counselors in the alcohol and drug fields might need to focus on how they work with women. Ask each group to present its guidelines to the group as a whole. These guidelines should include the following:

- Examining agency's written and unwritten policies and attitudes toward treating substance-abusing women

- Developing training opportunities for substance abuse staff on women's issues

- Reviewing intake procedures and including alcohol and drug-related questions on the intake form

- Having an up-to-date referral file of substance abuse and women's services including inpatient, outpatient, residential, crisis services, and special needs services

- Being able to have a woman counselor available to talk with substance-abusing women who are uncomfortable talking with men

- Knowing the Alcoholics Anonymous and Narcotics Anonymous meetings in the area, and the ones that are welcoming to women, as general agency information

- Developing a library of literature on alcoholism and drug abuse, substance-abusing women, and women's issues

- Having ongoing consultation/supervision groups and case presentations around issues and concerns for substance-abusing women

- Doing outreach to different types of women such as women of color, mothers, lesbians, elderly, and adolescents

- Examining staffing within the agencies and links to minority communities

Activity 3: Preparing a Case Presentation for New Nonsober Clients and Newly Recovered Clients

Discuss the "Preparing a Case Presentation for New Nonsober Clients and Newly Recovered Clients" outline. This may be used in a variety of settings by counselors who wish to get help from each other about working with substance-abusing female clients. Stress the following points as important reasons to have regularly scheduled consultation/supervision. Consultation/supervision will help counselors in the following ways:

- Increase sensitivity to picking up alcohol and drug problems in women.

- Learn more about alcoholism and drug abuse.

- Learn when and how to raise the issue of drinking and drug use.

- Discuss healthy dependencies versus unhealthy dependencies.

- Learn more about family alcoholism.

- Discuss how to deal with the prescription of drugs for alcoholic women by therapists and doctors (e.g., "How can we intervene when we know this is happening?").

■ Learn about and discuss resources other than Alcoholics Anonymous and Narcotics Anonymous.

■ Have a place to express frustration in working with alcoholic or drug-abusing women.

■ Look at how our own attitudes about alcohol, alcoholism, and drug addiction affect our treatment with substance-abusing women.

Preparing a Case Presentation for New Nonsober Clients and Newly Recovered Clients

The following questions might help focus and guide a new counselor's treatment plans for new clients. They also might be useful for the counselor and supervisor to discuss together as a kind of progress report on client and counselor.

In preparing for a case presentation concerning a woman whom you suspect has an alcohol or drug problem, it might be helpful to address the following questions:

1.   How long has she been in treatment with you?

2.   Is she involved in other types of treatment? If so, then what?

3.   What makes you suspect that there is a problem with drinking or with drugs?

4.   Have you spoken to her about her drinking or drug use? What have you said? How has she responded?

5.   What is her view of the problem?

6.   What are her goals in treatment?

7.   What are your expectations and goals for working with her?

8.   How are you working with her on these issues?

In preparing for a case presentation concerning a woman in recovery (e.g., a sober woman dealing with her substance abuse), it might be helpful to address the following questions:

1.   How long has she been in treatment with you?

2.   Is she involved in other types of treatment? If so, then what?

3.   What is the length of her sobriety?

4.   What types of support systems does she have?

5.   What are her current issues in treatment?

6.   What is her view of the problem?

7.   What are her goals in treatment?

8.   What are your expectations and goals for working with her?

9.   How are you working with her on these issues?

Activity 4:   Enhancing a Woman's Treatment on a Community Level

A model of community treatment would include a comprehensive program specifically designed to meet the separate needs of substance-abusing women. At the present time, few communities have such programs in place, but it is helpful to have a clear understanding of what services are essential to provide holistic treatment for the alcoholic or drug-abusing woman. Review the recommended list of services in this chapter (Elements of a Comprehensive Women's Substance Abuse Program section) with your staff to see whether any are already established within your community. Discuss what would be the next small steps in developing one or more of these services out of existing programs. Questions to raise in the group:

- Is there an outpatient mental health service that would be willing to develop groups for substance-abusing women?

- What can an inpatient alcoholism program (e.g., a separate women's area, women counselors, women's group) do to make substance-abusing women feel safe and welcome?

- If you were going to develop a community task force on services for substance-abusing women, who would you ask to be on it?

It is important to stress that alcoholic or drug-abusing women are an underserved and overlooked population who need understanding advocates. Community change begins with individuals and agencies becoming educated and concerned about substance-abusing women. It is this concern that can lead to the first steps in creating a safe, nonsexist treatment system for women with alcoholism or drug abuse problems.

Resources

Center for Substance Abuse Treatment (CSAT)
Contact: Camille T. Barry, Acting Director
Address: Rockwall II Building, Suite 618, 5600 Fishers Lane, Rockville, MD 20857
Phone: (301) 443-5052
Hotline: (800) 662-HELP (662-4357) (drug information and treatment referral hotline)
Web: http://www.samhsa.gov/csat

(CSAT was established to direct and coordinate federal efforts to promote treatment of alcohol and other drug problems.)

Hazelden Foundation, Library and Information Resources
Address: Box 11, Center City, MN 55012
Phone: (651) 213-4411 (library), (800) 328-9000 (publishing)
Web: http://www.hazelden.org

(This is a residential treatment program that also provides education and training at its Minnesota Center and other sites. Its library will respond to questions from professionals.)

Join Together
Address: 441 Stuart Street, Floor 7, Boston, MA 02116
Phone: (617) 437-1500
E-mail: info@jointogether.org
Web: http://www.jointogether.org

(This is a national program to help communities fight substance abuse. Programs include Public Policy Panels, a National Leadership Fellows Program, a National Computer Network, a Communications Program, and Technical Assistance to Community Programs. Although Join Together does not have a formal information service, professionals respond to phone queries.)

National Association of Alcoholism and Drug Abuse Counselors (NAADAC)
Address: 1911 North Fort Myer Drive, Suite 900, Arlington, VA 22209
Phone: (800) 548-0497
E-mail: naadac@naadac.org
Web: http://www.naadac.org

(NAADAC is a national professional organization for alcoholism and drug abuse professionals)

National Council on Alcoholism and Drug Dependence (NCADD)
Address: 12 West 21st Street, New York, NY 10010
Phone: (212) 206-6770, (800) NCA-CALL (622-2255) (hotline for referrals)
E-mail: national@ncadd.org
Web: http://www.ncadd.org

(NCADD actively advocates government policies to reduce alcohol and other drug addictions and to provide for the treatment needs and rights of affected people.)

6

Pregnancy and Parenting Issues

The Centers for Disease Control and Prevention has reported an alarming increase in the rates of frequent drinking among pregnant women, from 0.8% in 1991 to 3.5% in 1995. This means that at least 140,000 pregnant women are drinking at harmful levels each year.[1] Because alcohol crosses the placenta freely, consumption of any amount of alcohol is potentially dangerous for pregnant women. Children who are born to women who drink alcohol have a serious risk of having fetal alcohol syndrome (FAS), which is the leading known cause of mental retardation.[2] The possible consequences to the child of an alcohol-abusing mother clearly are very serious.

FAS was first identified in 1973. A unique set of characteristics was identified in children of chronic alcoholic women that involved weight and growth deficiency at birth, distinctive facial features, and central nervous system impairment with developmental delay. According to the National Institute on Alcohol Abuse and Alcoholism, children with FAS frequently have learning, attention span, and memory problems. They also can suffer impaired coordination, speech, and hearing, and they often act impulsively.[4] As they grow up and pass through puberty, the physical features of the disease might lessen, but developmental problems endure such as those involving intellectual, behavioral, emotional, and social functioning.[5] FAS is the most severe end of the spectrum, however, and does not address the range of problems broader than FAS that have been correlated with heavy maternal drinking. For example, fetal alcohol effects is a term used for children who exhibit some FAS features but do not fulfill the entire diagnostic criteria.[6]

> The extent of damage caused by prenatal alcohol exposure depends on the stage of fetal development, biological and environmental variables, and the amount and timing of the mother's alcohol consumption.[3]

The more general term of alcohol-related birth defects (ARBD) is used to denote all known adverse effects of alcohol on the developing embryo and fetus in both humans and laboratory animals, whether the defects are mild or severe, neurobehavioral or anatomical.[7]

Effects of Alcohol and Other Drugs

Infants born of drug-abusing mothers are showing a range of effects equal in seriousness to the damage of alcohol. It is estimated that between 2% and 11% of babies born each year have been exposed in utero to drugs, not including alcohol or nicotine exposure.[8] The lifestyle of a pregnant drug addict produces a number of problems including lack of prenatal care, poor nutrition, and physical illness. Infants born to women who are opiate or polydrug dependent have significant problems.

Many women who are drug abusers might have ingested several different drugs during pregnancy, further complicating and endangering the lives of their children. Infants born to multiple drug abusers are at high risk for long-term effects of intrauterine drug exposure and a complicated withdrawal and abstinence syndrome after birth.[9]

The risk of exposure to HIV is a danger to unborn children of alcoholic or drug-abusing women, who constitute the largest group of women at risk. HIV can be transmitted from mother to fetus in utero, during childbirth, and through breast feeding. It is essential that HIV-positive women seek health care providers familiar with HIV and perinatal transmission of HIV. For example, invasive procedures such as amniocentesis increase the risk to the fetus of contracting HIV from the mother. A woman's immune system is naturally suppressed during pregnancy and then returns to normal after birth. At one time, it was thought that HIV-positive women would be at higher risk for developing AIDS and/or worsening symptoms during pregnancy due to the natural suppression of their immune system, but recent studies have found this not to be the case. See Chapter 7 for more information about HIV and pregnancy.

The long-term effects of perinatal cocaine exposure are yet to be established. The most consistent findings show obstetrical complications, low birthweight, smaller head circumference, abnormal neonatal behavior, and cerebral infarction at birth. Children with this exposure are easily distracted and passive, and they face a variety of visual-perceptual problems and difficulties with fine motor skills.[10]

Early Intervention Strategies

Early intervention is difficult to achieve but is extremely important. If a woman can become sober and clean during the early stage of her pregnancy, then the chances for a healthy baby are greater. Also, just as the alcoholic's denial becomes harder to penetrate during the later stages of alcoholism, a pregnant woman's denial can become greater as her pregnancy progresses, perhaps due to extreme guilt and fear about the baby's welfare. According to Little and Ervin,

> In general, women appear to become less amenable to intervention in the later months of pregnancy. Maternal concern seems to be highest in the first trimester. Later, as the pregnancy progresses, the woman turns inward and is less likely to reach out for help. For this reason, as well as because of the crucial importance of the period of organogenesis, pregnant drinkers should be reached as soon as possible after conception.[11]

Pregnant substance-abusing women require more than public health information to recover. Active and aggressive intervention and treatment is needed as early as possible in the pregnancy for both the mother and the child. The clinical and treatment issues in working with this group are challenging. Until recently, there were few treatment facilities that understood and could treat pregnant alcoholic or drug-abusing women. It is critical to have services appropriate to the needs of these women. Intervention and treatment of pregnant substance-abusing women could mean saving two lives, not just one.

The crisis of pregnancy can be a powerful tool in precipitating a woman's decision to get help for her drinking or drug abuse. There is a sense of urgency on the woman's part to gain information and reassurance, but this is combined with fear, guilt, and denial about her drinking or drug use. Active outreach to a woman at this point is essential. You need to confront the woman with concerns for the unborn child and risk the woman's anger and rejection. By recognizing the client's guilt without compounding it and offering a specific plan of action around alcoholism or drug abuse treatment and prenatal care, you will be giving the pregnant woman some clear choices of what the next steps are in getting help.

Intervention and treatment strategies for helping pregnant substance-abusing women involve a range of services. First, there needs to be outreach to and education of health care providers who work with pregnant women and women in their reproductive years. This group

> Although alcohol-abusing women might be particularly receptive to intervention strategies during pregnancy, they appear less likely to seek out treatment. This might be due to the stigma attached to alcoholism while pregnant or because residential programs frequently lack provisions for child care for their other children. . . . Active outreach is critical for locating women at highest risk for poor outcome, particularly because many at high risk might not use prenatal care.[12]

must learn to identify alcoholism and drug abuse in women and to understand the health risks to unborn children. They also should be aware of the network of services that are (or should be) available to pregnant substance-abusing women.

Unfortunately, there are few programs specifically geared to the needs of pregnant alcoholic or drug-abusing women. Few halfway houses accept pregnant women, especially those with children, and outpatient support services are scant. Pregnant substance-abusing women need a variety of services that include evaluation and diagnosis, medical and prenatal care, and substance abuse treatment that might include detoxification, self-help groups, pregnancy support groups, parenting skills, and individual and group counseling. When comprehensive services are not in place, it might be necessary to involve a number of community agencies to provide a full range of services to a pregnant woman with alcoholism or drug abuse problems. You will need to be an active advocate and case manager, helping the pregnant substance-abusing woman to address both her recovery needs and the needs of her unborn child.

Women of childbearing age who are at risk for the complications of alcohol or drug abuse in pregnancy need to understand the importance of abstaining from alcohol or drugs prior to and during pregnancy. Alcohol- and drug-related birth defects are preventable. The sooner a substance-abusing woman who is pregnant stops using alcohol and drugs, the greater the likelihood of her having a healthy baby. Even after birth, a mother who is breastfeeding should continue abstaining not only for her own sake but also because of the potential for transmission of alcohol or drugs to the nursing infant.

Understanding a woman's family situation is important for planning ARBD prevention. Social supports, role models, family values, alcohol availability, stress, and other variables related to alcohol use are linked to both a woman's family of origin and other living arrangement she shares as an adult.[13]

Before a client begins to reduce her use or stops using alcohol or drugs altogether, she will need to have counseling and assistance in place to help her deal with both the issues related to sobriety and the problems and fears she confronts due to her pregnancy.

The alcohol and drug recovery issues focus certainly is the primary framework for counselors to return to and keep foremost for clients. This will be just as true after the baby's birth, a critical time to keep recovery issues in the foreground. At the same time, however, a pregnant woman will need advice and support regarding health issues, child care, child development, and her own daily living considerations. Attending to both of these considerations—alcoholism/drug treatment and personal health/pregnancy—is strongly suggested and will provide more of a support and safety net for your client. The Staff and Client Training Activities at the end of the chapter will help staff and clients learn to effectively work through some of these issues.

Substance-Abusing Women as Parents

Parenting and mothering are major issues in women's lives. It is central to many women's identities and is the source of much anxiety and guilt. Whatever is "wrong" with the child is assumed to be the fault of the mother. When alcoholism and drug abuse are added to mothering and feelings about self, an already difficult area for many women is magnified and intensified. The guilt of the alcoholic or drug-abusing mother is reinforced both by the stigma of being a substance-abusing woman and by the real problems that her drinking or drug abuse may have caused her family. There are very few people for whom the words *alcoholic mother* do not evoke some negative image. Many counselors automatically feel anger at the mother and identify with the helpless child.

Mothering is a difficult enough task for many women, but for substance-abusing women in early recovery, the task can be overwhelming. Their feelings of inadequacy are grounded in the fear that they might fit society's stereotype of "bad mothers." They fear that they damaged their babies during pregnancy and that their older children were inadequately cared for during their drinking or drug abuse. To treat substance-abusing women who also are newly sober mothers as separate individuals without addressing their children's needs, the mother-child relationship, and the entire family unit is inadequate treatment at best. It asks the newly sober women to face an overwhelming task alone—to begin the painful process of recovery without assisting them in their relationships with their children.

Guilt and Recovering Mothers

Guilt is the prevailing emotion that counselors find when working with recovering women. These feelings are made worse if women have unrealistic expectations of themselves as parents. Many women, substance abusing or not, have two images of themselves as mothers. One is that of an "ideal mother." This perfect, available, all-nurturing stereotype comes from expectations and ideals that they had of their own mothers. It also is influenced by images and expectations of society reflected in family, the media, and their own children. The second image is that of the "bad mother." This image comes from the feelings that women have about alcoholic mothers and about themselves as mothers. This image often bears as little resemblance to reality as does the first image. The greater the distance between the idealized image and the negative image that women hold of themselves, the more they are prone to feelings of depression and self-hatred. The guilt about parenting that most alcoholic or drug-abusing mothers feel once in treatment, which is exacerbated if their children have any serious physical, emotional, or learning problems, can be overpowering and can lead to feelings of hopelessness and helplessness and to a possible relapse.

Therefore, it is important to help an alcoholic or drug-abusing woman in treatment to understand that both she and her family have been victims of alcoholism and drug abuse and not of her deliberate or intentional behavior. Parenting is a learned behavior for which many adult daughters of alcoholic parents never had positive role models, and during that period of active drinking or drug use, options are limited. It is important that a woman expresses her guilt and shame and also learns to forgive herself. Women's support and therapy groups are invaluable in helping women with these issues. It is essential to assist a recovering woman to believe that if she abstains from alcohol or drugs, she can regain control of her life and become the mother she would like to be. She also needs reassurance that a counselor will help her to find the tools she needs to be able to parent successfully through services such as parenting classes and mothers' groups.

Issues for Mothers, Children, and Counselors

There are specific treatment issues that differ if a woman still is drinking or abusing drugs, is newly sober, or has long-term stable sobriety. If mothers still are actively drinking or abusing drugs, then their alcoholism or drug abuse must be confronted separately or as part of evaluations of their children's emotional and physical safety. Discussion of their children's welfare and (occasionally) the threat of loss of the children can be a motivating factor in helping women get into treatment. For newly sober women, the issues are different. They may either rush to fix everything immediately or deny that their children have been affected. They are fragile and vulnerable at this time, and it might be prudent for you to respect and nurture their defenses instead of doing detective work. If the children are in crisis, then the children's needs should be addressed with sensitive counseling for the mothers. Finally, for mothers with long-term stable sobriety, you should encourage the women to express and work through their guilt. They need to come to terms with their pasts as actively drinking or drug-abusing mothers and must learn to forgive themselves.

It is important to consider your own attitudes, which may include anger at the substance-abusing mothers, concern for the children, and/or reluctance to discuss alcoholism or drug abuse with the mothers at all. You might need help to work through your own attitudes, especially if you come from an alcoholic family. The mothers' own ambivalence toward having children and keeping children also might require consideration. Guilt or exasperation over child care responsibilities may compound these feelings. Reestablishment of mother-child attachment will take time. Sometimes, there is involvement of other family members or foster families who might be angry and untrusting of sober mothers' capacity to care for children. A third issue is the reluctance of mothers to include their children in their treatment. Denial and fear of losing children might keep women out of treatment as well. As mothers establish trust with an agency, however, they will begin to include their children. Offering specialized groups around parenting issues and sober mothers' groups can give a women permission to include their children in recovery. Offering concurrent children's groups will encourage this.

Practical Considerations for Mothers in Recovery

Alcoholic or drug-abusing mothers need support and encouragement as well as openly available child-oriented treatment services to help them overcome the guilt and stigma they feel as they become involved in recovery. Mothers in recovery from alcoholism or other drug dependencies will benefit greatly from drawing on the variety of ready-made support systems that are available and, in most cases, free of charge. Many mothers might have had negative experiences with health, legal, and social service institutions and might need time to develop trust in positive relationships with supportive systems. Alcoholic Anonymous (AA), Narcotics Anonymous (NA), Al-Anon, Parents Anonymous, Families Anonymous, mothers' groups, and women's support groups can be excellent referrals.

Sometimes, attending a group for herself becomes low priority due to a mother's other responsibilities, lack of babysitting, or lack of support from spouse or family. Low attendance and absences may be legitimate or may be due to a mother's resistance. Be sure to explore where resistance is coming from, taking into consideration the mother's point of view and perhaps helping her frame an alternative self-care plan.

Asking for help. Mothers in particular might need encouragement to ask for help from others due to feelings of failure or shame. Asking for help is an important skill in a solid recovery program. Simplify and talk through this process with your client by exploring the following components of asking for help:

a. Become aware of her needs, validating their importance.
b. Learn to recognize who and who not to ask. Sober friends who can listen, an AA or NA sponsor, and a counselor all are possibilities for asking. Friends or loved ones who are actively drinking or using drugs and family members who bear negative attitudes toward the client are not good people to ask for help. Help the client to move away from rejections and toward respectful treatment.
c. Push past difficulty in asking for help. What is in the mother's way? Pride? Fear? Trust issues? How can you address those blocks? Asking for help does not mean being rescued, although that might be the client's expectation—and a dangerous one.
d. Each of us has a different style of asking for help. Role-play and practice can help to work out a comfortable or an acceptable style for the client.
e. Realize that asking for help is an ongoing process.
f. Other issues to discuss with the client about asking for help are whether she can receive help when it is offered and how she will respond when others ask her for help.

Guilt and reality checks. Issues of guilt, whether verbalized or not, are ever-present for most mothers in recovery. Allow for the expression of guilt, but make certain to follow up with reality testing. Include ongoing factual education and information about the disease of alcoholism and how substance abuse impairs women's ability to be present for and available to children. AA's messages of hope can be helpful including the focus on one day at a time and staying in the current 24-hour period. The Twelve Steps also offer a way in which to make amends for past mistakes. Other ways to help mothers work on guilt can be found in the Staff and Client Training Activities.

References

1. Centers for Disease Control and Prevention, *NCADI Fact Sheet on Fetal Alcohol Syndrome*. Available: http://www.cdc.gov/od/oc/media/fact/fetal.htm (retrieved 13 November 1998)

2. P. S. Cook et al., *Alcohol, Tobacco, and Other Drugs May Harm the Unborn*, DHHS Publication No. (ADM) 90-1711 (Washington, DC: Government Printing Office, 1990), 17.

3. National Institute on Alcohol Abuse and Alcoholism, *Eighth Special Report to the U.S. Congress on Alcohol and Health* (Rockville, MD: NIAAA, 1997), 204.

4. National Institute on Alcohol Abuse and Alcoholism, *Fetal Alcohol Syndrome*, Alcohol Alert No. 13 (Rockville, MD: NIAAA, 1991), 1.

5. U.S. Department of Health and Human Services, *Ninth Special Report to the U.S. Congress on Alcohol and Health*, NIH Publication No. 97-4017 (Washington, DC: Government Printing Office, 1997), 229.

6. National Institute on Alcohol Abuse and Alcoholism, *Ninth Special Report to the U.S. Congress on Alcohol and Health* (Rockville, MD: NIAAA, 1997), 193; National Institute on Alcohol Abuse and Alcoholism, *Alcohol and Birth Defects: The Fetal Alcohol Syndrome and Related Disorders*, DHHS Publication No. (ADM) 87-1531 (Washington, DC: Government Printing Office, 1987), 12.

7. National Institute on Alcohol Abuse and Alcoholism, *Women and Alcohol: Issues for Prevention Research*, NIH Publication No. 96-3817 (Rockville, MD: NIAAA, 1996), 94.

8. Cook et al., *Alcohol, Tobacco, and Other Drugs*, 3.

9. Jane E. Brody, "Cocaine: Litany of Fetal Risks Grows," *New York Times* (September 6, 1988).

10. Substance Abuse and Mental Health Services Administration, *Identifying the Needs of Drug-Affected Children: Public Policy Issues*, DHHS Publication No. (ADM) 92-1814 (Washington, DC: Government Printing Office, 1992), 3.

11. Ruth E. Little and Cynthia H. Ervin, "Alcohol Use and Reproduction," in S. Wilsnack and L. Beckman, eds., *Alcohol Problems in Women* (New York: Guilford, 1984).

12. U.S. Department of Health and Human Services, *Ninth Special Report*, 214.

13. National Institute on Alcohol Abuse and Alcoholism, *Women and Alcohol*, 109.

▨ Staff Training Activities

Activity 1: Feelings and Attitudes About Alcoholic or Drug-Abusing Mothers
Activity 2: Guidelines for Approaching Substance-Abusing Mothers in Different Stages of Illness and Recovery
Activity 3: Dealing With a Substance-Abusing Mother's Guilt in Treatment
Activity 4: More Ways in Which to Help Mothers Work on Guilt
Activity 5: Parenting Issues for Your Client
Activity 6: Parenting Issues for Substance-Abusing Mothers Who Are Adult Daughters of Alcoholics

Activity 1:   Feelings and Attitudes About Alcoholic or Drug-Abusing Mothers

Ask your staff to think about how they feel when they hear the words *alcoholic mother* and how they might imagine the mother herself feels.

How the Counselor Might See the Woman

    Ambivalent
    Deprived
    Irresponsible
    Unfeeling
    Inconsistent
    Immature

How the Woman Might See Herself

    Negligent
    Unfit
    Bad
    Undeserving
    Dirty
    Guilty

Discussion:

▨ Both counselors and clients have internalized negative societal attitudes, but the woman herself has them to an extreme.

▨ Counselors might feel anger toward the woman and identify with the helplessness of the child.

▨ A woman needs external support to build a positive self-image in sobriety because of her guilt and self-hatred. A counselor with extreme negative attitudes can undermine a client's recovery.

▨ Counselors from alcoholic families might need to seek help for themselves in Al-Anon, adult children groups, or therapy if their personal issues interfere with working with alcoholic or drug-abusing mothers.

Activity 2:   Guidelines for Approaching Substance-Abusing Mothers in Different Stages of Illness and Recovery

a.   Mothers who still are drinking or abusing drugs

    ▨ Confront the alcoholism or drug abuse at every opportunity with the woman.

■ Evaluate the child(ren)'s emotional and physical safety.

■ Use the leverage of the woman's concern for her child(ren) as a motivator toward treatment.

■ Work with other adult family members (e.g., spouse, lover, parent) to encourage them to get help in learning about alcoholism or drug abuse.

■ Provide a mother with treatment options that include child care and allow her to have access to her child(ren). Maintain a resource list of such referrals.

b. Mothers who are newly sober

■ Do not encourage the woman to rush into fixing everything immediately or to deny any possibility of problems with the child(ren).

■ Concentrate on the mother's sobriety and accept her denial as a way of protecting an ego that still is fragile and vulnerable.

■ If a child needs evaluation for special intervention, then you might need to take a strong case management role.

■ Meeting the immediate needs of the mother usually is the best approach at this stage if a child is not in crisis.

■ Newly sober women might need help to lower their expectations of how things will change in early sobriety and to be prepared for a "long haul."

c. Mothers in later sobriety

■ Do not shield the woman from the knowledge that her drinking or drug abuse has affected her child(ren).

■ Listen to her story as well as to what she is *not* saying.

■ Help a mother to express and work through her guilt and shame.

■ Be able to face painful parenting issues with her and to talk about incidents of abuse or neglect.

■ Help a mother talk with her children about her illness, what happened, and the pain it caused. Role-playing with a mother can be helpful.

■ Prepare her to be able to listen to her child(ren)'s hurt, pain, and anger by having the mother fully explore her own.

Activity 3:   Dealing With a Substance-Abusing Mother's Guilt in Treatment

Guilt is the most central emotion for all substance-abusing mothers. Read and discuss the following points:

1. Help the mother to understand that both she and her child(ren) have been victims of alcoholism or drug abuse, not her deliberate or intentional behavior.

2. Listen with compassion to what she feels she did wrong. Without conscious expression, guilt can be misdirected into anger toward herself and others.

3. Help her to realize that during active drinking and drug abuse, options and choices in parenting were limited.

4. Convey hope. If she stays sober, then she can regain control of her life and realistically work toward the person and mother she would like to be.

5. Timing of working through guilt is important. It might be necessary in early sobriety to support denial of her past parenting and to deal with tasks of living sober today.

6. Women's support groups are excellent vehicles for recovery. Even in women's groups, mothers might have difficulty in talking about their parenting guilt, and it might take time for them to do so.

7. There are real issues for children with substance-abusing mothers that might need to be faced at every stage of sobriety. Women will need strong support from counselors to face these problems.

8. As counselors, we sometimes need to compromise our goals for children because a mother's sobriety still is tenuous. Patience and acceptance of our own anger and frustration at someone else's parenting difficulties is an important part of the process of helping.

9. Long-term sobriety does not mean that family problems disappear. A substance-abusing mother needs to understand that children from nonalcoholic families act out and have crises as well.

Activity 4:   More Ways in Which to Help Mothers Work on Guilt

1. Is it really guilt that she is feeling, or is it sadness, anger, pain, or rejection?

2. Encourage your client to do something nice for herself so as to appreciate herself and her strengths.

3. Encourage her to write a letter (but not necessarily to send or give it) to her child(ren) expressing her guilt and amends.

Activity 5:   Parenting Issues for Your Client

Assess and examine your client's strategies for handling her child(ren) as a sober parent such as the following:

a. *Setting limits:* Is your client able to set clear limits? Aware of her bottom lines? Tolerant to a point and then overly harsh? Too lax?

b. *Anger:* Does she store up anger? Explode? Is she physically or verbally abusive? Is she self-abusive with anger? Are there ways in which she could be more direct and not let annoyances build?

c. *Communication skills:* Is she able to listen? Can she talk without blaming? Can she name her problems, her fears, and her expectations regarding her child(ren)?

    d. *Expectations:* Clarify the expectations that she has for herself and her child(ren). What skills and strengths does she see (e.g., practical parenting skills, time management skills, further counseling or parenting groups to help with expressing emotions in a healthy and beneficial manner)? If she has a spouse, lover, or coparent to help, then how are they as a parenting team? On the preceding issues?

Activity 6:   Parenting Issues for Substance-Abusing Mothers Who Are Adult Daughters of Alcoholics

Many substance-abusing women have one or two alcoholic parents. The following parenting issues are common and might need to be addressed in later sobriety. Discuss as a group:

■ Difficulty in setting limits

■ Difficulty in following through

■ Black-and-white thinking in developing rules

■ Avoidance of conflict

■ Emotional distancing

■ A need to be in control

■ A need to look good

■ High tolerance for inappropriate behavior

■ Fear of rejection

■ Difficulty in knowing what *normal* is

■ Difficulty in having fun

■ Little spontaneity

■ Consistent guilt about parenting and a belief that there is such a thing as a perfect parent

■ Consistent feelings of failure

■ Exaggerated response to alcohol or drug experimentation among their own children

■ Overprotection of children from their own grief issues

■ Not trusting own perceptions

■ Lacking an individual identity

■ Client Training Activities

Activity 1

With the client alone or in a group setting, use role-plays about how mothers might handle the following situations (whether they are single parents or both parents are present):

1. You find evidence that your teenager is using marijuana.

2. Your toddler has been sick and crying throughout the night and seems sicker in the morning. You make a doctor's appointment for him. Now, his 4-year-old sister is upset about having to cancel the plans you had made for the day, and she is crying.

3. Your children want to know why you are out so many nights each week. It is because you are attending Alcoholics Anonymous, but they do not know that. You decide to talk with them about your alcoholism.

4. Instead of a role-play, choose a topic that seems high stress to your client in relation to her situation so that she can get a sense of her strengths, plan for crises, and decide in advance how she can use her support network to get through the difficult situation.

Resources

National Association of Families, Addiction Research, and Education (NAFARE)
Address: 200 North Michigan Avenue, Suite 300, Chicago, IL 60601
Phone: (312) 541-1272, (800) 638-BABY (638-2229) (cocaine baby helpline)

(NAFARE is a national organization that hosts many programs, one of which is a helpline that provides information to professionals and the public on the effects of addiction on fetuses and babies including referrals for addicted women.)

National Organiztion on Fetal Alcohol Syndrome
Address: 418 C Street, N.E., Washington, DC 20002
Phone: (202) 785-4585
E-mail: nofas@erols.com
Web: http://www.nofas.org

(This is a nonprofit organization dedicated to eliminating birth defects caused by alcohol consumption during pregnancy and to improving the quality of life for those individuals and families affected.)

7

HIV, AIDS, and Women

The AIDS epidemic is increasingly becoming a crisis for women as well as men in the United States. Women are being infected with HIV, the human immunodeficiency virus that causes AIDS, at a faster rate than is any other group of people. As of December 1997, approximately 30.6 million people were living with HIV/AIDS throughout the world. This figure was expected to increase to about 40 million by the year 2000.[1] More than 75% of all adult HIV infections have resulted from heterosexual intercourse.[2]

Issues for Counselors

Counselors are confronted with a difficult and emotionally frightening situation in helping women with the complex medical, social, and ethical issues surrounding HIV and AIDS. Those caring for people with AIDS also are most often female.[3] Understanding the facts about AIDS and communicating risks and prevention information to clients is only part of the task for counselors. First, it is crucial to face our own fears and concerns about AIDS to deal effectively with our clients' needs. It is a terrifying illness that is easier to ignore than prepare for and confront. However, in our professional roles as counselors with access to high-risk populations of women, it is particularly important that we do what we need to do individually and as part of programs to inform and reassure our clients that there is hope.

Helping women involves creating a safe environment in which they can talk openly with counselors about their sexual histories and current practices and in which we can provide them with information about safer sex. We can encourage and teach them to be assertive in their sexual relationships to help ensure that they are protected as much as possible. For those who have tested positive to the HIV antibody or have a diagnosis of AIDS, we need to be equipped to help them sort through the myriad of issues that result. Most important, this means empowering them to value themselves and to care about their health and their futures. There are lots of choices in treatment options, support networks, and things you can do to help your clients to take care of their health in ways that effectively manage the disease for an extended period of time. Taking control of an HIV-positive situation as quickly as possible will help your clients to avoid early illness due to the disease and to exercise more control over their health and their lives.

Definition of AIDS and HIV

There is much information about AIDS that is technical and complicated. However, it is only necessary to be able to explain the basic facts to help a woman be safer and informed. AIDS stands for acquired immune deficiency syndrome, a condition caused by a virus that attacks the body's immune system and eventually destroys it. It specifically affects white blood cells that are known as helper T-cells or CD4+, which fight infections and antigens to which the body is regularly exposed. When the numbers of these particular T-cells drop, it is an indicator that the immune system's ability to fight infection is declining.

The virus that causes AIDS is called HIV, which stands for human immunodeficiency virus. The incubation period for AIDS, the time between exposure to the virus and development of symptoms, can be as short as 6 months or as long as 10 years or more. The average period of incubation is between 7 and 8 years. Once a person has been exposed to the virus, it generally takes from 6 weeks to 6 months to develop antibodies to the virus that then yield a positive response to the antibody test. This process is called *seroconversion*. Because of the time span from exposure to seroconversion, it is recommended that people who have been sexually active and who want to know their antibody status wait 3 months after possible exposure. If the test is negative, then it should be repeated 6 months later.

Transmission of the AIDS Virus

The transmission of the virus that causes AIDS occurs primarily through blood and semen. Sexual contact and direct contact with infected blood through intravenous drug use or blood transfusions are the main ways in which a woman can contract AIDS. It is estimated that transmission is eight times more likely to be from male to female than the other way around.[4] Vaginal secretions do not transmit the virus as readily as semen, and there is more exposed surface area in the female genital tract.[5]

Counselors working with clients need to present them with an accurate perspective about AIDS as well as important information on transmission. In the Client Training Activities section at the end of this chapter, a list of

During unprotected heterosexual intercourse with an HIV-infected partner, women in general appear to be more easily infected with the virus than do men. Studies in the United States and abroad have demonstrated that other sexually transmitted diseases, particularly infections that cause ulcerations of the mucosal surfaces (e.g., syphilis, chancroid), greatly increase a woman's risk of becoming infected with HIV. Anal sex also increases a woman's risk of becoming HIV infected.[6]

ways in which to prevent HIV infection is included. In our Resources section at the end of the chapter, you can find a number of excellent support and advocacy groups that can help to inform and reassure you and your clients.

Women-Specific Symptoms of HIV Infection

Women also experience HIV-associated gynecologic problems. These illnesses occur in uninfected women as well, but in HIV-positive women they generally are more frequent, persistent, and severe. Also, the standard medications do not always provide adequate relief. Some women-specific symptoms of HIV infection include the following[7]:

Vaginal yeast infections
Esophageal candidiasis (i.e., yeast infections of the windpipe)
Bacterial vaginosis
More severe incidents of gonorrhea, chlamydia, and trichomoniasis
Severe herpes simplex virus ulcerations
Idiopathic genital ulcers (a unique manifestation of HIV)
Human papillomavirus infections
Pelvic inflammatory disease
Menstrual irregularities such as amenorrhea (i.e., no menses within the past 3 months)

The Importance of Early Diagnosis

According to Project Inform, an information and advocacy resource for people living with HIV/AIDS, women with AIDS do not get sicker or suffer with more opportunistic infections, nor do they die more quickly, than do men with AIDS. People who do not know their HIV status or ignore their HIV-positive status, and who do nothing to manage their HIV with good, preventative health practices, are the ones who succumb earlier to the disease. Women might be more susceptible than men to ignoring or not taking care of themselves properly, possibly because they have a less stable support network or are more willing to deny the existence of the disease.

Female hormones could accelerate the course of the disease (as with alcoholism). The barriers to health care, especially for women who are low income and/or often involved in an intravenous drug abuse subculture,

In a study by the Terry Beirn Community Programs for Clinical Research on AIDS (CPCRA) of more than 4,500 people with HIV, HIV-infected women were one third more likely than HIV-infected men to die within the study period. The CPCRA investigators could not definitively identify the reasons for excess mortality among women in this study, but they speculated that poorer access to or use of health care resources among HIV-infected women as compared to men, domestic violence, homelessness, and lack of social supports for women might have been important factors.[8]

might prevent those women from being diagnosed early and treated as aggressively as are men. According to the Boston Women's Health Collective, there are a variety of reasons that put women more at risk:

> Because of the myriad insensitivities of health and medical institutions to women, especially to women of color and lesbians, many of us seek care for HIV or AIDS only at the later stages of illness. Or, we may go without treatment for STDs [sexually transmitted diseases] or vaginal irritations, which can increase our risk of being infected by HIV if we are exposed.[9]

HIV Testing

There is pressure on women, particularly pregnant women from high-risk groups, to be tested for HIV. As counselors, it is important for us to explore the advantages and disadvantages of testing with women and to help them make their own decisions. First, a woman needs to be able to look honestly at her past and present to see whether she is in a group at high risk for AIDS. Any woman who has shared needles, "injecting drug works," cotton, or syringes to use an injected drug is at high risk for AIDS. Any woman who has received blood transfusions or blood products between 1979 and 1985 also is at high risk. Finally, any woman is at high risk if she has had sexual contact with the following: gay or bisexual men since 1979, men or women who have histories of intravenous drug use, men or women whose sexual histories are unknown, and men or women who have received blood products between 1979 and 1985. Women who can identify with having any of these risk factors might wish to think about testing for the HIV virus, especially if they are pregnant. Other factors that make alcoholic or drug-abusing women at especially high risk for AIDS are the lack of judgment about sex partners and safer sex practices while under the influence and low self-esteem that makes it hard to be assertive in sexual relationships.

Testing for HIV usually is done with two tests performed on a blood sample: the EIA and Western Blot tests. Used together, the tests are more than 99% accurate. A positive test result means that a woman has been exposed to the virus and can transmit the virus to others (e.g., lover, fetus, newborn). A negative result is more ambiguous. It might mean that a woman is not infected with HIV or that she has not made antibodies yet. A woman with a history of unsafe high-risk behavior who receives a negative result probably should be tested again. Tests for AIDS may be performed in physicians' offices, clinics, or hospitals, although confidentiality of test results is not always guaranteed. In some states, anonymous and confidential alternative testing sites have been established. Confidentiality is a major issue around antibody testing, and the risks of disclosure need to be discussed with women.

> Legislation related to HIV antibody testing is enacted by state governments. For information on state laws concerning mandatory HIV antibody testing, contact your state legislature, which usually is listed in the blue pages of your phone book.[10]

Counselors need to understand and present the pros and cons of testing to women to allow them to make informed, voluntary decisions for themselves. Some clients might need to talk about their fears, need help in reality testing risk factors, or need physical examinations and chances to look at overall health issues. A negative test result can leave a woman with a false sense of security and is not a substitute for changing sexual and drinking/drugging behaviors. Learning safer sex habits and adopting a sober and drug-free lifestyle is the best defense against AIDS. Test results alone do not lead to behavior change. In fact, a positive test could affect a newly sober person disastrously. Whatever the test result, a counselor needs to help a woman continue to focus on her sobriety and to develop a safe and healthy lifestyle.

High-Risk Groups

AIDS is now considered pandemic; it is everywhere. Women of color are at much greater risk of contracting AIDS than are white women. In 1996, HIV became the second leading cause of death among Hispanic women between 25 and 44 years of age, and over the past decade, the proportion of cases each year among Hispanics infected heterosexually has increased from about 30% to 60%.[12] This means that more than two thirds of women with AIDS are minorities during their childbearing years. The overwhelming majority of children who are being diagnosed with AIDS are black or Hispanic.

Women involved in alcohol- or drug-using subcultures are women at extremely high risk for contracting HIV and developing AIDS. Among women diagnosed with AIDS in the United States in 1997, most acquired HIV infection through sexual contact with

During 1997, the rate of new AIDS cases per 100,000 population in the United States was 83.7 among blacks, 37.7 among Hispanics, 10.4 among whites, 10.4 among American Indians/Alaska Natives, and 4.5 among Asians/Pacific Islanders.[11]

men with or at risk of HIV infection (38%) or through injection drug use (32%).[13] This can result from women's sexual involvement with infected intravenous drug-abusing partners and the difficulties women might have in setting limits and practicing safer sex in what can be dangerous and abusive relationships.

AIDS and the Lesbian Population

Lesbians have been ignored as a group at risk for AIDS. Although they are a lower risk population, they also are susceptible to AIDS through their own or their partners' intravenous drug use. They also may be at risk from past or present sexual relationships with other women or men from a high-risk group. Lesbian sex often includes contact with vaginal secretions, menstrual blood, and other body fluids that may transmit the HIV virus. Frequently, lesbians have experienced the social ramifications of AIDS through the illnesses and deaths of friends, the effects of the AIDS hysteria on lesbian and gay rights, and the limitation of insemination choices.

At first, lesbians were thought to be "low risk" so far as the dangers of exposure, and some of this denial continues to persist. Stereotypes of lesbians come into effect here as well, as Lee notes that

> many health care providers believe that lesbians do not ever have sex with men and, thus, assume that they are not at risk for sexually transmitted diseases and do not need Pap smears. However, the majority of lesbian women have had sexual relationships with men at some stage of their [lives], and a significant minority report injecting drugs or otherwise putting themselves in danger of infection with HIV or hepatitis.[14]

Until recently, women testing positive for HIV were not asked whether they had sex with other women because lesbian sex was not considered a high-risk behavior. Thus, statistics have not acknowledged the existence of lesbian and bisexual women among women with HIV illnesses.

Lesbians are now becoming proactive in educating their peers and preventing denial about transmission of the disease. Certainly, the range of immune system diseases from chronic Epstein-Barr virus to AIDS has encouraged a trend toward holistic health and safer sex, and alcohol and drugs have been implicated as interfering in achieving both. Substance abuse puts all women at risk for exposure to HIV, through intravenous drug use or through unprotected, unsafe sex with partners (male or female) who have been exposed to the virus, because options, decision-making skills, and self-care are limited by intoxication.

Pregnant Women and HIV/AIDS

Birth control, pregnancy, and childbirth are critical issues for women at risk for contracting the AIDS virus. There is some evidence that oral contraceptives might be associated with a greater likelihood of becoming infected, possibly because women on the pill are less likely to use condoms. Pregnancy can present dangers both to the mother who tests HIV positive with no symptoms and to the unborn child. An increasingly critical issue for women who have the virus is the very real possibility of transmitting it to a child in utero, during childbirth, or while breast-feeding. According to the National Institutes of Health (NIH), "Mother-to-child (vertical) transmission has accounted for more than 90[%] of all HIV infections worldwide in infants and children." The NIH also notes, "HIV-infected women who used heroin or crack/cocaine during pregnancy were also twice as likely to transmit HIV to their offspring as [were] HIV-infected women who did not use drugs." Early zidovudine (AZT) therapy (during pregnancy and given to the baby after birth) can help to reduce HIV transmission from mother to child by two thirds. Statistics show that 25% of HIV-positive pregnant women not using this therapy will pass on HIV to their newborns.[15]

Women Testing Positive for HIV or Diagnosed With AIDS

Women who are diagnosed with AIDS need caring and practical support to carry on with their lives. Their needs are great and include having support people and advocates when dealing with doctors and hospitals to better understand and make decisions about treatments and drug protocols. Women might need help with children; financial and legal issues; household chores and meals; and transportation to medical appointments, stores, or movies. Emotional support is invaluable in maintaining a balance between optimism and the limitations of illness. It also is important to pay attention to holistic health concerns such as nutrition, exercise, and stress management. Women need help connecting with other persons with AIDS as well as other supportive community resources. Counselors can play an important role by being a reassuring and supportive guide to help them manage the treatment of their illness by working to provide them with a stable network of support, information, and encouragement.

References

1. Office of Communications and Public Liaison, *How HIV Causes AIDS* (Bethesda, MD: National Institute of Allergies and Infectious Diseases, 1998). Available: http://www.niaid.nih.gov/factsheets/howhiv.htm

2. Ibid.

3. "People with AIDS" and "persons with AIDS" are terms preferred by those living with the disease because the terms emphasize that there is more to a person's life than being relegated to "victim" or "patient" status.

4. Center for AIDS Prevention Studies, *What Are Women's HIV Prevention Needs?* (San Francisco: UCSF AIDS Research Institute, 1998). Available: http://www.caps.ucsf.edu/women-rev.html

5. N. S. Padian, S. C. Shiboski, S. O. Glass, et al., "Heterosexual Transmission of Human Immunodeficiency Virus (HIV) in Northern California: Results from a Ten-Year Study," *American Journal of Epidemiology* 146 (1997): 350-57. Available: http://www.caps.ucsf.edu/ women-rev.html; Center for AIDS Prevention Studies, *What Are Women's HIV Prevention Needs?*

6. Office of Communications and Public Liaison, *Fact Sheet: Women and HIV* (Bethesda, MD: National Institute of Allergies and Infectious Diseases, 1998). Available: http://www.niaid.nih.gov/factsheets/womenhiv.htm

7. Ibid.

8. Ibid.

9. Boston Women's Health Book Collective, *Our Bodies, Ourselves: For the New Century* (New York: Simon & Schuster, 1998), 360.

10. National Center for HIV, STD, and TB Prevention, *Evaluation of Testing* (Atlanta, GA: Centers for Disease Control and Prevention, 1998). Available: http://www.cdc.gov/nchstp/hiv_aids/hivinfo/vfax/260300.htm

11. Centers for Disease Control and Prevention, *HIV/AIDS Surveillance Report* 9, no. 2 (1997): 1-44, as cited in Office of Communications and Public Liaison, *Fact Sheet*. Available: http://www.cdc.gov/nchstp/hiv_aids/stats/hasrlink.htm

12. Office on Women's Health, *Information Sheet: Hispanic Women and HIV/AIDS* (Bethesda, MD: U.S. Public Health Service, 1998). Available: http://www.4woman.gov/owh/pub/ fshis-aids.htm

13. Centers for Diseases Control and Prevention, *HIV/AIDS Surveillance Report*.

14. C. Lee, *Women's Health: Psychological and Social Issues* (Thousand Oaks, CA: Sage, 1998), 167.

15. Office of Communications and Public Liaison, *HIV/AIDS Statistics* (Bethesda, MD: National Institutes of Health, 1998). Available: http://www.niaid.nih.gov/factsheets/aidsstat.htm

Staff Training Activities

Activity 1:   Personal Sharing About Feelings, Thoughts, and Experiences With AIDS

Activity 2:   Positive and Negative Responses to AIDS

Activity 3:   Important Terms Related to AIDS

Activity 4:   Risk Factors for Women in General as Well as for Alcoholic or Drug-Addicted Women

Activity 5:   Prevention of HIV Infection

Activity 6:   Role-Play: Talking With a Woman About AIDS

Activity 7:   Ways in Which to Convey Information and Concern

Activity 8:   Client Education

Activity 9:   Issues Involved In Antibody Testing

Activity 10:   Overview of HIV Antibody Testing

Activity 11:   Guidelines for Pretest Counseling

Activity 12:   Test Sites

Activity 1:   Personal Sharing About Feelings, Thoughts, and Experiences With AIDS

Ask each person to share some of her or his thoughts and feelings about AIDS. Most people have concerns and fears about personal risks and risks to their loved ones. Encourage everyone to express how she or he feels about working with women on AIDS issues. What makes it hard for counselors to consider addressing these issues with clients? Develop a list and discuss.

Activity 2:   Positive and Negative Responses to AIDS

Make a list of some positive responses to AIDS:

■ Formation of volunteer and service organizations

■ Support groups for persons with AIDS and HIV-positive persons

■ Community fund-raisers

■ Emotional and caring support from family and friends

■ Schools teaching students about sexuality and sexually transmitted diseases

■ Creation of an AIDS memorial quilt worked on by thousands of lovers, friends, and family members of people who have died of AIDS

■ Plays, poetry, and novels written with AIDS as the central theme in a way that humanizes the epidemic

Make a list of some negative responses to AIDS:

■ Discrimination in areas of housing, employment, health, and life insurance

■ Increased fear of gay people and drug addicts

■ Mandatory testing of certain groups of people

■ Banning children from school who test positive to the antibody or have AIDS

■ Slow process of approval of drugs that could perhaps lengthen survival and decrease suffering of persons with AIDS

Activity 3:   Important Terms Related to AIDS

■ *AIDS:* AIDS stands for acquired immune deficiency syndrome. This condition is caused by a virus that attacks the body's immune system and eventually destroys it. The virus that produces AIDS is called HIV, which stands for human immunodeficiency virus. People with AIDS suffer from a wide range of opportunistic infections because they have no way in which to resist them. Having the virus does not mean that someone has or is going to develop AIDS.

■ *Seroconversion:* After someone has been exposed to the AIDS virus, seroconversion is the point at which antibodies are produced and become detectable in the blood. Seroconversion usually occurs within 3 months after infection with the HIV virus. However, for some people, it might take a little longer to develop the antibody.

■ *Seropositivity:* Seropositivity indicates a positive reaction to the AIDS antibody test.

■ *Transmission:* The virus is found primarily in blood and semen. It has been isolated in very small amounts in other body fluids such as saliva and tears, but transmission by any means other than sexual contact or direct contact with infected blood never has been demonstrated. Cervical and vaginal fluids contain enough virus to allow transmission in some instances. In general, male-to-female transmission is easier. A woman with the AIDS virus can transmit it to her child in utero, during childbirth, and possibly while breast-feeding.

Activity 4:   Risk Factors for Women in General as Well as for Alcoholic or Drug-Addicted Women

Ask the group members to share what they know about risk factors for all women and for substance-abusing women.

Women in general who are at risk:

■ Any woman who shares needles, injecting drug works, cotton, or syringes to use injectable drugs

■ Any woman who received blood transfusions or blood products between 1979 and 1985

■ Any woman who has had sexual contact with the following: men who have had sex with other men since 1979, women who have had sex with gay or bisexual men since 1979, men or women who have histories of intravenous drug use, men or women whose sexual histories are unknown, and men or women who have received blood products between 1979 and 1985

Alcoholic or drug-addicted women and special risks for AIDS:

■ Might be using intravenous drugs

■ Might be in relationships with intravenous drug-abusing men or women and subject to violence and intimidation regarding instituting safer sex practices

■ Lack of judgment about partners and safer sex practices while under the influence

■ Might be particularly hard to be assertive in sexual relationships due to low self-esteem

■ Possible suppression of a woman's immune system by alcohol or drugs, which can be cofactors in the development of AIDS

Activity 5: Prevention of HIV Infection

To prevent HIV infection, remember the following:

■ Do not have sex with an infected person.

■ Do not share needles with an infected person.

To prevent the spread of HIV infection, avoid behavior that might result in contact with blood, semen, vaginal secretions, or body fluids with visible blood. Specifically, avoid sex with anyone who might be infected with HIV and do not share injecting drug works. The following prevention measures apply to personal sex practices and injecting drug use:

■ To prevent sexual transmission of HIV, abstain from sex with an infected person.

■ Ask about the sexual histories of current and future sex partners.

■ Reduce the number of sex partners to minimize the risk of HIV infection.

■ Always use a condom from start to finish during any type of sex (vaginal, anal, or oral). Use latex condoms rather than natural membrane condoms. If used properly, latex condoms offer greater protection against sexually transmitted disease agents including HIV.

■ Use only water-based lubricants. Do not use saliva or oil-based lubricants such as petroleum jelly or vegetable shortening. If you decide to use a spermicide along with a condom, it is preferable to use spermicide in the vagina according to the manufacturer's instructions.

■ Avoid anal or rough vaginal intercourse. Do not do anything that could tear the skin or moist lining of the genitals, anus, or mouth and could cause bleeding.

■ Condoms should be used even for oral sex.

■ Avoid deep, wet, or "French" kissing with an infected person. Possible trauma to the mouth might occur, which could result in the exchange of blood. It is safe, however, to hug, cuddle, rub, or "dry kiss" your partner.

■ Avoid alcohol and illicit drugs. Alcohol and drugs can impair your immune system and judgment. If you use drugs, then do not share injecting drug works. Do not share needles, syringes, or "cookers."

■ Do not share personal items such as toothbrushes, razors, and devices used during sex that might be contaminated with blood, semen, or vaginal fluids.

■ If you are infected with HIV or have engaged in sex or needle-sharing behaviors that lead to infection with HIV, do not donate blood, plasma, sperm, body organs, or tissues.

SOURCE: National Center for HIV, STD, and TB Prevention. Available: http://www.cdc.gov/nchstp/hiv_aids/hivinfo/vfax/260040.htm.

Activity 6: Role-Play: Talking With a Woman About AIDS

Ask the group to do a role-play in which a counselor and client talk about AIDS. This can be done either with the whole group using two volunteers or in small groups of three or four people with two people doing the role-play and the other(s) observing. Address the client's fears, risks, and dread of finding out that she has HIV-positive status. Follow-up questions:

■ What did it feel like to be the counselor? To be the client?

■ Has anything similar come up for counselors working with women about HIV/AIDS?

■ Is it hard to initiate discussion and confront a client even when you are knowledgeable about HIV/AIDS? What are the issues that are hardest to discuss?

Activity 7: Ways in Which to Convey Information and Concern

Ask the group to come up with ideas:

■ Inform without overwhelming the woman.

■ Convey hopefulness.

■ Identify the woman's strengths, coping skills, and supports that can help with behavior changes.

■ Provide a client with reassurance.

■ Work together to identify what to change now.

■ Create a safe environment in which a woman can express her feelings and fears.

■ Be practical, sensitive, and open-minded.

Activity 8:   Client Education

A structured AIDS education program is an essential part of long-term treatment of substance-abusing women. Go over the following outline for client education that was developed for a residential program for alcoholic or drug-abusing women and discuss:

1.   Education about AIDS and transmission of HIV

    a. Myths/realities/AIDS anxiety

    b. HIV as a health concern and not a moral punishment

    c. Stigma and an AIDS diagnosis

2.   Defining high-risk behaviors for developing AIDS

3.   Education on how to lower the risks of exposure to and transmission of HIV

    a. Safer sex education

    b. Mother-to-child transmission (e.g., breast-feeding, in utero transmission)

    c. For intravenous drug users, cleaning of injecting drug works and message not to share needles and works

4.   Preventive health measures to lessen stress on immune system

    a. Stress management techniques including relaxation exercises, meditation, and visualization exercises

    b. Importance of positive health habits to support healthy immune system including good nutrition, sleeping habits, and cessation of alcohol or drug use and cigarette smoking

5.   Fostering awareness of support systems for people with AIDS diagnoses or who have tested positive for HIV (and their family members)

    a. Services that are women specific and offered by AIDS service organizations and community health centers, among others

    b. Support services for family members at same locations

Activity 9:   Issues Involved in Antibody Testing

Go over the following issues involved in testing and have people fill out arguments for and against testing and then share with the group or brainstorm as a large group.

Arguments for testing:

- To save lives, assuming that a woman will alter sexual behavior once her test result is known

- To provide medical intervention at an early point if test is positive

■ If woman is in a committed relationship and she and her partner wish to engage safely in unprotected sex, for example, if neither is infected and they have sex only with each other

■ If a woman is showing symptoms

■ If a woman is obsessed with fear and this fear is interfering with regular life activities (so long as she understands the ambiguity of results)

■ If a woman has had high-risk behavior and is considering pregnancy

■ If a woman knows that she has had sexual contact with an AIDS-infected person

■ If a woman is required to undergo mandatory testing (e.g., for the military or Job Corps) and wishes to know first on an anonymous basis

Arguments against testing:

■ A false sense of security that can result from a negative result

■ Issue of changing sexual or drugging behaviors not addressed

■ Effect of a positive result on a woman's emotional well-being and ability to stay sober without counseling and support

The choice to be tested needs to be a voluntary, informed decision. Women need to decide whether they can handle knowing that they might be positive even if they are perfectly healthy now. A counselor's role is to help the client look at all the issues of testing in a neutral atmosphere.

Activity 10: Overview of HIV Antibody Testing

Concerning HIV antibody testing, remember the following:

■ Counseling and early diagnosis are important to help prevent the spread of HIV.

■ Laws about testing are made by each state legislature.

■ HIV antibody tests are extremely accurate.

■ HIV-2 testing of all blood donations became mandatory on June 1, 1992.

Targeted counseling and testing programs represent one effective method of controlling the transmission of HIV. Counseling and testing for HIV is being expanded rapidly in hundreds of locations, in cooperation with state and local public health agencies, to reach persons at risk of HIV infection.

Counseling and early diagnosis of HIV infection are recommended for the following persons:

Persons who consider themselves at risk for infection

■ Women of childbearing age who are at risk of infection

■ Persons attending sexually transmitted disease clinics or drug abuse clinics

■ Spouses and sex- or needle-sharing partners of injecting drug users

■ Women seeking family planning services

■ Tuberculosis patients

■ Selected patients who received transfusions of blood or blood components between early 1979 and mid-1985.

SOURCE: National Center for HIV, STD, and TB Prevention. Available: http://www.cdc.gov/nchstp/hiv_aids/hivinfo/vfax/260300.htm.

Activity 11:   Guidelines for Pretest Counseling

Go over the following steps for pretest counseling. Discuss each step as a group to explore the process of helping a client to think about the issues related to testing:

1.   Review the client's risk of infection.

   ■ Why does the client want the test?

   ■ What information does she hope to gain?

2.   Explain the test and clarify its meaning.

   ■ What information can she actually get from the test?

3.   Caution the client about potential misuse of test results.

   ■ Discrimination

   ■ Confidentiality violations

   ■ Unsettled issues of reproductive rights (e.g., forced abortion, sterilization, pressures not to get pregnant)

4.   Help the client to think about possible reactions to the test and who should be told.

   ■ Will it devastate her or interfere with her day-to-day functioning?

   ■ Will it prove to be something that enhances her life?

5.   Help the client to reach a decision.

The client should be encouraged to take time to make a decision about testing and not to make a decision after the first time it is discussed. She needs to know all the facts about AIDS and issues surrounding testing to make her own voluntary informed decision.

Activity 12:   Test Sites

Have on hand a list of anonymous or confidential test sites to distribute to staff and/or clients.

Client Training Activities

Activity 1

As part of an ongoing relationship with a client, sex and sexuality eventually will be addressed in the context of treating the whole woman. The issue of AIDS prevention can be broached within the discussion of contraception and birth control methods. Women can be asked about safer sex, and whether they understand what that means in relation to HIV infection, as readily as they can be asked about the prevention of other sexually transmitted diseases.

Activity 2

Have on hand a variety of pamphlets and posters that make visible your willingness to discuss AIDS-related issues and your commitment to providing prevention and education. Remember that although a majority of people understand risk factors and the mechanics of transmission, they do not know how to incorporate concrete behavior changes into their lives.

Activity 3

If a client indicates a desire to be tested, then make sure to go over the pros and cons of the test-taking procedure. Help her to think through her need to know her health status. If she decides to take the test, then explain the importance of undergoing anonymous testing (labeled and identified as such) and the confidentiality issues involved including the protection of her test results.

Resources

Canadian HIV/AIDS Clearinghouse
Address: Canadian Public Health Association, 1565 Carling Avenue, 4th Floor, Ottawa, Ontario, Canada K1Z
     8R1
Phone: (613) 725-3434
E-mail: aids/sida@cpha.ca

(This agency serves AIDS educators across Canada and throughout the world, offering free publications, a lending library, and information and referral services in English and French.)

National AIDS Hotlines
Phone: (800) 342-AIDS (342-2437) (English), (800) 344-SIDA (344-7432) (Spanish), (800) AIDS-TTY (243-
     7889) (deaf)

National AIDS Information Clearinghouse (CDC NAC)
Address: CDC National Prevention Information Network, P.O. Box 6003, Rockville MD 20849-6003
Phone: (800) 458-5231, (800) 243-7012 (TTY)
E-mail: info@cdcnpin.org
Web: http://www.cdcnpin.org

(The Clearinghouse has been incorporated as a part of the CDC National Prevention Information Network. A reference, referral, and publication distribution service for HIV and AIDS information, the Clearinghouse offers information on all aspects of HIV/AIDS prevention, care, and social support.)

National AIDS Network
Address: 2033 M Street, N.W., Suite 800, Washington, DC 20036
Phone: (202) 293-2437

(This is a national resource center for community-based service and education organizations supporting those with AIDS, specializing in telephone referral to local groups.)

8

Dual Diagnosis Issues Among Women

Dual diagnosis is a condition in which both substance abuse and a mental health disorder exist.[1] Although dual diagnosis is relatively common in both the general substance-abusing and mentally ill populations, certain forms are particularly common among women. Some of the most commonly occurring psychiatric disorders that may occur with an alcohol use disorder are antisocial personality disorder, bulimia, depression, and anxiety. Studies have found that depression is more common in alcoholic women and that antisocial personality disorder is more frequent in men.[2] Posttraumatic stress disorder also is quite frequently found in women substance abusers, particularly women who have histories of childhood physical or sexual abuse.[3] A similar study concluded that women treated for dual diagnosis tend to report having been crime victims.[4]

It is quite difficult to identify clients who need treatment because it often is the case that symptoms deriving from substance abuse could be identical to symptoms associated with an organic or a psychiatric illness.[5] Dually diagnosed women can be particularly at risk for relapse and even suicide due to the severity of their mental health disorder. Therefore, it is essential that the dually diagnosed woman be assessed accurately for

> Treatment for co-occurring illnesses in persons with alcoholism should be a standard part of every alcoholism treatment program. Unfortunately, many patients with such illnesses fall through the cracks; for example, alcoholic patients with psychiatric problems may be rejected by both alcoholism programs and mental health programs. . . . Because of the increase in the frequency of polydrug abuse, alcoholism treatment programs must be aware of and be prepared to deal with this problem in their patients. It should be noted, however, that the most common pattern of abuse in the United States is still alcoholism alone.[6]

her other diagnosis and, if need be, obtain psychopharmaceutical medications as well. The substance abuse clinician should collaborate with other treatment providers with which the woman is involved to ensure that her mental health disorder is receiving the necessary attention.

Guiding Principles in Working With Dually Diagnosed Clients

Following is a list of guiding principles for working with clients who are dually diagnosed.

1. Never forget that dual diagnosis means that each diagnosis is of equal importance. When dually diagnosed clients present for treatment, they might minimize one or both of the disorders, especially if they are using a substance to medicate their feelings or symptoms of their mental health disorder.

2. Do not be afraid to ask questions relative to either disorder directly. The goal of a good assessment is to gather as much information as possible regarding both disorders. If a client does not want to answer the question or cannot as a result of trauma, then the client will avoid answering as a protective measure.

3. We, as counselors, must make sure to explore our own feelings about the use of substances and issues of mental health while treating clients. Our own feelings will affect how we perceive clients as well as the content and process of the treatment experience.

4. It is important for dually diagnosed women to be assessed accurately for the diagnoses in question. It often takes time to make accurate diagnoses because you must wait until the client has sufficient "clean time" from any substances to see what mental health symptoms persist. With time, however, you eventually will figure out, with the help of other providers in the picture, the range of clinical issues that you are treating. Moreover, clients often present at assessment with previous diagnoses that may or may not be accurate. Therefore, it is important to reassess each case even when a thorough evaluation has been conducted in the past. Also, it is common during early recovery for clients to feel anxious, panicky, and/or depressed. Their sleep, appetite, and sexual functioning also may be affected. These symptoms may or may not be indicative of a second primary diagnosis. It is important to assess whether these symptoms represent part of the recovery process or form a secondary clinical mental health diagnosis.

5. For many clients with anxiety, mood, and depressive disorders, it is crucial to obtain a psychopharmacological evaluation. Counselors should develop a network of local psychiatrists who are specialized in the field of treating clients with histories of addiction. An addictions psychiatrist will best be able to decide when and how to medicate a client with a history of both disorders. This can be particularly tricky when a client is actively drinking and/or drugging. However, there are many specialists whose expertise in this area has successfully helped clients to achieve sobriety. CASPAR Inc. has seen many successes in clients who were able to achieve sobriety after receiving psychopharmacological help for their second disorder.

6. Do not forget to encourage clients to be patient when beginning a psychopharmacological treatment. Clients often will experience a worsening of symptoms, side effects of the medications, and a sense of either being overwhelmed or having failed. If a certain medication does not achieve the desired

Research findings highlight the need for specialized intensive services for patients with dual diagnoses, who often have cognitive and social deficits that limit their ability to participate productively in standard substance abuse treatment programs. It has been suggested that long-term, flexible programs that combine elements of substance abuse (such as relapse prevention and training in social and problem-solving skills) and psychiatric treatment (such as nonconfrontational style and medication management) may optimize outcomes in patients with dual diagnoses.[7]

result after a few weeks, then a client always has the option of modifying the dosage or switching the medication.

7. It is highly recommended that all treatment providers working with a particular client collaborate to form a treatment team. This team, often comprised of substance abuse clinicians, psychiatrists, behavioral medicine specialists, mental health clinicians, primary care physicians, and representatives of the legal and protective service community, should work together to share information and develop joint treatment plans.

8. All counselors should remember to assess these clients' suicidal potential on a regular basis because they are at increased risk for harming themselves.

Eating Disorders and Substance-Abusing Women

Because eating disorders are so pervasive among women, especially alcoholic or drug-abusing women, you should include an eating history as part of a comprehensive assessment of a client. This may be done at some point during the first 6 months of sobriety or at the point of intake if there are some clear signs of an eating problem. Taking an eating history helps to break the taboo around talking about eating disorders, places the eating problem in a larger context, and educates the client that a preoccupation or concern with food is a legitimate problem. The denial about eating disorders might be even greater than that about alcoholism or drug abuse. Facing an eating disorder produces anxiety and fear, especially for women who never have discussed their eating behavior. Women often are deeply ashamed about their obsession with food and are guilty about their eating behavior, especially when it involves vomiting and laxative abuse. If you can express concern without being judgmental, then you might be able to explore with a woman what overeating, vomiting, fasting, or laxative abuse *does* for her. Does it produce isolation, physical problems, or mood swings? Have any crises or episodes of depression been connected with an eating episode? By approaching the eating disorder as a response to pain, it allows the counselor to ally herself or himself with the client in beginning to open up a dark and secret part of the client's life. A woman who reports physical cravings for certain foods, similar to alcohol and drugs, and an inability to stop eating them should be made aware of the addictive properties of sugar and refined carbohydrates.

The prevalence of eating disorders in women is an issue of increasing concern for counselors in alcoholism and drug abuse treatment facilities. Certain outpatient, residential, and inpatient treatment programs now are offering groups and counseling for women around eating disorders as well as alcohol and drugs. For some women, the eating disorders might have preceded their alcoholism or drug abuse, starting in childhood or early adolescence. For others, a preoccupation with food and an inability to control it might surface precipitously at the time they stop drinking or taking drugs.

Substance-abusing women with eating disorders can present a complicated treatment challenge. When a woman has alcoholism and an eating disorder, the alcoholism usually needs to be treated first. However, if the eating disorder is severe, then it might need to be treated concurrently. You can benefit a client during treatment by educating and informing her about food as a serious and legitimate concern and by letting her know that there is help available for any problems or trouble she might be having about food and eating.

Anorexia Nervosa

Anorexia, bulimia, and compulsive overeating are the three categories into which most eating problems are divided. Each of these may range in severity and frequency in an alcoholic woman's life so that a careful assessment is necessary on each client.

Anorexia (anorexia nervosa) is a disorder characterized by a relentless pursuit of excessive thinness. Those suffering from this disorder are frantically preoccupied with food and not eating. These women consider self-denial and discipline their most important values, and they condemn satisfying their needs and desires as shameful self-indulgence. They experience and see themselves as too fat when, in fact, they are starving themselves and are severely underweight. Anorexia is commonly seen in female adolescents. However, women who stop drinking or abusing drugs might revert back to or continue patterns of self-deprivation learned in adolescence. A medical assessment should be done at once on any severely underweight sober woman. Anorexia can be life threatening in its extreme forms, and medical hospitalization might be the best treatment alternative.

Bulimia

Bulimia is an eating disorder that is becoming more and more widely recognized among substance-abusing women. A recent study showed that polydrug abuse is significantly more common among bulimics than among anorexics. Bulimics use alcohol, amphetamines, barbiturates, marijuana, tranquilizers, and cocaine far more often than do anorexics. The woman's age and the severity of her eating disorder did not make a difference in the outcome.[8] Bulimia is binge eating followed by some form of purge activity, vomiting, laxative abuse, fasting, or rigid dieting. Someone who is bulimic may be underweight but is more likely to be average or slightly overweight, so there will not necessarily be outward physical signs of this disorder.

Compulsive Overeating

Compulsive overeating involves binging in secret and rapidly ingesting large quantities of high-caloric food or eating all day long. In LeBlanc's book on overcoming compulsive overeating, she defines compulsive overeaters as people who continue eating after they are full and who eat anyway even when they know they should not. She explains, "Compulsive eaters don't give in [to this impulse] just once in a while. Giving in has become a way of life, a way of coping."[9] Compulsive eaters often are overweight (but not always) and involved in a continuous cycle of diets, weight gains, and weight losses.

Connections Between Eating Disorders and Substance Abuse

Eating disorders often are linked to prescription drug abuse, especially amphetamines and tranquilizers. All three types of eating disorders produce a characteristic set of personality traits over time. These include low self-esteem, difficulty with boundaries, fear of sexuality, extreme mood swings, a distorted body image, and social isolation. These characteristics also are associated with alcoholism. Moreover, the behaviors of women with eating disorders are similar to those of women who abuse alcohol or other drugs. The eating disorder syndrome has a life of its own, leading women with eating disorders to rationalize and deny their problems just as they would deny their drinking.

Eating disorders have been put in a broad cultural perspective by some researchers because of the concern and preoccupation with food, body image, and eating that exists among the majority of American women. As Lee suggests, the causes of these types of disorders can be traced to gender inequity, women's socialization, and the basically patriarchal structure of Western society:

> Discontent with one's body is regarded as normal and natural for women in modern society, and disordered eating may be viewed as an extension of this discontent. Explanations for women's socially sanctioned obsession with thinness vary greatly but tend to center on social restrictions on women's lives and on power relations between men and women, suggesting that wholesale changes in the position of women in society may be required in order to bring about any major change in women's relationships with their bodies.[10]

By the time of adolescence, dieting has become a way of life for many girls, and for some, the extreme conditions of anorexia and bulimia have begun to develop. A cultural pursuit of thinness and a concern about weight become a social and cultural norm that is reinforced through the media and in a woman's socialization process. Disturbances in eating might reflect a fundamental disturbance between a woman's self-development and the demands and values of society that are first encountered in adolescence. An eating disorder often develops at the stage of adolescence when a girl is struggling to separate from her mother and to know herself as an autonomous being. Turning to food or depriving herself of it might be a way of expressing her struggle with separation.

Alcoholic and dysfunctional family systems are seen as "breeding grounds" for eating disorders. Food can become a buffer and an escape for a girl living in an environment of conflict. Eating-disordered children can become obsessed with food just as alcoholics are obsessed with alcohol. They might look for "answers" in food or exert the only control they feel through their food intake. Children might eat a lot or eat nothing and become increasingly obsessed with food and calories. Not eating might become a valued behavior. In alcoholic families, there might be few tools and reinforcements for learning moderation. Eating patterns and concerns about food and mealtimes might become a lifelong preoccupation. Mealtimes often are filled with conflict and crisis, producing lifelong negative associations with and feelings about eating.[11]

Treatment Issues for Substance-Abusing Women With Disordered Eating

Timing is crucial in treating eating disorders with a substance-abusing woman. It often is too much for a woman to stop drinking and deal with an eating disorder at the same time. However, there are instances in which eating disorders such as anorexia, binging, and vomiting or abusing laxatives become so all-consuming and debilitating that they need to be addressed at the same time as a woman stops drinking. A guideline used by one alcoholism and drug abuse treatment program that also treats eating disorders is to address an eating disorder as part of treatment if a patient reports binging and vomiting more than three times a day. At this point, a woman might be experiencing a medical and psychological decompensation that could be seriously affecting her health. Anorexia also may produce a severely debilitated physical condition in early sobriety that can require hospitalization in a medical setting, depending on its

The psychological states associated with severely disordered eating have overlaps with other psychiatric diagnoses, particularly depression, anxiety, borderline personality disorder, and obsessive-compulsive disorder.[12]

severity. Extreme laxative abuse also may result in physical problems that need to be addressed by a physician.

Women who have begun to deal with eating disorders as well as alcoholism or drug abuse will need help to learn new coping skills and strategies. It might be harder for many women to change their eating behaviors than it was to stop drinking or abusing drugs because of the pervasiveness of food. Women might have developed eating disorders in childhood that are well established by the time they start drinking and have been part of their way of living even longer than has alcoholism or drug abuse. In addition, there are frequent cases in which women will "transfer addictions." When women stop drinking and taking drugs, their obsession and compulsion may become fused with their eating behaviors. Some women, for whom food was not an issue prior to getting sober, will report acting out addictive behavior with food, secret eating, binging, or vomiting often for the first time in their lives. This can be disconcerting to a newly sober woman.

Anorexia, bulimia, and compulsive overeating each requires a somewhat different treatment modality. An anorexic patient least fits a food addiction model. She often is in a life-threatening situation that needs to be medically stabilized. Her recovery might involve learning to eat again as well as intensive psychotherapy and family therapy to uncover the roots of her self-starvation. A bulimic woman might need help to learn to eat a moderate meal, experience fullness, and allow the food to stay in her stomach while tolerating the initial panic, guilt, and desire to vomit that (for her) accompany eating. A compulsive overeater needs structure and clarity around food. The concept of "the first compulsive bite" starting the overeating cycle is helpful for many compulsive overeaters whose eating patterns are most similar to patterns in other addictive diseases such as alcoholism and drug abuse.

Abstinence from an eating disorder is a starting point that might involve relapse, especially in the beginning. A food binge usually is preceded by dangerous high-risk behavior around situations that the client needs to begin to identify. The feelings that trigger the desire to escape into food often fall into a pattern that can be recognized and predicted. New coping skills take time to learn. If you approach your client's eating disorder with the same sensitive understanding as you approach her alcoholism or drug abuse, then you will positively influence her recovery.

Overeaters Anonymous (OA), a self-help program based on the principles of Alcoholics Anonymous (AA), might be a solution for helping clients who admit to having food problems and are willing to seek help. Abstinence in OA means developing a plan of eating (usually three balanced meals a day), avoiding binge foods (i.e., sugars and high carbohydrates), and developing a support network of people with the same problem. But abstinence is seen as only the beginning of a recovery process. Learning to express feelings, develop healthy relationships, and establish a spiritually based life are the goals of recovery in OA. Abstinence is a tool that may change and evolve as a woman starts to learn to let go of her food obsession and begin a new way of life.

Individual counseling and psychotherapy with a professional who respects the seriousness of eating disorders is another alternative to clients recovering from both substance abuse and eating disorders. Food usually is "the last drug to go" for a sober woman. Feelings and family issues surface without food preoccupation and excessive eating as a buffer and an escape. You can help your client to grieve for the loss of food binges and food obsession and can examine with her some of the dysfunctional rules and behaviors learned in her family of origin. Abstaining from destructive eating behaviors often means that an alcoholic or drug-abusing woman will need a lot of emotional support and permission to feel anger and grief for the first time, completely drug free.

References

1. "Dual Diagnosis: Part 1," *Harvard Mental Health Letter* (August 1991). (Harvard Health Publications, Boston) Available: `http://www.mentalhealth.com/mag1/p5h-dual.html`

2. National Institute on Alcohol Abuse and Alcoholism, *Women and Alcohol: Issues for Prevention Research,* NIH Publication No. 96-3817 (Washington, DC: Government Printing Office, 1996).

3. L. M. Najavits, R. D. Weiss, and S. R. Shaw, "Link between Substance Abuse and Posttraumatic Stress Disorder in Women: A Research Review," *American Journal on Addictions* 6, no. 4 (1997): 273-83.

4. L. Westreich, P. Guedj, M. Galanter, and D. Baird, "Differences between Men and Women in Dual-Diagnosis Treatment," *American Journal on Addictions* 6, no. 3 (1997): 311-17.

5. H. Doweiko, *Concepts of Chemical Dependency,* 3rd ed. (Pacific Grove, CA: Brooks/Cole, 1996), 269.

6. National Institute on Alcohol Abuse and Alcoholism, *Alcoholism and Co-occurring Disorders,* Alcohol Alert No. 14, Public Health Service Publication No. 302 (Bethesda, MD: U.S. Department of Health and Human Services, 1991).

7. U.S. Department of Health and Human Services, *Ninth Special Report to the U.S. Congress on Alcohol and Health,* NIH Publication No. 97-4017 (Washington, DC: Government Printing Office, 1997), 357.

8. M. W. Wiederman and T. Pryor, "Substance Use among Women with Eating Disorders," *International Journal of Eating Disorders* 20, no. 2 (1996): 163-68.

9. D. LeBlanc, *You Can't Quit 'til You Know What's Eating You: Overcoming Compulsive Eating* (Deerfield Beach, FL: Health Communications Inc., 1990), 9-10.

10. C. Lee, *Women's Health: Psychological and Social Perspectives* (London: Sage, 1998), 123-24.

11. Elizabeth Mansfield, "Eating Disorders and Alcoholism: Linking Family System Dynamics," *Focus on the Family* 7 (1984): 27.

12. Lee, *Women's Health,* 130.

▓ Staff Training Activities

Activity 1: Similarities Between Alcoholism and Eating Disorders
Activity 2: Treatment Model Based on Similarities Between Alcoholism and Eating Disorders
Activity 3: New Coping Strategies for an Alcoholic Woman Who Is Dealing With Her Eating Disorders
Activity 4: Vignettes of Alcoholic or Drug-Abusing Women With Eating Disorders

Activity 1: Similarities Between Alcoholism and Eating Disorders

List the symptoms of progression of alcoholism and compare them to progression with eating disorders. Discuss the following:

■ Why is it difficult for recovering alcoholic women to talk about eating disorders?

■ How might an eating disorder affect a woman's sobriety?

Activity 2: Treatment Model Based on Similarities Between Alcoholism and Eating Disorders

Discuss "Treatment of Eating Disorders" as a group. Go over the following intake questions in some detail to clarify their meaning for participants:

1. What were meals like growing up?

Many eating disorders start in childhood and initially might be a response to an alcoholic or dysfunctional family. Women remember conflict or tension or an extreme repression of feelings at mealtimes. For many girls, mealtimes became a battleground, especially if they refused to eat or overate. Meals became situations that they dreaded and came to avoid, even as adults.

2. Have you gone through weight changes?

Women with eating disorders frequently experience wide fluctuations of weight. They might swing from extreme thinness to obesity or might gain and lose the same 30 to 50 pounds again and again, year after year.

3. Is anyone in your family overweight or concerned about weight?

Eating disorders, as well as alcoholism, tend to run in families. A mother preoccupied with food and weight will pass this attitude on to her daughter as "normal." She might be deeply ashamed of an underweight or overweight child.

4. Have you ever stopped eating? Binged? Abused laxatives?

These behaviors often are deep and shame-filled secrets for women with eating disorders. Just by using the words and asking the questions, an alcoholic woman has permission to share her food behaviors.

5.   How do you eat now?

A woman might not be able to answer this readily if she is dealing with an eating disorder. The question allows her to think about her current behavior and gives her an opportunity to reflect on her eating. She might bring up her eating behavior in a later session once the subject has been raised.

Treatment of Eating Disorders

Treatment planning for suspected eating disorders in your client:

1.   Include an eating history with your initial assessment.

   a. What were meals like growing up?

   b. Have you gone through weight changes?

   c. Is anyone in your family overweight or concerned about weight?

   d. Have you ever stopped eating? Binged? Abused laxatives?

   e. How do you eat now?

Taking an eating history breaks the taboos about talking about eating disorders. It allows you, as the counselor, to express concern without being judgmental. It puts the eating disorder in a larger context and educates clients about eating disorders.

2.   Explore what overeating/vomiting/fasting/laxative abuse does for the client. Remember that the eating disorder is a response to pain; it is the best coping mechanism the person has. A person will not give away her coping mechanism unless she has another to replace it. Accepting that your client has positive reasons for eating the way she does accomplishes the following:

   a. Allows you to ally with the person

   b. Helps to break down the person's harsh self-judgment

   c. Helps you to decide what coping skills your client needs to learn

   d. Builds the stage for confronting denial

Help your client to see herself as she actually is. Look at the consequences of her eating disorder (e.g., isolation, physical problems, mood swings). Connect her crisis/depression with her eating disorder.

3.   Use your client's strengths to help her recover.

   a. What helped her to get sober?

   b. Help your client to talk to you and others about her eating disorder.

   c. Break her recovery down into smaller, more manageable chunks.

   d. Use "what if" clauses; consider an intervention with family and friends.

   e. Decide together what is acceptable and unacceptable behavior and what the consequences are for unacceptable behavior.

Counseling the client's recovery from an eating disorder:

1. Give support and build self-esteem. Your client does not know how courageous she is or what hard work she is doing unless you tell her. Just as she minimized her eating disorder, she minimizes her recovery (denial again).

2. Build new coping mechanisms. Your client needs to learn relaxation, rehearse dealing with everyday stresses, and practice how to relate to people.

3. Encourage Overeaters Anonymous, Alcoholics Anonymous, and Al-Anon involvement or other good group therapies.

4. Be prepared to be active with your client. Call if she misses her appointments.

5. Concentrate on what your client needs to do to stay abstinent today rather than on why she has an eating disorder. Avoid analysis; put first things first.

6. Help your client to deal with anger. She might have anger that she has an eating disorder, that others do not, that it took so long to recover, or that others seem to be recovering faster.

7. Help your client to cope with grief. Food or alcohol has been her best friend. She has lost a coping mechanism, a friend, and an identity.

8. Teach your client ways in which to set limits. Most people with eating disorders are perfectionists who cannot tolerate having limits or imperfections. Model being imperfect, making mistakes and acknowledging them, setting limits, and expressing feelings.

9. Teach your client about feelings.

10. Explore new ways for your client to have fun and to nurture and reward herself without involving food or alcohol substances.

11. Slow down your client. She will want to recover too fast.

SOURCE: Adapted from a model by Susan D. DeMattos.

Activity 3: New Coping Strategies for an Alcoholic Woman Who Is Dealing With Her Eating Disorders

This model is based on the work of Louis Sutherland of Beech Hill Hospital, Dublin, New Hampshire:

a. Cognitive restructuring

   ■ Work with the client on identifying and labeling feelings.

   ■ Practice relapse prevention by identifying feelings that lead to a binge or purge.

   ■ Involve the client with Twelve Steps in Alcoholics Anonymous and Overeaters Anonymous, using a sponsor and taking a personal inventory.

b. Decision making and problem solving

■ Discuss with the client specific problems around shopping for food, cooking, and planning meals.

■ Support her in developing some regular routines in how she deals with food each day.

c.   Assertiveness training

■ Encourage the use of the slogans of Alcoholics Anonymous and Overeaters Anonymous, for example, "First things first" and "Easy does it."

■ Give the client affirmations to write and say each day, for example, "I want good things to happen to me," "I expect good things to happen to me," and "I embrace good things happening to me."

■ Develop a feelings formula to use in communication, for example, "I feel [mad, sad, glad, scared] when you . . ., and I wish . . ."

d.   Behavioral techniques

■ Encourage the client to ask for help from others with eating disorders through meetings and the telephone.

■ Expand the client's resources to include others to support her in times of stress.

■ Encourage moderate exercise. Caregivers need to be clear about moderation because bulimics tend to overdo exercise and become obsessed with meeting goals.

e.   Ongoing assessment

■ Ask the client to keep a food diary for 3 months (see Client Treatment Activities).

■ Suggest that the client keep a journal as part of her recovery process to record her feelings and how she has been dealing with them.

f.   Bibliotherapy

■ For clients who wish to read, there are a number of excellent books on eating disorders and experiences in recovery. See the Resources section at the end of this chapter.

Activity 4:   Vignettes of Alcoholic or Drug-Abusing Women With Eating Disorders

Hand out the following vignettes. Break the participants into small groups of three or four people. Ask them to read through each vignette and to make a plan for the treatment strategies they would employ as next steps. For example, they might ask the client to keep a food diary or suggest that she attend an Overeaters Anonymous meeting. If there is time, discuss treatment plans in the large group after small group discussions.

■ Jane is a 32-year-old woman who has been sober for 8 months in Alcoholics Anonymous. She recently completed 6 months in a recovery home for alcoholic women and is now living with two sober roommates. She has come to outpatient treatment because she has started to binge secretly at night and then make herself vomit. She is afraid that her roommates will find out and "be disgusted."

■ This is the first time that Mary, 28 years old, has mentioned food or eating in the 1½ years that you have been seeing her in counseling. She has been sober for 3 years and came to see you to help her deal with feelings of anger and rage that started to surface after she had been sober for one year. You have noticed a weight gain of 50 pounds or more in the time you have been seeing her. Mary has carefully avoided the subject of eating and weight until this session, when she broke down and cried. Her brother is getting married in a month. She is afraid to go to the wedding and admits that it is not because of alcohol but rather because of how she feels about being fat and having nothing to wear.

■ Lee is 17 years old and was brought into treatment by her family because of a referral from a school psychologist. Lee has been suspended for alcohol and pill abuse. She recently has started attending some meetings of Young People's Alcoholics Anonymous and reports that her drinking has been "cut down." Your sessions together are dominated by Lee's preoccupation with her weight and body image. She is significantly underweight but constantly talks about dieting and being too fat. She expresses concern that if she stops drinking and taking pills, she will "blow up like a balloon." She admits that she has vomited after eating "once or twice." You suspect that an eating disorder, as well as drugs and alcohol, is a major problem for her.

Client Training Activities

Activity 1

Take a brief eating history from the client as part of an assessment either at intake or during the first 6 months.

1. What were meals like growing up?

2. Have you gone through weight changes?

3. Is anyone in your family overweight or concerned about weight?

4. Have you ever stopped eating? Binged? Abused laxatives?

5. How do you eat now?

Activity 2

If a client is ambivalent or unsure of whether she wants to address an eating disorder, then it is helpful to give her some open-ended questions. Remember, she might have a great deal of denial and fear.

1. What goals do you have regarding eating, food, or weight?

2. What behaviors would you like to change?

3. What benefits have you gotten out of binging, vomiting, fasting, undereating, controlling your weight, and being preoccupied with food or weight?

4. What ill effects have you had from the preceding?

Activity 3

For a client who is willing to address her eating disorder openly, go over "Eating Disorders: Warning Signs, Danger Signs, and Addiction." Approach these signs with the client in an open, nonjudgmental way, letting her know that many women have problems with food and that she is not alone. Stress that eating disorders are considered illnesses just like alcoholism and that she is not to blame.

Activity 4

Ask the client to keep a food diary for a week or more and to bring it to the next session to discuss. This might be difficult for her to do at first. Reassure her that whatever she is able to record will be valuable.

A food diary should consist of the following:

a. Food and liquid consumed

b. Time of day

c. Context (e.g., social set and setting, alone or with others)

d. Feelings (e.g., scared, mad, glad, sad)

e. Did you binge? Vomit? Use laxatives? Fast after eating?

Activity 5

As a client is able to become more open about her eating disorder, it is appropriate to begin to help her practice new coping strategies. This might involve many months of trust building and frequent relapses in the beginning. An understanding, nonjudgmental counseling relationship can be invaluable to an alcoholic woman dealing with an eating disorder for the first time.

Activity 6

Discuss with the client the prospect of attending self-help and support groups as soon as it is appropriate. Make the connection to how a self-help group might be helping her to stay sober from alcohol and drugs.

1. *OA:* This is a self-help group based on the same principles as Alcoholics Anonymous. Groups meet in nearly every community, and information is listed in the telephone directory.

2. *Al-Anon or Adult Children of Alcoholics (ACOA):* For some women with eating disorders, family of origin issues might need to be addressed along with the eating disorders. Al-Anon and ACOA groups can be a great support.

3. *Anorexia-bulimia support groups:* Some mental health services and private practitioners now offer support groups for eating disorders. There also are outpatient groups associated with hospitals that treat eating disorders.

Activity 7

Severe, life-threatening medical and psychological problems are associated with both anorexia nervosa and bulimia. Inpatient treatment is strongly recommended in the following instances:

a. Electrolyte imbalances that are brought on by frequent vomiting

b. Malnutrition

c. Suicidality and despair; when the client feels unable to function

Resources

American Anorexia/Bulimia Association Inc.
Address: 165 West 46th Street, Suite 1108, New York, NY 10036
Phone: (212) 575-6200

(This agency provides information on eating disorders and treatment programs.)

Information Exchange Inc.
Address: 120 North Main Street, New City, NY 10956
Phone: (914) 634-0050

(This is a private nonprofit agency that provides training and consultation services to mental health, alcohol/drug abuse, and other professionals nationwide and abroad, especially in the areas of dual problems of mental disorder and substance abuse.)

Overeaters Anonymous, World Service Office (OA)
Address: P.O. Box 4020, Rio Rancho, NM 87174-4020
Web: http://www.overeaters.org

(OA is a self-support, self-help, Twelve Step group for individuals who want to stop eating compulsively.)

PART III

Trends and Considerations for Special Populations

Young Women: Prevention, Intervention, and Treatment

Women's treatment programs report treating younger and younger women each year. Not only has teenage alcohol and drug abuse become widespread, but the primary group of women seeking treatment in centers are in their early 20s and early 30s. Some of these young women are highly skilled professionals, some are high school dropouts, and others are young mothers. Many have been drinking or drugging heavily for quite a while, perhaps since their early teens, and come from alcoholic families. Children from alcoholic families are more likely to abuse alcohol or other drugs during adolescence.[1]

Most surveys also show increasing alcohol use among teenage girls, so that their use of alcohol almost (but not quite) equals that of teenage boys. This is a dramatic change that, accompanied by other changes in women's roles, might portend future increases in drinking problems among women. Regular drinking is now common among high school girls, and a sizable number engage in heavy drinking. Many studies show that adolescents are more likely to engage in unprotected sex when they drink alcohol than when they do not, increasing the risk of sexually transmitted diseases and HIV to young drinkers.[2]

Results of the 1998 Back to School Teen Survey from the National Center on Addiction and Substance Abuse (CASA) at Columbia University indicate that between 12 and 13 years of age, tobacco, alcohol, and drugs become a significant issue for youths. After 13 years, teens are three times more likely to know someone their age who sells drugs; offers them drugs; or uses acid, heroin, or cocaine.[3]

In another study of youths by CASA, the center reports even more serious problems for teenage girls:

Teen boys and girls exhibit different symptoms of substance abuse. Boys tend to be outer directed, displaying symptoms such as drunk driving, fighting, and truancy. Girls are [more likely] to be inner directed, displaying anxiety, depression, and lack of self-esteem as signals of substance abuse. Girls who abuse drugs are more likely to have suffered sexual abuse than [are] boys. The rate[s] of substance abuse among boys and girls [are] becoming increasingly similar. Women become intoxicated more quickly than men and addicted more rapidly than men. Tragically, girls who are high on alcohol and drugs increase their risk of being raped, and most teen pregnanc[ies] occur when one or both teens are high or drunk.[4]

The role of male peer pressure in the onset of adolescent and college-age women's drinking can be a significant factor. Some observations on alcohol problems in adolescent females suggest that girls who begin drinking during early adolescence have more opportunities to drink heavily, live with heavy-drinking parents, and make personal efforts not to be traditionally "feminine." These young women might be at high risk for drinking problems and early onset of alcoholism.[5]

Clinicians find that adolescent and young adult women often hide emotional immaturity and sometimes an extreme lack of knowledge about themselves and their bodies with a tough, pseudo-mature facade. Although they might have had many "adult" or traumatic life experiences (sexually, with the law, or with family), few people acknowledge that underneath they are frightened children still needing guidance appropriate to their age. An adolescent treatment program described a group of its female clients as being possessive and territorial about their belongings and jealous of other girls. The girls showed extreme ignorance about their bodies and also exhibited a great need to belong and feel accepted within the group.[6]

The close link between alcohol or drug use and interpersonal relationships for adolescent girls and young women is supported by research that looks at the needs of adolescents and college-age women for affiliation and connection. Adolescence is a time of transitions and changes in the context of relationships and connections in a young woman's life. These can create stress and emotional isolation despite seemingly successful competitive achievement and social adjustment. With women for whom the process of expanding their relationships is difficult and painful, alcohol and drug abuse (as well as eating disorders) might emerge when emotional needs are unmet and a sense of connection is sought through the use and abuse of substances.

Prevention Issues for Adolescent and College-Age Women

Prevention with adolescent and college-age women needs to address their knowledge, attitudes, and decision-making skills around alcohol and drugs as well as their feelings and self-concepts. Young women also need validation for their ongoing need to make connections and affiliations that empower them. Developing and maintaining relationships with friends and lovers is a central task for young women. One recent study of college women found that their decisions regarding drug use influenced them as they looked for, kept, and ended relationships.[7] Counselors can educate young women about how to make responsible decisions and about how to maintain relationships without resorting to alcohol or drugs for acceptance or control.

Young women from alcoholic or dysfunctional families might need opportunities to build self-esteem and explore positive coping strategies. Ongoing support groups for young adult women that focus on women's issues, assertiveness, and sexual identity are important to develop, particularly for women in college settings. A review of lifestyle and health of college-age women noted that although women (especially in college) frequently are supported by their peers in their decisions, the behavioral norm of the group might prove more influential than a woman's personal desire to change her behavior.[8]

Intervention occurs when an adolescent or young adult woman begins to experience life problems as a result of her drinking or drug use. Counselors can help to make the connection between her current life problems and her use of alcohol or drugs. The painful nature of transitions in relationships during adolescence and young adulthood is important to acknowledge and support. The counselor can help by showing how alcohol and drugs will only make relationships more difficult and unworkable. Intervention often is done most effectively in a group setting with peers. Peer-based counseling programs in high schools and colleges have been an effective model for reaching young women beginning to experience problems with alcohol or drugs. The role of a counselor might be to develop such a program. Young women also need groups that focus on feelings and self-esteem as an integral part of developing a life free of alcohol and drug abuse.

Treatment for alcohol-abusing young women often results from intervention by family, friends, or school or college authorities. There are treatment services available in many areas for adolescents, far fewer solely for adolescent girls. Some women's services will accept young women in inpatient and residential care. Many communities and college campuses have support groups for young alcoholics and addicts. There are young people's Alcoholics Anonymous groups, sober dances, and outings. Age-appropriate activities that foster friendship and connection are important for an adolescent or college-age woman who is trying to recover. A number of young women are coming into treatment programs in communities where ongoing outreach continues to be done and where programs are set up that support young women's need to feel safe and accepted by others.

Prevention, Intervention, and Treatment Services for Young Women

Prevention Services

Alcohol and drug classroom education. There are comprehensive programs taught by trained teachers reaching adolescent women in the classroom. Role-plays and activities allow a girl to practice refusal skills and to learn about friendships and protection in peer relationships. Alcohol and drug education programs that foster cooperation and communication are especially helpful to adolescent girls.

Peer-led education activities. Peer leadership programs in high schools and colleges have been a new development in which young women have played an active part. Becoming a peer leader gives a young woman a caretaking and nurturing role and also a strong sense of affiliation with others. Participating in peer-led activities often is perceived as safe and nonthreatening to young women, especially when the peer leaders are young women like themselves.

Children from alcoholic families groups and services. Younger adolescent women can benefit from Alateen groups in the community. Older adolescents and young adult women from alcoholic families may join Adult Children of Alcoholics support groups. These are available in most communities as part of Al-Anon. Individual counseling and group supports that focus on self-esteem, assertiveness, and exploring sexual identity often are helpful to young women who are working to overcome the impact of family alcoholism on their lives. This also is an important prevention measure for these young women who are at high risk for developing substance abuse problems themselves.

Intervention Services

Student assistance programs. High schools and colleges have developed counseling and referral programs for students who are identified by school authorities, parents, or others as in trouble with alcohol or drugs. These programs usually provide an alternative to suspension or expulsion, and they require counseling and group services (and sometimes inpatient treatment) as a condition of remaining in the school or college system. Young women have successfully entered these programs. A limitation of these programs is that adolescents usually are treated as a homogeneous group without an acknowledgment of the needs of young women. Just as with adult women, adolescent and young women might feel safer in women's groups or working with women counselors.

Outpatient support groups for young women questioning their drinking. Adolescents and young women might recoil from the diagnosis of alcoholism but be willing to think and talk about their alcohol or drug problems by exploring or questioning their behavior in a safe, nonjudgmental support group. Both short-term and open-ended women's groups focusing on the context and issues surrounding a young woman's drinking may help a young woman either make more responsible decisions around alcohol and drug use or seek treatment as a next step.

Treatment Services

Adolescent inpatient programs. There are an increasing number of separate adolescent treatment programs in hospitals and alcoholism facilities. Most are for males and females together and involve at least a month of inpatient care with psychiatric, medical, and addictions services. There often is a strong focus on the family. Family counseling and active family participation usually are required. Some of these programs provide separate services for adolescent and young adult women in women's groups.

Residential programs. Residential programs for adolescents and young adults usually last 6 months to 1 year after completion of an inpatient treatment program. Adolescent residential programs are not available everywhere. Halfway houses for women sometimes will treat adolescent women. Most treat women from 18 years of age and upward. In the United States, residential programs solely for teenage girls are scarce. Residential treatment gives young women an opportunity to develop new self-conceptions, explore conflicts about themselves as women, and establish new and satisfying interpersonal relationships, especially with other women.

Outpatient programs. More women's alcoholism services are developing groups and treatment services for adolescent and young women. The high incidence of alcohol and illicit drug abuse among younger women and the early onset of drinking and resulting psychosocial problems, especially unwanted pregnancy, can make it valuable to have a special focus on young women's issues and concerns. Their needs often are complex and varied, demanding much from the counselor.

References

1. U.S. Department of Health and Human Services, *Ninth Special Report to the U.S. Congress on Alcohol and Health,* NIH Publication No. 97-4017 (Washington, DC: Government Printing Office, 1997), 34.

2. Ibid., 266.

3. National Center on Addiction and Substance Abuse, *1998 CASA National Survey of Teens, Teachers, and Principals* (New York: Columbia University, CASA, 1998). Available: http://www.casacolumbia.org/pubs/sept98/contents.htm

4. National Center on Addiction and Substance Abuse, *Adolescence and Alcohol, Tobacco, and Other Drugs: A Dangerous Mix* (New York: Columbia University, CASA, 1998). Available: http://www.casacolumbia.org/pubs/aug97/part2.htm

5. Kevin Thompson and Richard Wilsnack, "Drinking Problems among Female Adolescents: Patterns and Influences," in Sharon Wilsnack and Linda Beckman, eds., *Alcohol Problems in Women* (New York: Guilford, 1984), 59.

6. Keith McMillen, *The Addiction Letter* (Williamsburg, PA: New Beginnings at Forge Cove, August 1987), 1-2.

7. K. M. Williams, "Learning Limits: College Women Constructing Meaning about Drugs in Their Relationships," *Dissertation Abstracts International* 58, no. 12 (1998): 4586-A.

8. K. M. Hendricks and N. H. Herbold, "Diet, Activity, and Other Health-Related Behaviors in College-Age Women," *Nutrition Reviews* 56, no. 3 (1998): 65-75.

▉ Staff Training Activities

Activity 1: Exploring the Reasons Why Adolescent Girls Drink Alcohol
Activity 2: Transitions in the Lives of Young Women
Activity 3: A Relational Model of Alcohol and Drug Use
Activity 4: Diagnosing Alcohol and Drug Use in a Young Woman
Activity 5: Role-Play Talking With a Young Woman in a College Setting About Her Drinking

Activity 1: Exploring the Reasons Why Adolescent Girls Drink Alcohol

Brainstorm reasons why young women start to drink. Ask the group to think of girls separately from adolescent boys during this activity even though many of the reasons are the same for both.

Reasons why girls drink:

Peer pressure	Lose inhibitions
Acceptance	Rebel
Rite of passage	Low self-esteem
Accompany boyfriend	Escape from feelings
Act grown up	Experiment
Maintain a relationship	Be sexy and glamorous

Discussion:

■ Look at each of these reasons and explore where it comes from (e.g., media, emotional insecurity, family, friends).

■ How does each reason reflect a young woman's concern for maintaining and enhancing relationships?

■ Which of these reasons empower a young woman and which give the power of choice to others?

Activity 2: Transitions in the Lives of Young Women

There is evidence that women tend to turn to alcohol and drugs at moments of transition or upheaval. These often are times of disconnection and change. Outline some of the major transitions in young women's lives that could make them vulnerable to abuse of alcohol or drugs. Do this exercise as a group activity.

■ Parental divorce or separation during adolescence

■ Loss or rejection by a boyfriend or peer group

- Geographic change in school or community

- Going away from home to go to college or work

- Separation or estrangement from parents and/or siblings

- Teenage pregnancy

- Death of a parent or close friend

Activity 3:   A Relational Model of Alcohol and Drug Use

This model was developed by Sybil Hendrickson, IMPACT, Center for Addictions Studies, Cambridge, Massachusetts. It was inspired by the Stone Center of Developmental Studies, Wellesley College, and by Blythe McVicker Clinchy, Nancy Rule Goldberger, Mary F. Belenky, and Jill Mattuck Tarule, eds., *Women's Ways of Knowing: The Development of Self, Voice, and Mind* (New York: Basic Books, 1997). Outline for the group the following motivations for a young woman's alcohol or drug use based on her need to maintain and preserve relationships:

1. *Bartering:* Young women will use alcohol or drugs as a way of maintaining relationships with boyfriends or lovers who drink and use drugs. A relationship becomes centered around drinking or drug taking, not necessarily for the substances but rather as an attempt by a young woman to keep the relationship going. Drinking is motivated mainly by the belief that it keeps the relationship intact. The young woman's greatest fear, if she stops drinking or drugging, is that she will lose the relationship. A college student might want to study on weekends but will drink with her boyfriend instead and willingly suffer the loss of education.

2. *Sociocultural use:* Young women will drink and use drugs as a way in which to maintain the traditional stereotype of compliant females. Alcohol or drug use puts many young women in a submissive and powerless position. They comply with the wishes of boyfriends and lovers, remaining the "good girls" and not challenging or confronting their significant others. There also is the opposite phenomenon, however, of young women who drink and drug to rebel against the culturally defined female stereotype.

3. *Feelings:* Young women will use alcohol to deal with pain and to overcome feelings of isolation and discomfort in relationships. Drinking or drugging becomes adaptive and allows a young woman in a relationship to act sexually and emotionally in ways she could not if sober. Young women gain a sense of ease and lose inhibitions, which gives them the illusion of closeness and intimacy. Young women from alcoholic or dysfunctional families might be drinking or taking drugs to avoid the painful memories of childhood emotional and physical neglect and·abuse. Turning to alcohol or drugs might be a familiar pattern learned from parental role models.

Activity 4:   Diagnosing Alcohol and Drug Use in a Young Woman

Discuss "Young Women's Alcohol and Drug Questionnaire":

- It is important to remember the relational focus of a young woman's drinking or drug use and to ask about the context of her drinking.

■ Answering *yes* to some of these questions might mean a pattern of trouble with alcohol but not necessarily alcoholism.

Young Women's Alcohol and Drug Questionnaire

___ Do you drink/use drugs because you have problems with relationships?

___ Do you drink/use drugs when you get mad at friends, boyfriends, or your parents?

___ Does drinking make you feel more attractive, less inhibited sexually, like a different person?

___ Do you drink/use drugs because you sometimes have problems:

    ___ Facing up to stressful situations?

    ___ Going out on a date or socializing with friends?

___ Do you drink/use drugs to lose your shyness and build up self-confidence?

___ Does your drinking/using drugs make you feel accepted by others:

    ___ Your boyfriend and his friends?

    ___ Your friends?

    ___ Strangers at parties?

___ Do you drink/use drugs to escape painful feelings?

___ Has your drinking/drug use changed during the past year? Please describe how it has changed:

_____

_____

_____

___ Have you experienced any of the following:

    ___ Drop in grades or school attendance?

    ___ Change in personal priorities?

    ___ Change in athletic performance or commitment?

    ___ Desire to spend time alone?

    ___ Problems with parents or friends because of drinking/drug using?

    ___ Guilt or shame over your drinking/drug use?

    ___ Needing to drink or use drugs more than you used to so as to feel the effects or the "high"?

    ___ Drinking/drugging when you did not intend to or drinking/drugging more than you intended to?

    ___ Remorse or regret over situations that have occurred while you were drinking or using drugs?

___ Do you at any time worry about your drinking/drugging and think that it might be causing trouble for you or someone else?

_____

_____

_____

_____

_____

Activity 5: Role-Play Talking With a Young Woman in a College Setting About Her Drinking

Divide people into groups of three or four. One person will play the role of the alcohol-abusing student, and another will play the student adviser. The remaining small group members will be observers (or they may switch roles). Read the following scenario:

Janet is 21 years old. She is in her third year of college. She lives with her boyfriend, Bill, in an off-campus apartment, and she works in a local student tavern "to help pay for college expenses." Janet came to college with a full 4-year scholarship. This year, she is on academic probation and has only one semester to pull up her grades or else she will lose her scholarship and might be unable to graduate with her class. Ever since Janet moved in with Bill last spring, her academic work has suffered. She complains that Bill likes to drink and party on weekends and that she cannot find the time to study. You have been her student adviser since she came to the college, and you are concerned about the changes in Janet. She looks depressed and is withdrawn. You have suspected that she might be drinking too much since she started her relationship with Bill, and you are concerned about her welfare. She has come to your office late, most unusual for her. You are going to talk to her about her drinking.

■ Ask each group to role-play the meeting between Janet and her adviser.

■ Discuss the role-play in the small group and then in the group as a whole.

Questions:

■ What was the adviser feeling? What was Janet feeling?

■ Was Janet's drinking affected by her living situation? How?

■ Do you suspect that Janet has a drinking problem or not?

■ What suggestions can the adviser offer her?

■ How does the importance of a relationship measure up against the need for academic success when alcohol is involved in Janet's life? Why?

▓ Client Training Activities

Activity 1

Go over the "Young Women's Alcohol and Drug Questionnaire" with the client. Let her know that this is a tool to help both of you explore her drinking or drug history. She might need to be reassured that you are approaching her with an understanding and nonjudgmental attitude. It might be the first time she has shared this important part of her life with someone else.

Activity 2

Work with the young woman to develop a list of activities and interests as alternatives to socializing with alcohol or drugs to help build her self-esteem.

Activity 3

Help your client to feel comfortable refusing an offer of drugs or alcohol. Role-play a situation at a party in which she might feel pressured to accept alcohol or drugs.

Activity 4

Help your client to devise ways in which to deal with her feelings and bolster her coping skills. Help her to identify her support network and people she can talk with in times of stress. She might need help in sorting out priorities and in learning to set short-term achievable goals.

Activity 5

With the help of a family tree or by taking an anecdotal history, establish the role that alcohol and/or drugs have played in the client's family. This might further define the importance of her being able to identify a substance abuse problem in herself and to intervene early. It also will help to identify areas with which the client will need help such as expression of feelings, being able to ask for and seek support, trust issues, and recognizing and acknowledging personal needs. She also might need referral to Al-Anon (or Alateen) and Adult Children of Alcoholics support groups.

Resources

Do It Now Foundation
Address: P.O. Box 27568, Tempe, AZ 85285
Phone: (602) 491-0393
Web: http://www.doitnow.org

(This is a nonprofit private organization aimed toward educating the public, especially the 13- to 30-year age group, regarding drug abuse, alcoholism, and other health-related issues from AIDS to eating disorders.)

Parents' Resource Institute for Drug Free Education (PRIDE)
Contact: Thomas Gleaton, President
Address: 3610 DeKalb Technology Parkway, Suite 105, Atlanta, GA 30340
Phone: (404) 577-4500
E-mail: prideprc@mindspring.com
Web: http://www.prideusa.org

(PRIDE is a nonprofit organization devoted to alcohol, tobacco, and drug prevention that offers information to the public as well as programs for parents, youths, educators, businesses, and governments.)

10 Women of Color and Multicultural Counseling

Women have multiple identities, and we must recognize that they cannot be neatly categorized. Never assume that you know how a woman will identify herself by basing your opinion either on her outward appearance or on superficial information about her such as the gender of her current partner. Each person has the right to define herself or himself, and women may do this in surprising ways.

Part of your role as a counselor might be to work with your client to integrate all aspects of her identity. You will need to work hard to find out how the woman understands the different parts of her identity including identity as an alcoholic or a drug abuser. What parts make her proud? What parts have caused her problems in life? What parts would she like to develop further? What parts does she wish that she could disown? Explore her ambivalence. How does she see the different parts of her identity fitting together (or not fitting together) in her life? Understand that the process of "categorizing" is itself disempowering and that many women have been categorized by society in ways that might feel stigmatizing, isolating, and/or fragmenting. This manual discusses different populations to help you understand some of the cultural factors that might emerge during counseling.

Cultural Diversity

Counselors who are concerned about providing alcoholism services to women face an even greater treatment challenge in providing quality treatment to women of color. African American, Hispanic, Native American, and Asian women represent the largest groups of ethnic and cultural minority women in the United States. We must be able to provide services that can effectively serve this diverse and growing population. Each of these four groups is itself multicultural and highly heterogeneous, comprising many languages, customs, and ethnic and tribal backgrounds. By the year 2000, African Americans are expected to comprise about 13% and Hispanics about 10% of the total U.S. population. Asian Americans (including Pacific Islanders) are expected to comprise about 4% and Native Americans about 1% of the total U.S.

population.[1] Dividing people of color into four major ethnic groups masks an enormous amount of within-group diversity.

Research has not yet made clear how drinking practices and alcohol problems differ in women with regard to race and ethnicity. A 1984 survey by the Alcohol Research Group was one of the first to oversample ethnic minorities to get a more accurate picture. Among the group's original findings, African American and Hispanic women abstained more than did white women, and Hispanic women were less likely to drink heavily than were black or white women.[2] However, more recent analyses of the data from this study revealed, for example, that among three Latino groups (Mexican Americans, Cuban Americans, and Puerto Ricans), Mexican American women had the highest rates of abstention *and* the highest rates of heavy drinking.[3]

Among Native American women, recent studies have found that among tribes, there are very different drinking norms according to tribal culture and socialization:

> Where social integration is high and drinking norms require nonuse or minimal use of alcohol, as in the Pueblo Indians of the Southwest, most women tend to drink little, if at all. Those few women who do drink heavily in violation of traditional norms may rapidly escalate to extreme drinking behavior in response to social ostracism and stigmatization. Less highly integrated groups, including Southwestern Plains Indians such as the Apache or Ute, typically have less differentiated gender roles, greater variations in women's drinking, and relatively weaker stigmatization of heavier drinking by women.[4]

These types of findings reveal the impossibility of assessing a client's drinking behavior based on her racial/ethnic category; the diversity of people and their circumstances within each category is too great. However, it is important for counselors to learn as much as possible about how women are socialized within their own culture and how their acculturation into the dominant society affects their drinking behavior.

Myths and Stereotypes

Inaccurate stereotypes and prejudicial assumptions about women of color have hindered attempts to learn more about the nature of their drinking problems and to identify and treat their alcoholism. Women of color continue to suffer disproportionately from discrimination, unequal access to educational opportunities, unemployment, and social prejudice. They also suffer from a lack of culturally sensitive alcoholism treatment services and from counselors who usually do not understand their clients' needs.

Women of color who are alcoholics often find fewer alcoholism services available for their specific needs than do men. A survey in Massachusetts showed women of color to be the least represented of all groups in state-funded inpatient, outpatient, and residential treatment programs.[5] For a woman of color who also is a lesbian, the problem is further compounded. Women of color usually find themselves alone or in a small minority either in

Myths, stereotypes, and lack of cultural awareness play a major role in the inability of counselors to bridge the gap between themselves and alcoholic women from ethnic/cultural groups different from their own. A myth is an ill-founded belief given uncritical acceptance by members of a group, especially in support of existing or traditional practices. A stereotype is a standard mental picture held in common by members of a group, representing an oversimplified opinion.

programs dominated by men or in women's programs dominated by white women.

It also is likely that women of color face additional or different barriers to treatment. A study investigating the similarities and differences in the difficulties faced by white and African American women who enter treatment reported that African American women face more financial difficulties (e.g., lower income, lack of access to insurance coverage for alcoholism), are more likely to be polydrug abusers, and experience a greater sense of alienation than do white women.[6]

There are no shortages of stereotypes around women of color and alcohol. It often is falsely assumed that African American women tend to be either abstainers who dominate in a matriarchal society or hard-drinking prostitutes. Another stereotype is that cultural sanctions keep Hispanic women from drinking at all. A third is that Native American women are so busy taking care of their alcoholic husbands that they do not fall prey to drinking problems themselves. Asian women might be stereotyped as docile, submissive, and nondrinking. Clients, depending on their awareness, fall into a continuum of interpersonal styles that might either confirm or transcend these cultural stereotypes.

Acculturation

Women of color present different interpersonal styles based on how integrated they are into mainstream white society. An acculturated woman of color, for example, has pride in her racial/cultural identity and yet is comfortable operating in the dominant society as well. A more traditional woman of color tends to operate within the rules of her own culture and has chosen to reject most of the dominant society's values and norms.

The acculturation process itself, as well as lack of support systems for women of color, can lead to abuse of alcohol and drugs. One can speculate that the balancing act of an already multifaceted role is an overwhelming ongoing task. The following summaries present a brief overview of some of the major issues about alcoholism for women of

Women who are more acculturated to U.S. society have a fivefold increased chance of being frequent heavy drinkers than women who are considered to be less acculturated. Overall, the association between drinking patterns and acculturation is stronger and more consistent for women than for men.[7]

color from Asian American/Pacific Islander, Hispanic, African American, and Native American communities.

Asian American and Pacific Islander Women

Asian Americans and Pacific Islanders[8] comprise more than 60 ethnic/racial groups including Chinese, Japanese, Korean, Filipino, Vietnamese, Cambodian, Laotian, Hmong, and Thai. Obviously, this is an extremely diverse population of people with many different languages and dialects and religious practices, coming from all parts of the world and acculturating to the dominant culture of the United States to varying degrees. About 67% of the members of this population are immigrants, many of whom are refugees from Southeast Asia. Through the early 1990s, the Asian American/Pacific Islander population in the United States grew faster than all other racial/ethnic groups and had a projected population of 41 million people by the year 2050.

As this population acculturates and assimilates into the United States, the risk for substance abuse begins to increase. This is because in the process of acculturation, some of the traditions, social norms, and values of a person's original culture become replaced by social norms and values of American culture. According to the National Center on Addiction and Substance Abuse at Columbia University, few Asian American women report heavy drinking, but as they acculturate to U.S. society, drinking rates increase. The center suggests

Immigration: Recent immigrants can experience language and cultural barriers; unemployment or underemployment; educational, social, and health difficulties; the pressures of being new, poor, and a minority in an unfamiliar community; and feelings of loss, grief, separation, and isolation as they adjust to a different way of life.

Intergenerational conflict: The children of immigrant parents often cope more readily with, and adapt more quickly to, the American culture and language than do their elders. This can put them in conflict with the cultural traditions, beliefs, values, and practices of their parents, grandparents, and countries of origin as well as cause communication problems.

Family stress: Children and adolescents also might be asked to serve as translators and intermediaries between their families and their new communities. For some teenagers, prematurely assuming adult roles and responsibilities can result in rebellious or other alienating behavior. Such stresses on the family can make all family members more vulnerable to substance abuse.

that many communities (Asian as well as Hispanic) do not approve of women drinking and so discourage women from drinking, which might encourage these women to hide their substance use.[9]

Besides acculturation, other stress factors for this population that may increase the risk for substance abuse include immigration, intergenerational conflict, and family stress.

Some general characteristics of the Asian American population include a reverence for authority, a sense of pride/shame, and an emphasis on family decision making (similar to Hispanic cultures). When Asian Americans have difficulty in communicating in English, they might avoid seeking care, especially for a problem as stigmatizing as substance abuse or HIV/AIDS. Studies have documented that Chinese Americans, in particular, avoid seeking mental health services.

> One study of Asian Americans in Los Angeles found that among women, Japanese Americans were the most likely to report being drinkers (73%), followed by Chinese (49%) and Koreans (25%). High rates of alcohol consumption also have been noted among persons with one Asian and one white parent. Filipino women are least likely to report the use of alcoholic beverages.

African American Women

Socialization in the African American family is an important part of understanding the identity of alcoholic African American women. For many, there is a strong orientation toward God and the church dating back to early childhood, intense loyalty to the extended family, strong vows of privacy, and respect for the family unit (especially the "mother figure").[10] An African American female who develops alcoholism or drug dependence loses status and power in the family and might even lose her emotional and financial support if she seeks professional help because she has "exposed" the family. In the absence of support of blood relatives, it is important to help the recovering African American woman make connections with understanding people in her extended family and in the African American community. Having a spiritual base to her recovery might help support her sobriety.

African American women report feeling uncomfortable in white, predominantly male Alcoholics Anonymous (AA) meetings unless they can find other African American women who can be role models. However, a spiritually based self-help program with an African American-oriented focus often is an important part of an African American woman's recovery. As important as African American-oriented support groups are for recovering African American women, so too is the availability of female therapists, especially African American ones. African American alcoholic women feel alone and uncomfortable in treatment settings, even those that are exclusively for women. They share the concerns and burdens of all women entering treatment, but they also fear opening up in a setting predominantly oriented toward white women.

Hispanic Women

Hispanic women are an extremely heterogeneous group with respect to country of origin, race, education, income, age, religion, marital status, years in the United States, language, acculturation, and cultural values. All of these factors play a part in understanding the culture and the community of the Hispanic woman who is having problems with alcohol or drugs. Generally, Hispanic women look toward the family as the center of culture. Everything that defines a woman and gives her a sense of belonging, confidence, identity, and pride is encompassed by and affects interpersonal family relationships. Being female in Hispanic culture carries values of responsibility to husbands or other significant males (e.g., father, brother) as well as being faithful, submissive, obedient, and humble. Family relationships are dictated by a definite authority structure of age, sex, and role.

Hispanic women have begun to work outside the home and are gaining a measure of education that was unequaled before. The Hispanic woman might be the head of the household, but she probably will expect her children to follow the traditional values of respect for a significant male. She might have lacked proper role models and be confused about her place in society, so she might resist assimilation of new behaviors more vigorously than do women of other ethnic groups. There might be a significant male who could influence her use of drugs (i.e., her use or abstinence).[11] Counselors will find that understanding individual, family, and community perceptions of gender prescriptions is necessary in providing services to Hispanic women.

Hispanic alcoholic women can be affected by guilt and shame, in part because of strong sanctions within Hispanic culture against women's drinking. There is a tendency for Hispanic women to be influenced by their families to stay away from alcoholism treatment because of the shame that it will cause the families. Hispanic women are more likely to seek help from medical or mental health services first and, therefore, are at risk for developing addictions to prescribed drugs. Treatment for alcoholism rarely is sought voluntarily unless there is a physical illness associated with it.

Language is a key factor in reaching Hispanic women. Having multilingual female counselors available to Hispanic alcoholic women is essential to attract them into treatment. Even if a women speaks English, it might not be the language in which she is most comfortable expressing her feelings. The subtleties of the values and traditions that make up Hispanic people are transmitted through the language. If the woman speaks Spanish or Portuguese primarily, then there might be a reluctance to speak any English even if the woman can speak broken English. If the client is bilingual, then she might choose to speak in English, Spanish, or Portuguese.

Counselors should pay particular attention to the following:

- Building a strong bond of trust or rapport before delving into highly personal matters that might damage a woman's dignity or respect

- Avoiding direct confrontation of a woman with her problems

- Allowing the woman to express problems when she feels safe in her interaction with the therapist

Depending on a Hispanic woman's past experiences with helping services, she might be more or less receptive to seeking help outside of her cultural environment. Counselors might need to adapt traditional treatment methods to reach the Hispanic population. Service providers might be more successful with this population by considering the following:

- Establishing informal at-home meetings with the family to develop rapport and *confianza* (trust)
- Assessing the roles of the individual members of the family, particularly with reference to the use or nonuse of traditional roles
- Including the male authority figure of the family in all important decisions
- Reinforcing the female-headed household's accommodation of new roles and values
- Assessing the support or nonsupport of communications within the family
- Determining the dominant language used in communications within the family (Spanish, Portuguese, or English)
- Assessing the need for outside resources for the family (e.g., Medicaid, food stamps, welfare, dental)

These methods are general guidelines for helping counselors to recognize significant differences among Hispanic alcoholic women. There is no one right way in which to provide effective service delivery to such a culturally diverse population. Counselors and social service professionals must make themselves aware of the uniqueness of the Hispanic populations they hope to serve by developing a better understanding of the social, cultural, economic, and political contexts in which their clients operate.

Native American Women

Unlike other special populations, Native American women who live on reservations often are living under a situation of forced prohibition. Alcohol frequently is outlawed by local option, and the penalties for drunkenness are less severe than for possession, which encourages drinking until the supply is gone. Weakened group controls against drunkenness reflect the forbidden and limited availability of alcohol in the immediate community and the lack of institutionalized sanctions. Alcohol has been associated culturally with loss of inhibitions and, for many women as well as men, with a sign of emotional rebellion against personal and institutional oppression.

Native American women have suffered under damaging stereotypes that have both contributed to their alcoholism and hindered their recovery. Many recovering women are in the process of discovering their own individual needs and strengths as they develop their identities separately from these stereotypes.

There is within-group diversity in Native American culture among Native American tribes and nations. Native American women may have different languages, cultures, traditions, and spiritual beliefs that need to be respected in developing culturally sensitive alcoholism services for them. Spirituality, as part of Native American tradition, is a very important aspect of recovery. How much a woman identifies as a Native American and as a member of a tribe is important in understanding how closely her recovery needs to be part of that cultural and social framework. She might have a different framework based on whether she grew up in an urban setting or on a reservation. Mistrust of agencies and helping professionals who represent the white culture needs to be addressed. Other Native American women in recovery can be important role models to the Native American woman trying to get sober. Barring this, women of all colors are needed to help Native American women develop new identities and a network of support with other sober women.

A review of counseling strategies offers these suggestions for understanding the Native American perspective:

> When counseling Native Americans, researchers recommend studying the client's specific cultural and family context, keeping in mind that individuals vary in the degree to which they reflect tribal culture. Each client is unique and must be approached as an individual. Most treatment will take place in a nonreservation or urban setting, so considerations of urban Indian lifestyles must be incorporated in[to] prevention and treatment. Recognizing differences between Indian and non-Indian healing models may offer more insight into a traditional client's view of the counseling process. To gain the trust of the client and better ensure a return after the first visit, counselors are advised to take the lead from their clients by matching their silent language and considering community-based therapy that incorporates native beliefs and practices.[12]

Strategies for Creating Sensitive Treatment Programs

Bringing women into treatment is not feasible until a system is in place to offer them sensitive, effective, nonracist treatment. The alcoholism field, which historically has preferred the dictum "Keep it simple" and has attempted to see alcoholism as the "great leveler" of people, has begun to move beyond this to appreciate and become comfortable with differences in sex, race, and beliefs. Counselors should not negate the existence of differences or pretend "color-blindness." As in the case of women (and therefore women of color), "equal treatment" often is itself discrimination, a failure to design programs and policies that really meet the needs of the different people who are being served. It is important that both the agency and individual counselors understand the sociopolitical forces, such as racism, discrimination, and oppression, that have affected minority women. Culture, class, and language factors can be barriers to effective counseling. A client's worldview or cultural identity plays an important role in the counseling process.

Five basic interpersonal styles have been outlined by Bell and Evans to describe white counselors and African American clients that are relevant for working with all women of color. These five styles are overt racism and hostility, covert (hidden) prejudice, cultural ignorance, color-blind denial of cultural differences, and culturally liberated awareness and understanding of racial/cultural differences.[13] Most counselors who have reached the point of being culturally liberated have studied and practiced the dynamics of cross-cultural counseling and are capable of expressing both regard for an alcoholic woman and communication across racial lines. The culturally liberated counselor acknowledges the reality of racism without allowing it to be an excuse for the client's self-destructive behavior.

The separateness and uniqueness of women in treatment who come from a variety of cultural and ethnic backgrounds demand efforts on the part of both agencies and counselors to learn as much as they can about the minority groups represented in their communities. A commitment to hire and train women of color to be available to women coming into treatment who are African American, Hispanic, Native American, or Asian is imperative to give an agency credibility and to develop trust with women of color seeking treatment. Outreach into racial/ethnic minority communities often is the first step in bringing women of color "out of hiding." This is best done through developing close links with existing social support systems in minority communities such as churches, health clinics, and social clubs. These provide services that are safe and visible for women in a world they already know.

This part of the book has not paid specific attention to the experiences of dominant groups. This is because most of what is written about women's treatment is, in fact, specific to the dominant group, even when it claims to be culturally neutral. The decision to focus on disenfranchised groups in this part does not indicate a belief that a membership in a dominant group is somehow not an identity. Perhaps belonging to a dominant group might be less problematic for the individual, and most likely will be less examined, but it still needs to be understood within the context of diversity. Understanding the minority position is not enough when the goal is to work across difference. The majority position also must be understood as a culturally specific position.

Much of the work done in multicultural treatment settings wrongly assumes that the counselor belongs to the dominant group and is working with a minority client(s). Yet, this is only one of the many possible permutations of relationships within a multicultural agency. Even in counselor-client relationships that are "matched" in terms of one or more cultural factors, you never should assume that difference will not be an issue.

Our experience has been based on an all-female model—women counselors working with women clients—and there are many benefits to this model such as increased feelings of safety for the clients and the chance to become empowered as women. However, male counselors often are in the position of working with female clients—one more example of working across difference—and it is hoped that this part of the book, in particular, will be helpful for those male counselors who are committed to the recovery and empowerment of their female clients.

This part of the book challenges the standard AA claim that alcohol is "the great equalizer." Although facing addiction might give straight, white, middle class women a taste of some of the oppressive forces that other women face, it is more likely that such women will have more social supports and greater opportunities, once they are clean and sober, to return to a higher quality of life. It is true that having race or class privilege does not "protect" one from addiction, but we ignore real differences in power at the peril of truly authentic relationships across difference and at the peril of social change. The myth of the great equalizer is, at its base, an attempt to achieve color-blindness, and ultimately it renders invisible the realities of oppression and obscures the real differences in power that exist.

The rest of this book is only an introduction to some of the issues that might arise in working across difference. It is by no means all-inclusive, nor does it let you off the hook from doing more extensive research into understanding your clients' (and your own) perspectives in all their complexity. It is strongly recommended that you make ongoing multicultural awareness training a priority within your agencies. The next few chapters continue to explore the experiences of various disenfranchised groups of women and the issues that can arise in working with women across different populations.

References

1. U.S. Department of Health and Human Services, *Healthy People 2000,* PHS 91-50213 (Washington, DC: Government Printing Office, 1990).

2. National Institute on Alcohol Abuse and Alcoholism, *Women and Alcohol: Issues for Prevention Research,* NIH Publication No. 96-3817 (Washington, DC: Government Printing Office, 1996), 34; R. Caetano, "Findings from the 1984 National Survey of Alcohol Use among U.S. Hispanics," in W. B. Clark and M. E. Hilton, eds., *Alcohol in America: Drinking Practices and Problems* (Albany: State University of New York Press, 1991), 293-307.

3. National Institute on Alcohol Abuse and Alcoholism, *Women and Alcohol,* 35.

4. ibid., 36.

5. Massachusetts Division of Alcoholism and Drug Rehabilitation, *Report from the Task Force on Minority Women and Substance Abuse* (Boston: Massachusetts Division of Alcoholism and Drug Rehabilitation, 1987).

6. Hortensia Amaro, Linda Beckman, and Vickie Mays, "A Comparison of Black and White Women Entering Alcoholism Treatment," *Journal of Studies on Alcohol* 48 (1987): 220-28.

7. U.S. Department of Health and Human Services, *Ninth Special Report to the U.S. Congress on Alcohol and Health,* NIH Publication No. 97-4017 (Washington, DC: Government Printing Office, 1997), 52.

8. Information in this section was retrieved from *Prevention Primer: Asian/Pacific Islander Americans.* Available: http://www.health.org/multicul/asian/apubs.htm

9. National Center on Addiction and Substance Abuse, *Substance Abuse and the American Woman: The Difference* (New York: Columbia University, CASA, 1996). Available: http://www.casacolumbia.org/pubs/jun96/womchap2.htm

10. Material about black women was adapted from Carolyn S. Carter, "Treatment of the Chemically Dependent Black Female: A Cultural Perspective," *The Counselor* 6 (1987): 16-18.

11. Material on Hispanic women was adapted from *CTRC Update,* newsletter of the Community Training and Resource Center, an organization whose purpose was to develop and expand alcoholism treatment services to special populations in Massachusetts.

12. M. L. Robbins, "Native American Perspective," in J. Gordon, ed., *Managing Multicultural Substance Abuse Services* (Thousand Oaks, CA: Sage, 1994), 173.

13. P. Bell and J. Evans, *Counseling the Black Client* (Center City, MN: Hazelden Foundation, 1981).

Resources

American Indian Institute
Address: 555 Constitution Street, Suite 237, Norman, OK 73072-7820
Phone: (405) 325-4127
Web: http://www.occe.ou.edu/aii/index.html

(This is an information resource on Native Americans.)

African-American Family Service (A-AFC)
Contact: Kathy Boese, Information Specialist
Address: 2616 Nicollet Avenue South, Minneapolis, MN 55408
Phone: (612) 871-7878

(Formerly the Institute on Black Chemical Dependency, A-AFC provides information on substance abuse and other family services serving the African American population.)

Indian Health Service
Alcoholism and Substance Abuse Program
Address: Room 5A-20, 5600 Fishers Lane, Rockville, MD 20857
Phone: (301) 443-4297
Web: http://www.tucson.his.gov

(This is a government agency directed toward alleviating the substance abuse problems of Native Americans.)

Mass Alliance of Portuguese Speakers (MAPS)
Address: 92 Union Square, Somerville, MA 02143
Phone: (617) 628-6065

(MAPS is a bilingual organization providing individual, group, and family counseling; acupuncture detox; and substance abuse education and prevention programs.)

National Asian Pacific American Families Against Substance Abuse (NAPAFASA)
Address: 300 West Cesar Chavez Avenue, Suite B, Los Angeles, CA 90012
Phone: (213) 625-5795
E-mail: napafasa@apanet.org
Web: http://www.emory.edu/nfia/about/partners/napafasa.html

(NAPAFASA is a nonprofit coalition that works with Asian and Pacific Islander populations, families, and professional service providers regarding substance abuse and related issues including promoting health, wellness, and social justice.)

National Coalition of Hispanic Health Services Organization (COSSMHO)
Address: 1501 16th Street, N.W., Washington, DC 20036
Phone: (202) 387-5000

(COSSMHO is an organization founded to represent and advocate for the mental health needs of the diverse Hispanic communities.)

National Congress of American Indians (NCAI)
Address: 2010 Massachusetts Avenue, N.W., Washington, DC 20036
Phone: (202) 466-7767
Web: http://www.ncai.org

(NCAI is a government organization providing information on all aspects of Native American life.)

Office of Minority Health Resource Center (OMHRC)
Address: P.O. Box 202, Washington, DC 20013-7337
Phone: (800) 444-6472, (301) 565-4020
Web: http://www.omhrc.gov

(OMHRC is a national resource for minority health information that provides information, resources, and publications on health-specific topics that target African American, Asian American, Alaska Native, Hispanic/Latino, Native American, and Pacific Islander peoples.)

11 Lesbians and Bisexual Women: Outreach and Treatment Issues

The lesbian alcoholic seeking help to stop drinking or abusing drugs can face a multitude of barriers to treatment, both internal and external. Certain barriers are in the nature of the disease of alcoholism such as recurring denial and the potential for relapse, and are part of the arduous struggle that every alcoholic faces. Unfortunately, many times the barriers to treatment are the result of the fear of and prejudice toward lesbians present in the agency or counselors. These attitudes interfere with establishing an atmosphere that is conducive to support, self-disclosure, and the connections so necessary to helping a woman recover. This chapter discusses some of the issues and considerations important in working with lesbians and provides a framework for sensitizing treatment services and counselors to the needs of lesbian clients.

The importance of knowing about and being sensitive to lesbian issues is underscored by the fact that 10% to 15% of the population is made up of gays and lesbians.[1] Lesbians are women whose primary emotional, affectional, social, and sexual bondings are with other women. It also is important to remember that a lesbian's identity extends beyond her sexual orientation, her attractions, and her sexual behavior.

Although sexual orientation ordinarily is used to designate a person's sexual behavior, its wider, more comprehensive application involves human relationships and emotions. The term refers not just to what people "do in bed" but also to who they are as complete human beings. And because people are complex and not static, they do not always fit neatly into distinct categories of sexual/affectional orientation. The world is not divided into separate camps of 90% "pure" heterosexuals and 10% "pure" homosexuals. Rather, there is a wide range of experience, a broad continuum of sexual/affectional orientation, into which human beings fit.[2]

Sexuality is not static, and over the period of a woman's life, she might shift positions on the continuum of sexual/affectional behavior. The term *sexual orientation* covers not only sexual attraction and behavior but also fantasies, emotional preference, social preference, and lifestyle. This points out the incompleteness in assigning only a sexual definition to lesbians; emotional bonding, social and friendship networks, and a lifestyle with a strongly woman-identified emphasis also are part of a lesbian's existence. Women who identify themselves as lesbians also might continue to relate to men as friends or occasional sexual partners or might bond in a primary emotional way with women but never choose to sexualize the relationships.

There is no "typical" lesbian, and counselors must be aware of the diversity of the lesbian experience; each woman is unique. Even the term *lesbian community* can be a misnomer because of the heterogeneity of the group being described. Lesbians are found in every socioeconomic class, ethnic/racial/cultural group, religion, and region of the country. Among women who knew at a young age that they were lesbians or were attracted to girls or women, some acted on these feelings and some denied or dismissed them. Other women marry and have families, and later in life they begin to realize that they have feelings for women or stop denying insights they might have had but repressed at a younger age. Many lesbians are mothers with children from heterosexual marriages, by adoption, or through artificial insemination, and they are raising the children in a variety of family settings.

Some lesbians are comfortable acknowledging their sexual orientation openly; others prefer to remain "in the closet" or hide their identity due to fear of legal, societal, or familial repercussions. Women use a variety of words to describe themselves because not all women are comfortable with the word *lesbian*. Some prefer to identify as *gay* and some as *homosexual*. Many women have begun to use the term lesbian when referring to themselves because the term gay is more associated with male homosexuals, whereas the term lesbian is more woman identified. Use of the different words by men and women also stresses the differences between lesbians and gay men, which are many. Although lesbians and gay men share certain struggles and solidarity, lesbians have as much in common with all women and women's issues.

As with other oppressed groups, stereotypes and myths have come to represent lesbians in the minds of the dominant culture. Unlike other minority groups, lesbians face unique consequences if their lifestyle becomes known such as rejection by family of origin, loss of the custody of their children, job discrimination or loss of job, housing discrimination, and even physical violence. This fact has caused many lesbians to hide, or "pass," in the larger society, denying important aspects of themselves and their lives. Tensions can exist within a lesbian partnership when one partner is more open about her identity than is her lover. This can prove stressful in situations such as socializing with coworkers, deciding how the couple will spend holidays, and making arrangements with landlords. It also influences how women with children may choose to, or be able to, relate to the outside world, such as parent-teacher associations and teachers, and it affects coparenting.

Homophobia

Homophobia, externalized and internalized, is a source of stress and conflict to lesbians and plays a leading role in the high rates of alcoholism found in lesbians. Homophobia is the fear, dread, and hatred of lesbians (and gay men), the "particular blend of all these things that work to keep homosexuals as a hidden (closeted) underclass of society, discriminated against, treated as deviants, sinners, maliciously perverted, sick, and abnormal."[3] Those most hateful and fearful might call for the death, jailing, or "curing" of lesbians by changing their orientation through controlling and invasive means. Those more "tolerant" might insist that lesbians stop "flaunting" their sexuality and stay hidden or invisible. The negative attitudes are, to a greater or lesser degree, expressed in every aspect of the culture—in the media, in the medical and psychiatric establishment, in religious teachings, and in the legal system. Negativity, even hidden under the lip service of tolerance, can have its consequences, as Lee explains in her book, *Women's Health: Psychological and Social Perspectives:*

> Even those health care providers who are not actively hostile or pathologizing in their attitudes towards lesbians tend to assume that all clients are heterosexual and thus fail to be sensitive to lesbians' needs. . . . Many lesbians prefer not to reveal their sexual orientation unless they can be sure of a non-hostile response . . ., and because of the power differentials inherent in the health care provider-client relationship, it is necessary for health care professionals to convey a positive attitude of respect.[4]

When a lesbian chooses to pass, the stress can be great from trying to present herself as heterosexual, denying or omitting important aspects of her life to try and fit into society. The outer world and inner world can be quite disparate, affecting her self-image and self-esteem. Cultural sanctions against same-sex relationships attempt to undermine the fullest development of romantic and sexual relationships. Homophobia and internalized homophobia (hatred turned inward) also replicate certain aspects of codependence such as the denial of self, denial of feelings, lack of boundaries, and obsession with seeking and maintaining the approval of other people.

"Coming out" is the process by which a lesbian comes to terms with, admits, and accepts her identity. This often involves a transformation from viewing herself negatively and with stigma to a positive state in which she refuses to accept the validity of the stigma and, in fact, takes pride in her identity. Coming out entails more than a sexual experience or a single disclosure to an important friend or family member. This is a long process, and a woman can become stuck at various points. Alcohol and drugs can hinder the coming out process. Knowing where a client is in her coming out process will help in understanding her and in empowering her to build a strong support network. Coming out gives others the chance to truly know and accept a woman for herself and, therefore, allows a lesbian to feel that acceptance can further her own self-acceptance. There is a serious psychic toll exacted by not coming out that negatively affects a lesbian's emotional health.

Women who are lesbians drink alcohol or take drugs for the same reasons that other women do so—to relax, socialize, even to escape. Historically, the lesbian or gay bar has served as a meeting place and primary social outlet, the only place a woman could go to be herself, meet other women like herself, and feel like she "belonged." Alcohol and drugs were a large part of this social scene and once were viewed as a symbol of a freer counterculture. The bar was a place to escape and, more important, a place to belong:

> The positive aspects of being a part of a gay [lesbian] community reinforce drinking patterns. Drinking is not used to escape from something; rather, it is used to join something. Initial socialization into a gay [les-

bian] community often occurs by attending gay bars and by enacting the drinking roles perceived as essential for a gay [lesbian] identity.[5]

Alcohol and drugs become an escape or a relief from problems and stresses present because of societal views toward lesbians. Some lesbians might feel that it is "easier" to stay drunk or drugged or to appear crazy than it is to be a lesbian in this society. Some have no idea what their lives would be like without alcohol- or drug-centered activities and perhaps believe that drinking or using drugs is synonymous with being a lesbian. Older lesbians might enter treatment fearing that they will be entirely alone, unaware of the numbers of older lesbians and older women in general in Alcoholics Anonymous (AA). These mistaken beliefs are understandable if the lesbian bar has become a woman's world and pseudo-family or if one cannot find lesbian and gay AA meetings locally.

According to a review of current research, one of the latest government research monographs on women and alcohol states that we still do not have enough data to make clear estimates on how much lesbians suffer from alcohol and drug abuse compared to the general population. However, some general patterns regarding lesbians' alcohol use have been documented.

Many agencies and counselors are not aware or willing to acknowledge that they are serving lesbians because of both staff and client discomfort surrounding lesbianism. Often, counselors mistakenly rely on certain practices in approaching lesbian clients— denying completely the presence of lesbian clients in their caseloads, "curing" or attempting to dissuade a woman of her sexual orientation, discounting the importance of a client's intimate relationships in providing family systems treatment, isolating lesbians from other clients, or telling a lesbian in a group that her sexuality is "irrelevant" when a heterosexual client's marital or family issues would be considered as a matter of course. Some lesbian clients have been denied services or, if their identities were discovered, made to feel so uncomfortable that they have left treatment. A lack of agency commitment to providing in-service training on lesbian issues makes a statement to staff that these issues are unimportant. The lack of knowledge might leave well-meaning staff to rely on old stereotypes or fears when working with lesbian clients.

General Patterns of Lesbians' Alcohol Use

1. Although rates of heavy drinking among lesbians appear comparable to rates of heavy drinking among heterosexual women, more lesbians than heterosexual women report alcohol problems.

2. More lesbians than heterosexual women drink alcohol (i.e., fewer lesbians are abstainers).

3. Among lesbians, rates of drinking, frequency of drinking, and alcohol problems do not decline with age as they do among women in the general population.

4. Alcohol use in general, and reliance on bars for socialization in particular, may be declining in the lesbian communities.[6]

Stereotypes such as the following can be extremely harmful: Lesbians really want to be men; all a lesbian needs is a good man to "fix" her; alcoholism causes lesbianism, so a sober lesbian really wants to be heterosexual. Treatment approaches founded in these myths might discourage a lesbian from ever seeking treatment again, particularly if she feels that her recovery depends on changing her identity to meet a counselor's or program's ideal. One lesbian client describes her experience as follows:

> I was so grateful to be admitted into recovery home treatment [because] I knew my drinking was killing me and I wanted help. I was assigned to a room alone (although there were empty beds in other dorm rooms). Then, a few hours after admission, the house manager took me aside and said I was just lucky to be there at all and that if I even looked like I might "cause trouble," I would be asked to leave immediately. I decided to leave the house that night, and it was several months later before I again had the courage to ask for help.[7]

The most helpful treatment strategy will be founded in a perspective that sees a lesbian as a whole person and her lifestyle as one that fits within the definition of a healthy and viable option. The main goal of treatment in this perspective is to help a woman live to her fullest potential and to have healthy and affirming relationships with the people in her life. Counselors who feel uncertain about how to relate to lesbian clients can do best when approaching a woman from this framework. Empathy, concern, and support are necessary ingredients, as with any other counseling situation, to make room for the client to be herself. Striving to create a safe, comfortable, and nonjudgmental treatment setting is the goal.

Agency intake forms and posted agency policies protecting sexual orientation can make a lesbian client feel welcomed. Instead of asking questions about marital status, which assumes heterosexuality and so makes homosexuality seem unacceptable or out of the question, counselors can routinely ask, "With whom do you have important relationships? Is your current partner male or female?" Or, a counselor can inquire about which family members the client wishes to include in treatment by asking about significant relationships, boyfriends or girlfriends, or husbands or female lovers. To ask the same questions of all clients gives a message about an agency's openness and commitment to treating all clients, regardless of sexual orientation. There are times when a client might not feel safe answering affirmatively that she has a female partner, but eventually she might feel comfortable and accepted enough to be able to disclose this important truth about herself and her life.

Working with women in treatment requires the inclusion of family for the best outcome. When working with lesbians, family must be defined in a more expansive and inclusive way and not only as existing through blood, adoption, or marital ties. It is vital to include those people who the client identifies as her family system such as her lover, her roommate(s), her children, her lover's children, a coworker, her therapist, and perhaps her ex-lover.

Complicated issues can exist between a client and her family that are unrelated to the alcoholism. Due to being disowned for her sexual orientation, a lesbian might be estranged from her family of origin. She could be outed to a sibling but not to her parents and might want to keep this a secret. She might be hiding her lifestyle from her children and husband or ex-husband to stay out of a custody battle because lesbian mothers have little or no protection from a legal system that can declare them "unfit mothers" based solely on life-style or sexual orientation. Despite "unanimous" research stating that lesbian parents raise children who are socially and psychologically well adjusted, this continues to be a problem for lesbians who are or wish to be mothers.[8]

The lesbian client in treatment for her alcoholism or drug abuse might have a lover and be in a primary relationship that has all the commitment and love found in a heterosexual marriage but none of the legal protection or vali-dation. Sometimes, the lover might choose not to participate in family treat-ment for fear of making her sexual preference known, fearing lack of confidentiality or staff judgments. This hinders total treatment and further entrenches the partner's codependence and isolation. Isolation can be doubly hard for lesbian codependents because similar issues apply: "How do I tell my Al-Anon sponsor or group that the alcoholic in my life is my female lover?" Trying to involve a closeted older lesbian's support system can be difficult be-cause her lover also might be extremely private about her identity and because other family members might not be aware of her orientation or could be es-tranged or dead. The lover and the sober woman's friends also might be un-aware of, in denial of, or enabling her substance abuse, making some form of outreach critical.

Group support and outreach to lesbian codependents is a critical part of any family outreach program, and couples counseling can be an important ad-junct to treatment, particularly during the early stages of recovery when both partners need education and help with communication skills. Lesbians not in narrowly defined primary relationships also have important family ties that need to be honored and provided for in the range of family services that are of-fered.

Sexual issues can be of concern to a lesbian client in the same way as sex is a concern to any recovering substance abuser. Damage from alcoholism or drug abuse might have affected sexual functioning or caused gynecological problems and neglect of health. Addressing issues of sexual dysfunction al-lows clients to share their concerns. Knowing that removing the alcohol or drugs will improve the situation also helps. A client might be in a couple rela-tionship but experiencing sober sex for the first time, as might her partner. Discussing fears in counseling can prevent relapse in some cases.

The specter of AIDS has had a great impact on lesbians. At first, lesbians were thought to be "low risk" so far as the dangers of exposure, and some of this denial continues to persist. Stereotypes of lesbian women come into effect here as well. Lee notes,

> Many health care providers believe that lesbians do not ever have sex with men and thus assume that they are not at risk for sexually transmit-ted diseases and do not need Pap smears. However, the majority of les-bian women have had sexual relationships with men at some stage[s] of their li[ves], and a significant minority report injecting drugs or other-wise putting themselves in danger of infection with HIV or hepatitis.[9]

Until recently, women testing positive for HIV were not asked whether they had sex with other women because lesbian sex was not considered a high-risk behavior. Thus, statistics have not acknowledged the existence of lesbian and bisexual women among women with HIV illnesses.

Lesbians, long active in caregiving and support roles during the AIDS crisis, now are becoming proactive in educating their "sisters" and preventing denial about transmission of the disease. Certainly, the range of immune system diseases, from chronic Epstein-Barr virus to AIDS, has encouraged a trend toward holistic health and safer sex, and alcohol and drugs have been implicated as interfering in achieving both. Substance abuse puts all women at risk for exposure to HIV, through intravenous drug use or through unprotected, unsafe sex with a partner (male or female) who has been exposed to the virus, because options, decision-making skills, and self-care are limited by intoxication.

As women become sober, they actually might be facing their sexual orientation for the first time. If their identities have been shaped primarily in the bar scene, or if their friendships and socializing are primarily alcohol or drug centered, then they might experience questions about sexual identity for the first time. It is vital that counselors stay neutral with clients who are questioning their sexual identity, particularly during early recovery. Questioning indicates that as a woman is "clearing up," or looking at and exploring basic life issues for perhaps the first time, and does not necessarily indicate that she is not a lesbian. Once the buffers are removed, women might experience societal prejudice and internalized conflicts in a new way, without substances to numb these messages. The lesbian in treatment and sober will be sensitive to the presence or absence of support and to judgmental and homophobic attitudes, and in the process she might bury some important issues that she needs to discuss. She might feel that a part of her is "unacceptable," leading to internal stresses and secret keeping that can be isolating and a setup for relapse.

It is necessary for treatment providers to understand and address their own limitations in working with lesbian clients. Staff might need supervision and training to identify, prevent, and defuse their own attitudes that might hinder clients. Counselors can develop a working knowledge of area resources and referrals for lesbians and can inform themselves as well as post a list of phone numbers of support groups, professional groups, political organizations, and women's health centers.

In addition to knowing about area resources for lesbians, counselors must be aware to which AA and Narcotics Anonymous (NA) meetings it is appropriate to refer lesbians. Some meetings might be more supportive to women in general, and some meetings could be geared specifically to lesbians and gay men. The issues of self-disclosure and honesty with others can be threatening to a lesbian as she ponders how members in her AA group or her AA or NA sponsor will respond if she comes out to them. It is not always possible to attend gay and lesbian meetings of AA/NA at which these issues are discussed or become moot points. Not all lesbians choose to attend gay meetings, even if they have the choice. At some point, attendance at a gay and lesbian meeting might be important for the sense of community, belonging, and hope that it can provide.

The proliferation of special-issue Twelve Step program meetings (including AA, NA, Al-Anon, and Adult Children of Alcoholics [ACOA] meetings) begun by and for lesbians or gay people in general is one instance of how substance abuse is being addressed as a critical health care issue within the lesbian community. During the past two decades, the number of alcohol- and chemical-free social alternatives has multiplied. Women's music festivals offer space for chemical-free camping and continuous AA meetings. Lesbian social groups and professional organizations sponsor sober dances. Lesbian cultural figures, including several popular musicians, have written songs addressing alcoholism or their own recoveries from addiction or codependence, providing important role models and raising the issues with audiences around the world.

In recent years, education and prevention efforts have grown within the lesbian community to address the prevalence of alcoholism and substance abuse among lesbians. Although several urban areas in the United States offer specialized treatment programs for lesbians, the reality is that the bulk of the services have to be provided by non-lesbian-specific agencies. Therefore,

> it is critical that traditional alcohol treatment programs and other social service settings begin a dialogue with their respective homosexual communities. It is imperative that these agencies either hire lesbian staff or provide their non-gay staff with opportunities for education and attitudinal change.[10]

Not all lesbians will be able to see a lesbian clinician, nor might all choose to do so.

Reaching out to lesbians requires many considerations, especially given that there is no "one type" of lesbian, and approaches and services need to be varied. Outreach requires, first, a commitment and philosophy on the part of an agency that must be coupled with adequate, sensitive, knowledgeable, and nonjudgmental services once clients present for treatment. Treatment providers must realize that they already have lesbian clients in their caseloads, women who do not feel safe enough or supported enough to come out or who fear rejection if they do.

Improving the feeling of being welcome within an institution can be accomplished in very simple but direct ways such as by posting confidentiality and antidiscrimination policy statements and by displaying lists of lesbian resources or AA meetings on waiting room bulletin boards.

The alcoholic or drug-abusing lesbian, like any substance-abusing woman, needs the counselor's support and understanding. She has a right to unbiased, informed, and sensitive services that seek to arrest her addiction and support her in her struggle for sobriety.

Counselors must work through their own biases and stereotypes about lesbians. Some clients might have faced discrimination in previous treatment settings due to homophobia, and this must be discussed because this could damage counselors' ability to foster trust building. The Staff and Client Training Activities at the end of this chapter will help clinicians learn how to advocate for lesbian and bisexual clients.

References

1. H. Doweiko, *Concepts of Chemical Dependency,* 3rd ed. (Pacific Grove, CA: Brooks/Cole, 1996), 268.

2. D. Finnegan and E. McNally, *Dual Identities* (Center City, MN: Hazelden Foundation, 1987), 21.

3. S. Pharr, "Two Workshops on Homophobia," in K. Lobel, ed., *Naming the Violence,* National Coalition against Domestic Violence (Seattle, WA: Seal Press, 1986), 209.

4. C. Lee, *Women's Health: Psychological and Social Issues* (Thousand Oaks, CA: Sage, 1998), 166.

5. P. Nardi, "Alcoholism and Homosexuality," in T. Ziebold and J. Mongeon, eds., *Gay and Sober* (New York: Harrington Park Press, 1985), 18.

6. National Institute on Alcohol Abuse and Alcoholism, *Women and Alcohol: Issues for Prevention Research,* NIH Publication No. 96-3817 (Washington, DC: Government Printing Office, 1996), 327.

7. B. Weathers, *Alcoholism and the Lesbian Community* (Washington, DC: Gay Council on Drinking Behavior, Whitman-Walker Clinic, 1981), 7.

8. Lee, *Women's Health,* 169.

9. Ibid., 167.

10. S. C. Anderson and D. C. Henderson, "Working with Lesbian Alcoholics," *Social Work* 30 (1985): 523.

◼ Staff Training Activities

Activity 1: The Power of Names
Activity 2: Myths and Facts
Activity 3: Coming Out Issues

Activity 1:   The Power of Names

Ask the group members to give all the names they have ever heard lesbians called, and list these on a blackboard or flip chart so that all can see. Examples:

Dyke	Femme	Amazon	Man-hater	Pervert
Queer	Witch	Lezzie	Feminist	
Butch	Faggot	Spinster	Gay	

A short discussion is sufficient. Group members might at first be reluctant to contribute, so the leader might wish to start, perhaps using a more inflammatory term, such as diesel dyke, to give group members permission to be open.

◼ Show how the words demonstrate the following:

– Not being the norm (e.g., queer, pervert)

– Not fitting traditional sex roles (e.g., butch, spinster, Amazon)

Discuss ways in which sex roles and their extremes are used to control all of us. Words such as feminist and man-hater are used to control women who become *too* assertive or independent. Words such as witch and faggot remind us of the ultimate means of control (death); faggots were the bundles of wood used to burn witches and others at the stake.

◼ You also might find, as the group members do this exercise, that there is a silence that reflects the invisibility of lesbians. Invectives for gay men are perhaps more well known. Point out to the group how such a silence about lesbians discounts and stigmatizes a lesbian lifestyle.

Activity 2:   Myths and Facts

This exercise allows participants the opportunity to challenge preconceived notions about lesbians. By providing five myths, a spectrum of information can be covered. Frame the exercise by helping the group to examine how these myths came into being and what purpose they serve. List the myths on a prepared handout or flip chart, with space between each to add the factual information.

Myth: Women become lesbians because they have had bad experiences with men.

Fact: This assumption is grounded in the view that lesbianism is a sad, reactionary, inferior choice made out of fear, that is, a negative choice. In fact, there is no single lesbian identity. Some women have been in relationships with men and then experience a shift in attraction and affinity to women. Some women feel that they always have been lesbians. If this myth were true, then there would be more lesbians given that violence against girls and women is at an all-time high in this society.

Myth: Lesbians want other people's children because they cannot have children of their own.

Fact: One out of three lesbians is a mother, and lesbians do have children and are having children through adoption or artificial insemination. This myth feeds the stereotype that lesbians are lonely, barren women and that lesbians want to steal or seduce children into a homosexual lifestyle.

Myth: Lesbians want to do men's jobs.

Fact: This myth is used to oppress all women. Men's jobs usually pay better. Women seeking to work in certain trades or to attain executive or management positions can be perceived as threatening. Strong women are seen as being out of their traditional role.

Myth: Lesbians socialize in dark, dirty bars.

Fact: At one time, gay bars were the only places in which lesbians could find community and socialize in relative safety. This myth implies that all lesbians are alcoholic and sick, and it raises the issue of lesbians as "sordid" people needing to be hidden away.

Myth: Lesbian relationships do not last.

Fact: Although often against the odds and without social, legal, or familial support, many lesbians do value, develop, and maintain long-term committed relationships. Relationships may take a variety of forms and do not necessarily fit into a male-female heterosexual context.

- After completing these myths and facts, allow time for reactions and questions. Encourage participants to volunteer and discuss other myths and stereotypes.

Activity 3: Coming Out Issues

What can you do if you sense that your client is a lesbian? What if your client comes out to you and discloses that she is gay? Counselors often wonder how best to help lesbian clients feel safe to come out to them or whether they should ask about sexual orientation. The following concepts and suggestions might be helpful and can be presented after or in conjunction with a discussion of the preceding questions.

- Do not frame talking with a woman about her sexual orientation as a confrontation. Never push or force a woman to disclose her identity.

- Do routinely ask all clients about sexual identity and orientation in a caring, relaxed, and nonjudgmental manner. Find a style that is comfortable for you and explain that the questions are routinely asked of all clients. The important thing is not to demand that they label themselves one way or another. They might not be ready to open up to you. Suggested ways in which to ask questions include the following:

Do you have a partner/significant other right now?

Would you like to talk about your current sexual relationships?

The client might not be able to answer openly or honestly at that moment, but your questions have let her know that you would be a person she could choose to talk with in the future.

■ Make sure that you include information on homosexuality and lesbian health matters in sexuality lectures or health education groups.

■ Displaying lesbian and gay resource lists, posters, and books in your office will give the message that you are familiar with the issues about which a lesbian client might want to talk.

What if your client comes out to you, the counselor?

■ Rushing to "reassure" her by saying "That is not an issue here" or "We are only dealing with alcoholism, not your sex life" will actually close the door on the topic in a nontherapeutic manner. In reality, this is a very important issue and reflects her willingness to be open. It is more helpful to ask about how it feels for her to come out to you and what her fears might be.

■ Ask about her support system. Who else knows that she is a lesbian? How long has she been out? How comfortable is she with her sexual orientation? Does she have a sense of belonging to a community, or does she feel isolated?

■ Protect her confidentiality in patient records and in conversations with other staff members. Allow your client to be the judge of when and to whom she comes out.

■ Although it is important that you are aware of your own feelings, biases, and strengths in working with lesbian clients, you do not have to be an expert on lesbian issues. Remember that there are reasons that she has chosen to come out to you; you are caring, sensitive, and a good listener. Use the resources listed in this chapter to enhance your knowledge of particular aspects of a lesbian's lifestyle and world.

■ Client Training Activities

Activity 1

In initial sessions and when taking a sexual history with a client, it is important to use more inclusive terms in asking about her significant relationship. Instead of asking about a husband or a boyfriend only, use the term spouse, partner, or lover and use "he or she." Allowing for the possibility of the existence of types of relationships other than heterosexual marriages will give your client permission to be open about who she is. Such openness enhances recovery.

Activity 2

Help the client to identify and acknowledge the feelings that lead to less healthy behaviors. Are there any goals she can set around changing these behaviors? Any actions she can take?

Example:

The more afraid I feel that my lover will leave me, the more I try to control myself and not show any feelings.

Goal/action:

When I feel afraid, I will . . . [e.g., talk about my feelings with my lover, call my sponsor]. When I feel insecure about the relationship, I will affirm my own good qualities. If I am wondering about how my lover is feeling, then I have the right to ask.

Activity 3

Discuss the ways in which the client expresses and withholds anger. When is she comfortable expressing anger? Does she let it build, take it out on herself, and deny angry feelings? How was anger shown or not expressed in her family? Is it "okay" for her to be angry and express her feelings? Is direct expression, without blame or violence, a concept with which she needs help? Perhaps a role-play would work in which your client talks about her anger with you and practices how she would confront her partner, staying with "I" messages rather than blaming "you . . ." statements.

Activity 4

Establishing a sober support network is imperative for the recovering lesbian alcoholic or drug abuser. She might have little knowledge of how and where to socialize with other sober lesbians. Suggested issues to work on with your client include the following:

1. Where can she find alcohol and drug-free supports for lesbians in your community?

2. Is she aware of the available local or statewide resources for the lesbian and gay community? These include hotlines as well as religious, social, and political organizations that might be able to help with resources for sober lesbians. The organizations listed at the end of the book also can be used.

3. Help her identify and list the following, whether on paper, in a journal, or verbally:

    a. Where, and to whom, can the client go to feel safe and supported as a recovering alcoholic or drug abuser?

    b. With whom does she feel safe and supported to be herself as a lesbian?

c. Which names are on both lists? If none, then how might she go about combining both groups? Help the client to realize that she does not necessarily have to start a "new" life and that, instead, she can make positive changes in her existing social network.

Activity 5

The importance of doing outreach and providing information to an alcoholic or drug-abusing woman's family has been highlighted in previous chapters. Creativity and flexibility are required in defining "family" with lesbians. Ask your client to tell you which relationships are important in her life and be inclusive in the outreach and education you provide. The term family might include her roommates, lover, ex-lovers, therapist, and lover's children as well as adoptive or biological family. She might have different needs about confidentiality regarding her sexual orientation with the different family members, and this must be respected. Be able to offer information on Al-Anon or ACOA groups for lesbians and gays as well.

Activity 6

Special issues might arise around referral to Alcoholics Anonymous and/or Narcotics Anonymous. What often is termed "resistance to Alcoholics Anonymous" in heterosexual clients might be justifiable fears in lesbian clients. Lesbian recovering alcoholics or drug abusers could have the following concerns:

1. Do I tell my sponsor and group members that I am gay?

2. How do I reconcile anger, guilt, or fears of exclusion and rejection that I might feel due to religious teachings about lesbians with the Alcoholics Anonymous/Narcotics Anonymous notions of spirituality and a higher power?

3. What do I do if the only place I can socialize comfortably as an outed lesbian is in a gay bar, and my "straight" sponsor says that I have to stay out of bars?

If your client has not brought these issues up in treatment, then you might want to ask how she handles these hypothetical situations or feelings and whether or not they affect her sobriety. Remember that you might be the only person with whom your client believes she can be open about her sexual orientation. Helping her to carefully and safely expand this, particularly with other recovering people, is a treatment goal.

Activity 7

Helping clients to understand, identify, and work through their own homophobia often is critical in helping alcoholic or drug-abusing lesbians to achieve and/or maintain sobriety. Active substance abuse usually prevents women from integrating life experiences and accepting themselves, two dynamics necessary in the coming out process. Exercises such as the following can help to open up these issues and are beneficial in individual work and in a support group for lesbian recovering substance abusers once some sobriety has been established. Failure to address internalized homophobia can set up sober clients for isolation, loneliness, and self-hate, all of which can lead to relapse.

1. Ask the client what she heard about lesbians and gay people when she was growing up, who her role models were, and what she heard from family and friends.

2. Ask the client how she herself viewed lesbians when she was growing up. How do these ideas compare with how she views herself and other lesbians today?

3. What does it mean to the client to be a sober lesbian? Who are her role models for this?

Resources

Lesbian, Gay, Bisexual, and Transgender Specialty Center at the Lesbian and Gay Community Services Center
Address: 208 West 13th Street, New York, NY 10011
Phone: (212) 620-7310

(This agency addresses issues related to gays, bisexuals, transgender, and lesbians with respect to substance abuse.)

National Association of Lesbian and Gay Addiction Professionals (NALGAP)
c/o Progressive Research and Training for Action (PRTA)
Address: 440 Grand Avenue, Suite 401, Oakland, CA 94610-5012
Phone: (510) 465-0547
Web: http://www.prta.com/nalgap.html

(NALGAP is a national membership organization whose mission is to address and counteract the effect of heterosexual bias and homophobia on those affected by substance abuse and addictions through advocacy, training, networking, and resource development.)

12 Disabled Women and Substance Abuse

Women with disabilities constitute a diverse and largely overlooked special population within the field of substance abuse.[1] Disabled substance-abusing women come from all racial, age, ethnic, class, and cultural groups. They may have physical, hearing, learning, emotional, visual, or health disabilities. Some of these women think of themselves as disabled and others do not. A common ground that most disabled women share, however, is the discrimination faced by all people who are seen as "damaged" and different. A disabled woman faces handicaps and barriers, some imposed by society, some imposed by the environment, and others coming from the negative attitudes of the disabled woman herself—all of which make day-to-day living a serious challenge. Disabled men and women have been severely underrepresented in substance abuse treatment programs. There is substantial evidence that the proportion of disabled people with alcoholism is the same as (or greater than) that of the general population. The barriers to substance abuse treatment can be overwhelming for disabled women who already suffer from low self-esteem, the stigma of disability, and the discrimination that all women face. The past two decades have seen some pioneering advocacy work done on behalf of disabled men and women.[2]

It is clear that disabled women face the same barriers that all women face, only compounded many times over. Services designed for the disabled female population need to be especially sensitive to the economic and employment barriers that many of these women face as an ongoing part of their lives. The critical emotional issue for most women with disabilities is that of self-image and self-esteem. Several disabled women who authored a book on women and disability, titled *No More Stares*, describe their experiences:

> Disabled females are doubly disadvantaged. The problems facing disabled children in educational settings—those of access barriers, negative attitudes, and low expectations—are further compounded for disabled females by sex role stereotyping. This combination frequently results in low educational attainment and limited job experience. Though we are of different races and disabilities, we share a lot too. We've all been told—some more, some less—that we're not O.K., that we're not equal.

We've all been stared at; we have been kept out of schools, jobs, concerts, parties, careers, etc. We've been kept out by physical barriers (like stairs and the lack of aids for vision- or hearing-impaired persons) and mental or attitudinal barriers (excuses like "You'll upset the customers if we put you in the front office" [and] "A deaf person can't teach").[3]

Pressure to be physically attractive is present for all women in American society. Social norms, advertising, and a male-dominated fashion industry define the "ideal" woman. Women who do not fit the image are subject to the prejudices, fears, and hatred that are overtly and covertly expressed by both men and women in our culture through their attitudes and actions. Disabled women live with the reality of being different and the emotional and social isolation it produces. They are encouraged to hide their disabilities to make other people feel comfortable. They face stereotypes of being weak and less intelligent and of needing protection. Disabled women also are discouraged from being sexual, assertive, and independent.[4]

Studies of alcohol and drug problems among disabled populations demonstrate that the proportion of disabled women and men who have substance abuse problems is at least as great as that of the nondisabled population. Alcoholism and illicit and prescription drug abuse are present among all disability groups.

The lack of services for disabled women is part of a larger problem for all people with disabilities who are shut out of the alcoholism and drug treatment systems as they presently exist. Despite the pioneering advocacy work done with special populations for the past two decades, disabled persons still are not represented in significant numbers in most treatment programs.

Despite the changes in federal laws and handicapped legislation, public attitudes and lack of knowledge about disabilities and alcoholism stand in the way of most disabled alcoholic women receiving treatment. Few studies, if any, have been done on the additional barriers that disabled alcoholic women encounter in approaching treatment for the first time.

Women With Hearing Impairments

Many aspects of the deaf community and deaf culture have prevented the deaf substance-abusing woman from being identified, diagnosed, and treated. The stigma of alcoholism combined with the stigma of deafness is more than many deaf adults want to face. Due to the absence of communication with the hearing world, many deaf people lack basic information about alcoholism and drug abuse. They have not had an opportunity to learn about the disease concept of alcoholism, and they view alcoholism and drug abuse as moral issues. Women face the triple stigma of being "deaf, drunk, and female." Mistrust of the hearing community can increase the chances of a deaf or hearing-impaired person's lack of acceptance of information presented through the media and written English.

The major impediment for hearing-impaired alcoholic or drug-abusing women is that treatment agencies are designed to serve verbal hearing clients. Communication of concepts, ideas, feelings, and experiences are at the heart of substance abuse treatment. Recovering alcoholics describe alcoholism as the "disease we talk to death." Interpreters, an essential part of communication for those deaf people who communicate through signing, are unavailable as a matter of course in most treatment programs.

Until recently, education for the deaf has varied widely in method and quality from community to community. The controversy in deaf education among oralism, signing, and total communication (a philosophy of communication including gestures, speech, formal signs, finger spelling, speech reading, reading, and writing) has left many deaf adults deficient in the understanding of written and spoken English. In addition, American sign language (ASL), now recognized as a distinct language with its own syntax and vocabulary, does not include some of the abstract concepts and ideas that are used in English about alcoholism. The term alcoholism itself, as well as others such as blackout, sobriety, surrender, and powerlessness, has not had an expression in ASL. Alcohol and drug abuse programs need to appreciate cultural and linguistic differences inherent in communicating with deaf women. Programs can provide interpreters and also the materials developed specifically for deaf and reading-limited clients that explain concepts of alcoholism and the Twelve Steps of Alcoholics Anonymous (AA) through picture-ideas.[5]

One of the challenges of working with the hearing impaired is to provide the necessary tools for communication without making the issue of deafness the focus of treatment. Deafness can create low self-esteem, isolation, and loneliness, but it usually is not the sole determining factor in a woman's substance abuse. A woman's self-image and self-esteem as a deaf person depend on many factors such as onset and degree of deafness, how well integrated she is into the deaf community, her level of education, and whether her parents were deaf or hearing. Deaf children whose parents are deaf tend to show more social and educational adjustment than do children whose parents are hearing.[6] Deaf women also will have a wide range of abilities to understand and communicate in written and spoken English and to interact and be comfortable with hearing people. Discomfort with the hearing community is a common experience for deaf women who have strong affiliations in the deaf community.

Treating your client as a total person means learning to understand the many facets of the client—as a deaf person, as a substance abuser, and as a woman. The difficulties encountered in growing up as a deaf woman in a hearing culture are profound. A woman might lack social, emotional, and educational skills for communication. She might have a fear and distrust of helping resources that are primarily for hearing people. The counselor needs to understand the moral stigma of being an alcoholic or drug-abusing woman. The deaf woman needs to spend time (often more time than that spent by a hearing client) learning the disease model of addictions and understanding that women can have alcohol or drug problems. It is important to provide special services for deaf clients within the context of a larger alcohol and drug treatment program. Women need to be exposed to hearing women who are recovering. Deaf women will need one-to-one counseling and often longer stays in treatment. They will be facing a challenge of learning new, often difficult and abstract ideas about alcoholism and addiction. Repetition and feedback are important. Deaf women might have serious deficits in education and job skills that will mean a greater coordination of resources than hearing clients might require. A deaf woman in a residential recovery home, for example, will need to be connected to a variety of community resources. The deaf woman needs to be able to use community-based treatment, especially AA and Narcotics Anonymous (NA). Large urban areas are beginning to have signed AA meetings. Some AA telephone information hotlines have two text telewriter numbers. If there are no available signed AA or NA meetings, then this could be an important resource to develop as part of advocacy work with deaf women.

For many deaf women, the information and understanding they are receiving about alcoholism and drug abuse might be entirely new. The isolation of alcoholism and deafness can be devastating. It is broken through when treatment programs provide the tools for communicating with deaf clients. For many deaf women, the common bond of recovery connects them in a new way to the hearing community, transcending the loneliness of deafness. For example, recovering deaf women in a hearing halfway house begin to feel part of a new community of recovering women, both hearing and deaf.[7]

Women With Mobility Impairments

Mobility impairment can range from arthritis, to limb loss, to severe spinal cord injury. Unlike hearing impairment, which often is an "invisible disability," mobility impairments usually are highly visible. Most mobility impairments are the result of chronic illness or injury in which women have spent long periods of time in medical and rehabilitation settings. Many women who are mobility impaired have experienced long periods of isolation while institutionalized for treatment and have love-hate relationships with institutional settings. Prescription drug use and potential abuse is common among mobility-impaired women because of their long-term participation and experience with traditional pain management. For mobility-limited and disabled women, alcohol and drugs are an immediate response to the social isolation and stigma of disability. Depression, pain, low self-esteem, and limited resources increase the risk of alcoholism and prescription drug abuse in this population.

Spinal cord-injured clients, in particular, often suffer a devastating loss of freedom and crisis of identity in young adulthood, when they are most active and productive. For many severely mobility-limited women, drinking abusively can interfere with self-care and independent living and can create a range of other physical problems. The use of alcohol or drugs after injury also can interfere with the emotional adjustment to disability. Women who become sober and drug free might be facing their disability and its losses for the first time without substances. An important part of helping women with mobility impairments is working with them on their issues of self-esteem, sexuality, and identity. Assertiveness training and exploring recreational activities not involving alcohol or drugs need to be part of a long-term recovery process.

One of the most important things to remember is that your client is the expert on her mobility impairment. Ask and encourage her to communicate her needs. In a treatment care setting, the provider should make sure that the client's physical condition and limitations are adjusted for so far as they effect her comfort, safety, and ability to participate in the program.[8]

Women with mobility impairments should be allowed the necessary time to accomplish the tasks of daily living to allow them to fully participate in the program. Rearranging groups or counseling to start at 9 a.m. rather than 8 a.m., for example, gives the client an opportunity to bathe, dress, and eat—tasks that might take a long time to accomplish.

The need to make treatment not only physically accessible but also accessible in terms of the attitudes and behaviors of the staff helps to make the mobility-impaired woman feel a part of treatment and not isolated and separate. Some programs will be able to develop resource lists of other mobility-impaired recovering women who can help in providing role models and in encouraging the woman in treatment to begin to build self-esteem and hope. Centers for independent living and disability rights organizations are important resources to many women who are recovering. Most AA meeting lists will indicate which meetings are handicapped accessible. Helping a mobility-impaired woman to develop a treatment plan that can accommodate her special needs will mean involving a variety of community and alcoholism or drug treatment resources.

Women With Visual Impairments

A visually impaired woman who is encountering blindness as well as alcoholism or drug abuse in adulthood might need counseling and treatment in addition to skills training. Using a range of substance abuse services as well as services for the visually impaired should be part of a comprehensive treatment plan. Women with alcohol or drug problems who have adjusted to the physical challenges of blindness should be encouraged to participate in alcoholism or drug abuse treatment in inpatient, outpatient, and residential settings.

Women who have developed alcoholism or drug abuse problems prior to their visual loss might be coping with both disabilities simultaneously, compounding the stigma of blindness with the stigma of alcoholism and drug abuse. Other women might develop alcoholism after learning to live as visually impaired people and need treatment primarily for their substance abuse problem. Blindness and visual impairment separate people from objects, the tools of their culture and mobility. The stress of learning to function as a blind person in a sighted world produces frustration, anger, and fear—emotions that can be sedated by alcohol or drugs. A low sense of self-worth and an uncertain sense of her physical appearance may add to a woman's frustrations of blindness.[9]

It is estimated that 70% of women who are legally blind have some vision, although only 10% come close to having normal vision.[10] It is important to assess the degree of blindness when asking the client about her disability to introduce her to the most appropriate resources.

As with other disabilities such as deafness and mobility impairment, the visually impaired woman is best equipped to know how to deal with her disability. A thorough orientation to the location and physical layout of the program as well as to the daily routine is essential. Key program materials should be available on audiotapes or in Braille and large print. All emergency procedures should be thoroughly demonstrated, and the woman should become familiar with daily living areas such as bathrooms, meal sites, and coffee locations. Once the client is oriented physically, she will be better able to fully participate in the program.

Women With Developmental Disabilities

A developmentally disabled woman is one who usually manifests her disability before 22 years of age and who has a combination of physical and mental limitations with an IQ between 60 and 85. A woman with such a disability faces a severe and chronic challenge to self-care. She might have difficulty in speaking and understanding language. Her ability to socialize and to be financially and economically independent is limited. She is capable of learning only if information is presented in concrete terms.

Developmentally disabled women experience many of the same problems as do other women of average or better intelligence. Alcohol and other drugs affect their capacity to work and to relate to peers in community living situations, and they affect family life as well. Because of intellectual limitations, a developmentally disabled woman will lack information about alcohol and drug abuse and will be far slower in facing and dealing with her problem. She might have an inability to process certain types of information. She might tend to "parrot" (repeat what you say) or agree with what you say as a type of automatic response. She might have problems understanding abstract reasoning or generalizing information. She might remember things selectively. All of these tendencies contribute to a much slower grasp of treatment concepts and recovery. Substance abuse treatment provided to developmentally disabled women is best provided in close collaboration with community-based mental retardation services.[11]

Developmentally disabled women who are high functioning can benefit from alcohol and drug abuse services, especially if these services are willing to adapt their programs and materials to meet the different learning style of these clients. For some women, the concepts in AA are too difficult and abstract, and the verbal communication is too complex.

Common Ground in Working With Disabled Women

Whether the disability is cognitive, physical, verbal, or visual, a disabled woman will need flexible and adaptable treatment planning that will take into account her special needs. "Enable" is a concept in the alcoholism field that has negative connotations of unhealthy dependency. In the disability field, enabling means helping a disabled woman become empowered to function within the limits of her disability.[12] Disabled women will need advocacy and support to reduce the barriers between themselves and treatment. Many disabled women will stay away from alcoholism and drug treatment services because of problems such as lack of access to the building, inability to find out hours of operation, and fear of rejection. Disability awareness and education are essential for counselors in the alcohol and drug abuse fields, just as alcohol and drug assessment education should be required of professionals in the disability field. As attitudes change and education increases about alcoholism and disability, more doors will be open to disabled women for treatment and recovery.

References

1. Throughout this chapter, *disability* is used as the general term to describe a functional limitation that interferes with a person's ability to walk, see, hear, speak, lean, or lift. More specific terms are used for particular, physical, mental, or sensory conditions.

2. Alexander Boros, director of Addiction Intervention with the Disabled (AID) in Cleveland, Ohio, has originated a model for providing services to disabled alcoholics and drug abusers within existing alcoholism and drug programs.

3. A. C. Carrillo, K. Corbett, and V. Lewis, *No More Stares* (Berkeley, CA: Disability Rights Education and Defense Fund, 1982), 9-11.

4. Boston Women's Health Book Collective, *Our Bodies, Ourselves: For the New Century* (New York: Simon & Schuster, 1998), 37.

5. See note 2.

6. L. Jabobs, *A Deaf Adult Speaks Out* (Washington, DC: Gallaudet College Press, 1974), 42.

7. The Women's Alcoholism Program of CASPAR Inc., Cambridge, Massachusetts, provides a program for deaf substance-abusing women as part of its halfway house program for alcoholic and drug-abusing women.

8. *The Seed,* Newsletter of the Coalition on Disabilities and Chemical Dependency (Summer 1987): 4-5.

9. Edward J. Glass, "Problem Drinking among the Blind and Visually Impaired," *Alcohol Health and Research World* 6 (Winter 1980-81): 20-25.

10. L. Cherry, *Report on Surveys Conducted by the Bay Area Project on Disabilities and Chemical Dependency* (Coalition on Disability and Chemical Dependency).

11. Maine Department of Mental Health, *The Maine Approach: A Treatment Model for the Intellectually Limited Substance Abuser* (Augusta: Maine Department of Mental Health, 1987), 3-4.

12. *The Seed,* Newsletter of the Coalition on Disability and Chemical Dependency (Spring 1988): 3.

Staff Training Activities

Activity 1: Feelings, Biases, and Assumptions Commonly Held About Disabled and
                  Chemically Dependent Women
Activity 2: Different Models of Viewing Disability
Activity 3: Facts and Myths About Disabled Women

Activity 1:   Feelings, Biases, and Assumptions Commonly Held About Disabled and Chemically Dependent Women

Ask group members to share words, ideas, and experiences that come to mind when they think of a disabled alcoholic or drug-abusing woman.

Examples:

Mentally deficient	Living in an institution
Asexual	Alone
Helpless	Poor
Pitiful	In pain
Unable to work	Has no fun
Childless	Depressed

Ask people to share which disability (blindness, deafness, mobility impairment, or developmental disability) is the one they have the hardest time imagining for themselves and why.

What is the hardest issue you have to deal with in working with a disabled woman who also has a drinking or drug problem?

Do you have the same goals for treatment and recovery for a disabled woman as for a nondisabled woman? If not, how are they different?

Activity 2:   Different Models of Viewing Disability

1. *Religious model:* This was used by the church during the 19th century to explain the misfortune of disabled people. Their disabilities were understood as "acts of God" and something that they should accept.

2. *Social pathology model:* This was developed by social agencies during the early part of this century. Disabled people were socially deviant, were different from the norm, and needed to be trained and "reformed" so that they would fit into the nondisabled society.

3. *Medical model:* This has been the prevailing philosophy since the 1940s and still is in many parts of the world. The disabled person is seen as sick and medically needy. The disabled person is a

passive patient who will be helped by the physician's expertise. The patient's knowledge of her condition is considered inferior to that of the physician.

4. *Civil rights model:* This is the newest and most popular movement among a broad spectrum of disabled people. The disabled person is part of a minority group that deserves equal rights and opportunities to work and live just like any other group. Disabled people are seen as handicapped, not by their disabilities but rather by the attitudes and barriers existing in the dominant society. A major proponent of this philosophy is the independent living movement, whereby the person is considered the expert in dealing with her own disability.

Questions:

Which model do you use as a lens to see a person with a disability?

What messages do fund-raising drives such as the Jerry Lewis Telethon give about the disabled (e.g., helpless, fragile, needing to be cared for)?

How would you feel if a disabled woman questioned your treatment of her or access to your services?

Activity 3:   Facts and Myths About Disabled Women

Discuss each of these facts and myths as they relate to disabled women:

1. It could happen to me.

   (*True*) Disability can happen to anyone. It is an "open minority." Anyone can "join" at any time. Some people see disability as a form of premature aging in an ageist and death-phobic culture, which is why we fear it so much.

2. Disabled people are angry at those who are nondisabled.

   (*False*) Most people with disabilities will go through stages in which they feel angry. However, most disabled people have learned to live with their disabilities and do not resent the nondisabled.

3. It is not okay to talk or ask about a woman's disability.

   (*False*) Most disabled women appreciate the acknowledgment of their disabilities. Asking a woman about her disability is recognizing that she knows more about it than you do and that you appreciate this. She is the expert on her own disability, and this needs to be respected.

4. A woman with a disability never will lead a normal life.

   (*False*) Many disabled women have romantic relationships, have children, play sports, are capable of performing in many professions, and can live normal lives within the limits of their disabilities.

5. A disabled alcoholic or drug-abusing woman can get sober and drug free.

   (*True*) If disabled women are allowed to participate in substance abuse treatment and the barriers to treatment are removed, then they can recover just as well as can nondisabled women.

NOTE: Nicholas J. Zirpolo provided invaluable information and perspective in developing several of the Staff and Client Training Activities.

Resources

Coalition on Disability and Chemical Dependency (CDCD)
Address: 2165 Bunker Hill Drive, San Mateo, CA 94402
Phone: (415) 578-8047

(CDCD addresses the fact that people with disabilities frequently are chemically dependent or are at risk for becoming dependent, and it advocates increasing the accessibility of substance abuse prevention and treatment programs that do exist and to increase the number available.)

National Easter Seal Society
Address: 70 East Lake Street, Chicago, IL 60601
Phone: (312) 726-6200, (312) 726-4258 (TDD)
and
Address: 1350 New York Avenue, N.W., Washington, DC 20005
Phone: (202) 347-3066

(This is a nonprofit, community-based health agency dedicated to increasing the independence of people with disabilities, with 190 affiliates nationwide, available to disabled adults, children, and their families for direct services, screening, advocacy, public education, and research.)

Self-Help for Hard of Hearing People (Shhh)
Address: 7910 Woodmont Avenue, Suite 1200, Bethesda, MD 20814
Phone: (301) 657-2248 (voice), (301) 657-2249 (TDD)

(Shhh is a nonprofit private national organization whose goal is to educate consumers and professionals about various aspects of hearing loss.)

National Health Information Center
Address: P.O. Box 1133, Washington, DC 20013-1133
Phone: (301) 565-4167, (800) 336-4797

(This service of the U.S. Department of Health and Human Services welcomes inquiries from consumers and professionals interested in health-related disability issues and provides referrals to appropriate organizations.)

National Mental Health Association (NMHA)
Address: 1021 Prince Street, Alexandria, VA 22314-7722
Phone: (703) 684-7722

(NMHA is an active information center that refers callers to 1 of 600 affiliate centers across the country and provides fact sheets about various types of mental illness and mental health such as schizophrenia, depression, adolescent suicide, stress, and tension.)

Council of Citizens With Low Vision
Address: 1400 North Drake Road, Suite 218, Kalamazoo, MI 49007
Phone: (616) 381-9566

(This is a membership organization that serves as a clearinghouse on low vision and promotes education, research, legislation, and the elimination of barriers to the full use of residual vision.)

National Federation of the Blind (NFB)
Address: 1800 Johnson Street, Baltimore, MD 21230
Phone: (301) 659-9314

(NFB is a consumer group that answers questions about blindness and refers people to appropriate resources, among other activities.)

13 Homeless Women

"First one survives, then one goes on to live." This is the philosophy of a small shelter for alcoholics in Cambridge, Massachusetts. Its late director, Theresa Rowe, fully understood what it was to be a homeless alcoholic woman. She was a recovering alcoholic who had lived on the streets while she was actively drinking. She had experienced firsthand the danger and degradation of being an alcoholic woman, poor and abandoned. "They called me an *it*," she said. "No matter how many baths I took, I still felt dirty inside." Poverty, loss of connections and relationships, and often the death or removal of children can precipitate an alcoholic woman into the terror and isolation of living on the streets. The stigma of alcoholism is increased by the stigma of homelessness for a woman on the streets, causing Rowe to be victimized or rejected by most of the people she met. "I was beat up by men on the street, cursed by passersby, and treated like a criminal by the cops," recalled Rowe. "After a while, I began to believe I was no good." The emotional devastation of being an outcast and the physical dangers of being alone and unprotected create many hurdles for the homeless alcoholic woman to overcome in recovery. Achieving physical safety and achieving emotional safety are the first steps to survival for a homeless woman, and they open the way to recovery and the restoration of dignity.

Homelessness for alcoholic and drug-abusing women is related to broader issues of social change and its impact on the poor. Economic and social policy has had dire consequences for the poor and homeless in this country, especially women. From the Housing Rehabilitation Acts of the 1940s, to the Mental Health and Retardation Act of 1963, to the recent changes in welfare policies and budgets, one can trace the path to the homeless situation as it exists in America today.

One of the primary causes of homelessness over the past 20 years has been the failure of deinstitutionalization programs to provide adequate facilities for patients on their release from the state institutions of mental health. Deinstitutionalization began during the 1950s when behavior-controlling drugs became an effective form of therapy. It was not until the late 1960s that the trend toward noninstitutional treatment began in earnest and then peaked during the mid-1970s. Many women with both alcoholism and mental illness were excluded from community-based programs. Traditional alcoholism programs did not want them because of their mental illness and need for medication. Community-based mental health services rejected them because they were actively drinking. Emergency shelters frequently housed only men and were unprepared for the influx of homeless women with multiple needs and problems. A shelter for alcoholics in Cambridge reported an increase in the proportion of women clients from 2% to 8% from 1979 to 1985.

Another major factor affecting the lives of substance-abusing women and precipitating them into homelessness was gentrification of urban areas, compounded by the lack of and loss of low-income housing. Redevelopment and spontaneous conversions of rooming houses and multifamily dwellings to private residences have caused many poor alcoholic and drug-abusing men and women to live on the streets. Clearing slums to make way for private developers created a crisis for populations at high risk, especially indigent alcoholics, drug abusers, and women with children whose only hold on private shelter was in slum housing and rooming houses.

A final outside factor, one closely associated with substance-abusing women who are homeless, is the phenomenon known as the "feminization of poverty." This refers to the increase in poverty among women of all classes. Homeless alcoholic and drug-abusing women usually are women who have been progressively affected by a complex nexus of social, political, and economic forces that increasingly speak to the powerlessness of women. Substance-abusing women experience a progression of economic and social losses that, along with their disease of alcoholism and drug addiction, leaves them in a precarious state.

In the alcoholism field, the existence of homeless men has been studied in depth for more than 30 years. A study of the experiences of homeless alcoholic women done during the 1970s by Bahr and Garrett first revealed the differences in the backgrounds and drinking patterns between homeless alcoholic men and homeless alcoholic women. The lives of homeless women were found to be lonelier, more alienated, and more poverty stricken than those of homeless men. Homeless alcoholic women were more likely to have been married, to have had children, and to have begun their drinking later in life than homeless alcoholic men, and women found themselves on "skid row" at an earlier age. Women had fewer economic resources to keep them from homelessness once alcoholism took over their lives. For women, a marital crisis or abandonment most often was a precipitating factor into homelessness, whereas for men, it was the loss of a job.[1] According to the U.S. Department of Housing and Urban Development, an estimated 50% of homeless women and children are on the street due to violence in the home.[2] Once a woman becomes homeless, her drinking patterns and patterns of association differ dramatically from those of homeless men. Women tend to drink alone more than do men. Women do their drinking in more isolated settings such as parks, alleys, and abandoned buildings, avoiding bars and other public places. It is possible that homeless alcoholic women hide their drinking, in part, because of the stigma of female alcoholism. The lives of homeless women are described as lonely, vulnerable, and friendless. They are the most isolated and alienated of any of the inhabitants of skid row.[3]

Recognizing the Homeless Client's Feelings

The inner and outer world of the homeless alcoholic or drug-abusing woman is one of shame, despair, and abandonment. Within the context of women and relationships, a homeless woman has experienced the total disconnection and loss of important relationships in her life, and her self-esteem has been shattered. A home traditionally is an American woman's center of activity and relationship, the place in which she defines and fulfills her roles as daughter, partner, lover, mother, and friend. To be homeless is a tangible expression of the disruption and lack of meaningful relationships and roles in a woman's life. A substance-abusing woman who is homeless has lost her "protectors" and feels vulnerable. To have some protection from the loneliness and desperation of life on the streets, women often turn to men who abuse them and further damage their sense of self-worth and identity. Most homeless alcoholic and drug-abusing women experience rapes, beatings, and abuse in the streets and live constantly in the shadow of violence. Lack of sleep and food makes them even more at risk for abuse. They also might resort to prostitution, shoplifting, begging, and breaking the law to meet their needs for companionship, money, and protection. Living day to day on the streets is an all-consuming, full-time occupation for a homeless woman who also is caught in the cycle of addiction to alcohol or other drugs.

A new generation of women are entering the ranks of the homeless, that is, young women in their early 20s and even late teens who have experienced abandonment and powerlessness at an early age. Their drinking frequently is combined with the use of illicit drugs, with the use of both alcohol and drugs beginning during early adolescence. Alcoholism and drug abuse have removed the support of family and friends. These young women often find male "protectors," or fellow street alcoholics or addicts, and they might appear at shelters as "couples." Many of these women have experienced physical and sexual abuse, and they frequently look far older than their chronological age while emotionally they still are children. This group is at high risk for contracting sexually transmitted diseases including AIDS. In a recent study of 240 homeless and drug-recovering women, it was found that their closest source of social support most often consisted of friends who showed emotional distress and risky behaviors, suggesting the need for making available an alternative support system.[4]

Until recently, there have been sharp differences in the number and quality of treatment services for homeless substance-abusing men and women. Many shelters served men only, and publicly funded detoxification programs usually would have 2 or 3 women's beds compared to 20 or more men's beds. According to the National Law Center on Poverty and Homelessness, there is a great diversity to the homeless population. For example, 37% of the homeless are families with children, 25% are children, 25% to 40% work, and 40% have alcohol or drug dependency problems.[5]

Practical Treatment Considerations

The importance of shelter comes before all else for homeless women, whether drinking or sober. A room means, first and foremost, security, protection, and a place to rest and stay warm. The physical security of a shelter allows a woman to get the sleep and rest that she needs for her physical and mental well-being. Privacy is something that a homeless woman loses. A room affords the security of privacy and the ability to begin to build up basic self-respect. Many women start their recovery with simple daily rituals of bathing, dressing, eating, and beginning safe associations with others. Women need encouragement to work on their self-esteem through small symbolic acts of self-care. It might take a homeless woman in a treatment program a much longer period of time than it does other women to begin to restore her sense of self-worth and her trust of others as well as to explore her abilities to work. Homeless women have experienced the losses of alcoholism and other drug abuse as well as the devastation of homelessness and abandonment. A counselor would do well to lower her or his expectations of a homeless substance-abusing woman entering treatment. It is helpful to acknowledge the client's initial distrust, to anticipate relapse, and to allow her to enter the program more than once (if necessary). Homeless alcoholic women might have a myriad of physical and emotional problems that need to be addressed as they recover. Malnutrition, physical abuse, gynecological problems, lack of routine medical care, and dental problems need to be addressed as a first priority. Women who have dual diagnoses might need to be reevaluated and prescribed appropriate drug treatment for their psychiatric illness.

The effects of a life of alcoholism, drug abuse, homelessness, and poverty extend far beyond short-term treatment. The sense of powerlessness and apathy and a crippling attitude of hopelessness and resignation make recovering from alcoholism and drug abuse and staying sober and clean difficult. Women, even in their 20s, might seem tired out and drained of energy for many months. They might not be mentally or physically capable of facing work or education as soon as are other women clients. They might become overwhelmed with the losses in their lives and become severely depressed. For women who have been homeless and abandoned for many years, the loss of contact with children can be particularly painful.

Helping homeless substance-abusing women to trust themselves and other people is a long process that requires patience. It is important to begin with an understanding of how profoundly they have experienced rejection and abandonment, how low their self-esteem might be, and how much they need to repeatedly experience the security and safety of a homelike residence to grow and come alive. Although some women have found great help in inner-city Alcoholics Anonymous or Narcotics Anonymous groups where they meet other recovering persons who have formerly been on the streets, Brissett-Chapman points out,

> These programs generally do not offer sufficient treatment because these women often lack the commitment and trust needed to use a community support model. They are often socially isolated and lack the sophisti-

cated interpersonal skills and confidence to learn new behaviors and engage others in mutual and effective ways.[6]

As part of long-term treatment, women also will need job training and sheltered work experiences to help them regain a sense of confidence and financial independence. Older women and women with disabilities might need advocates to help them obtain the disability and medical benefits they have lost or never have been able to obtain on their own.

Although this chapter has focused primarily on homeless women themselves, it is important to remember that alcoholism and other drug abuse also plays a major role in the increasing numbers of homeless women with children. Alcoholic and drug-abusing women might go undiagnosed in family shelters and in shelters for battered women, where the focus is primarily on loss of housing and family violence. The alcoholism or drug abuse of a partner or spouse might mask the drinking or drugging problem of the woman seeking help with children. Staff working in these facilities need to be informed and educated about women's substance abuse issues.

References

1. H. M. Bahr and G. R. Garrett, *Women Alone: The Disaffiliation of Urban Females* (Lexington, MA: D. C. Heath, 1976), 135.

2. U.S. Department of Housing and Urban Development, *A Report on the 1988 National Survey of Shelters for the Homeless* (Washington, DC: Office of Policy Development and Research, 1989).

3. M. Sandmaier, *The Invisible Alcoholics: Women and Alcohol Abuse in America* (New York: McGraw-Hill, 1980), 195-96.

4. A. Nyamathi, J. Flaskerud, and B. Leake, *Nursing Research* 46, no. 3 (1997): 133-37.

5. National Law Center on Poverty and Homelessness. Available: http://www.nlcph.org/h&pusa.htm. Retrieved 2 December 1998.

6. Sheryl Brissett-Chapman, "Homeless African-American Women and Their Families: Coping with Depression, Drugs, and Trauma," in Cora Lee Wetherington and Adele B. Roman, eds., *Drug Addiction Research and the Health of Women,* NIH Publication No. 98-4290 (Bethesda, MD: National Institutes of Health, 1998), 507.

Staff Training Activities

Activity 1: Images of a Homeless Substance-Abusing Woman
Activity 2: Exploring the Needs of Homeless Alcoholic and Drug-Abusing Women
Activity 3: Hierarchy of Needs and Services for Homeless Substance-Abusing Women

Activity 1:   Images of a Homeless Substance-Abusing Woman

Ask the group members to spontaneously share adjectives and words that they think of when they hear the term *homeless alcoholic woman* or *homeless and drug-addicted woman*. Write down each response in a list.

Examples:

Prostitute	Abandoned	Sick
No good	Addict	Victim
Fallen woman	Lonely	Transient
Skid row bum	Dirty	Manipulative
Homeless	Outcast	Sad

■ Go over each word and discuss whether it is accurate or a stereotype.

■ Ask the group to examine the feeling content behind the words we use to describe the homeless alcoholic or drug-abusing woman.

■ What makes us feel this way (e.g., outcast among outcasts, our own fears of abandonment)?

Activity 2:   Exploring the Needs of Homeless Alcoholic and Drug-Abusing Women

Ask each person to put herself or himself in the place of a homeless substance-abusing woman. Address the following questions in a group discussion:

■ Where can she be found in the community, and where is she welcome?

■ What does she need to survive?

■ Where can she go in the community to get her needs met?

■ Where are the gaps in services for homeless women?

■ What needs will be met if the woman is drinking or drugging? If she is sober and clean?

■ How does she feel about herself?

■ What makes it most difficult for her to ask for help?

■ Where would you begin with her if she came to you asking for help?

Activity 3:   Hierarchy of Needs and Services for Homeless Substance-Abusing Women

Discuss the "Hierarchy of Needs and Services for Homeless Substance-Abusing Women" list. Ask people to think about what is available in their own communities for homelessness, alcoholism, and drug abuse. How are women's needs met in these services? Discuss ways in which to improve the service system to meet the needs of homeless women.

Hierarchy of Needs and Services for Homeless Substance-Abusing Women

1. *Food and shelter:* These include rest, privacy, emergency medical care, hygiene, referral, and clothing.

2. *Detoxification:* This involves safe, supervised withdrawal from alcohol or other drugs. This might take longer than 7 days and could take as long as a month.

3. *Medical and psychiatric evaluation:* This is evaluation of acute medical and psychiatric illnesses that need immediate treatment.

4. *Long-term residential placement:* This is a halfway house or residential treatment setting of one year or more that provides a safe and supportive atmosphere.

5. *Introduction to alcoholism or drug abuse recovery:* This is a program in which there are role models of other homeless men and women who are sober and recovering.

6. *Long-term work and job training:* After 6 months, if a woman is strong enough emotionally and physically, then it is time to begin exploring helping her to become either partially or fully self-supporting.

7. *Reconnection with family and friends:* A safe and sober foundation is needed before attempting to risk contacting those who have abandoned her or whom she has abandoned.

8. *Rebuilding of self-esteem:* All the previous steps begin a lifetime process of helping a homeless woman to regain her sense of integrity and sense of self. Counseling, involvement in Alcoholics Anonymous or Narcotics Anonymous, and a long-term solid support system might be necessary for a woman to begin to feel fully human and alive once again and to be able to live in the world in which she once was an outcast.

Client Training Activities

Activity 1

Evaluate the client's immediate needs and develop treatment plans that address these needs.

- Does the client feel safe?

- Does she have shelter, clothing, and food?

- Does she have medical needs? In this case, it is important for the woman to have a physical exam, including a gynecological exam, with a medical caregiver who is competent in treating alcoholism and drug abuse and who will be empathetic and reassuring during the exam. You might need to accompany the client to the physician's office to support her through her fears and to help advocate for her.

- Does she have mental health issues or a dual diagnosis? Psychological supports, including consultation, evaluation, and medication, should be available as backup to you and your clients.

Activity 2

Begin immediate education about the disease of alcoholism and other drug addiction including physiological effects and postacute withdrawal. As the client "clears up," maintaining time away from alcohol and drugs, she might begin to experience guilt, self-blame, depression, anger, and sadness over events that occurred while she was drinking. Therefore, she will need education on how active alcoholism and drug abuse remove the power of choice in decision making, cause disconnections and losses, and place women in dangerous situations where they are at risk for abuse and violence.

Activity 3

Assist the client in developing a basic routine of hygiene, self-care, and gradually increasing responsibility. Help her to incorporate daily supports into her day such as Alcoholics Anonymous and contact with a sponsor. Help her to go slowly and establish small and reachable goals.

Examples:

- Today I will attend one Alcoholics Anonymous or Narcotics Anonymous meeting, the 8 p.m. meeting at St. James Church.

- Today I will speak with one other person at my Alcoholics Anonymous or Narcotics Anonymous meeting, and I will start the conversation by introducing myself.

- I will eat three meals today.

Activity 4

Help build self-esteem by helping your client acknowledge and list her strengths and skills.

Examples:

- I am a survivor.

- I have stayed sober for 3 weeks, as difficult as this time has been for me.

- I am a high school graduate.

Activity 5

Feelings of grief, anger, and depression will arise in any substance abuser's recovery process. Complications can occur with homeless women whose losses as alcoholic and drug-abusing women were exacerbated by the devastation of homelessness and resultant loss of dignity and stigmatization. As grief and anger begin to surface, you must make room to listen at the same time as the woman continues to educate herself about alcoholism and other drug abuse. You can frame many of the past events in the disease concept and slow down a woman who is obsessed with immediately contacting family members or blaming herself for the loss of children. Women also need room to discuss any experience of physical or sexual violence. You can create an atmosphere of openness by letting clients know that you are aware of the violence that might have occurred in their lives. There also is the subtle abuse that women experience in dealing with bureaucracies that administer to the homeless, which will in some way affect your interactions, perhaps in the ways that you will work together to establish trust. A homeless woman needs your patience. In considering those actions that she feels she must undertake, help her by setting a timetable for goals she can work toward accomplishing and the basis for that timing.

Resources

National Coalition for the Homeless
Address: 1012 Fourteenth Street, N.W., Suite 600, Washington, DC 20005-3410
Phone: (202) 737-6444
Web: http://www2.ari.net/home/nch

(This is an advocacy group committed to ending homelessness.)

14 Elderly Women

Little has been written about the special problems and concerns of older alcoholic and drug-abusing women.[1] It is only recently that alcoholism and prescription drug abuse have begun to be recognized as major health problems among older Americans. Losses and changes in women's lives as they age are compounded by alcoholism and drug addiction. Ageism, sexism, and poverty converge to create many barriers to treating older women. Denial and misdiagnosis of alcoholism and drug addiction by medical and social service professionals have prevented older women from being introduced to treatment services. The problem often is the lack of awareness about substance abuse among the elderly by counselors; for example, counselors working with the elderly might not be educated enough about the symptoms and problems of substance abuse. Conversely, counselors providing substance abuse treatment might not know how to work effectively with the elderly. The growing population of aging women requires that health service providers improve their skills in diagnosing and treating substance-abusing elders. For older women who do enter treatment, the prognosis is good.

According to a recent report from the National Center on Addiction and Substance Abuse (CASA), there are approximately 25.6 million women over 59 years old living in the United States. Of these, 17% are addicted to nicotine, 7% abuse alcohol, and 11% abuse psychoactive drugs other than alcohol.[2] The elderly are the fastest growing segment of the U.S. population. By the year 2050, this population will be much more multicultural in nature, with one third of the elderly population comprising members of ethnic minority groups.[3]

Physicians, nurses, home health aides, and family often are the primary counselors for older people. When elderly people come to physicians about physical problems, the role and effects of alcohol often are overlooked and ignored. Some physicians are reluctant to give the diagnosis of alcoholism to an older patient because of the stigma associated with it. The symptoms of alcohol abuse often are incorrectly attributed to aging and/or chronic physical illness. In CASA's recent report on alcoholism and the mature woman, Califano points out,

The substance abuse and addiction of mature women is hidden in the shame, embarrassment, and denial of those who struggle with it. It is swept under the rug of denial and desperation of families and friends who can't accept the reality that mother or a dear aunt may be abusing alcohol or addicted to it or who simply don't know what to do about it. It gets lost in the shadows because so many physicians fail to identify substance abuse or addiction in their female patients, and some physicians who do ignore it because they don't believe anything can or should be done.[4]

Alcoholism is a progressive disease whose signs and symptoms might remain hidden for many years of a person's adult life. Life circumstances often change with age; retirement; loss of a spouse, siblings, or friends; and decreased economic resources. As a result, an older person's loss of control over alcohol can become evident to others as a new problem when, in fact, it has been present for many years. Physiological changes due to aging also can contribute to the seemingly "sudden" appearance of an alcohol problem. The aging process slows down the metabolism and elimination of alcohol from the body. Although the amount of alcohol consumed might be unchanged, the heavy drinking of a younger drinker can turn into a visible alcoholism problem as she grows older. In addition, problem drinking in the elderly can be precipitated by isolation, loneliness, bereavement, physical or mental infirmity, or a combination of these factors. More unscheduled time and fewer responsibilities after retirement can result in loss of self-confidence and withdrawal from friends and family. Women in particular can find retirement to be a stressful change. If they have limited family networks or few outside interests, then they might find that they cannot sufficiently replace their lost job-related social network.[5] Some older people turn to alcohol to cope with these changes.

The middle years appear to be an age of transition in drinking practices for women as well as a transition in family dynamics and other areas of their lives. Until recently, the majority of alcoholic women seen in treatment had been in their late 30s and 40s. For many of them, their problem drinking was precipitated by crisis events related to marriage, family, or female physiology. Problem drinking as a response to a traumatic event is much truer for women than for men, as a review of the clinical literature suggests.[6] Women in midlife, meaning the time when children are grown or soon will be, often experience a mix of emotions. For many, there is a sense of relief at completing their child care responsibilities but also some anxiety and fear at what the future holds. The loss of one's role as parent coupled with the uncertainty of taking on new roles can be a high-risk time for developing a range of unhealthy coping strategies including abuse of alcohol or other drugs.[7]

Women face social and economic pressures during the second halves of their lives that put them at risk for alcoholism and other drug abuse and also affect the normal process of aging. One of the cultural pressures affecting older women is the phenomenon of ageism. Ageism has been described as a belief that a person's worth and ability are determined solely by chronological age. According to the book *Our Bodies, Ourselves,* ageism in the United States springs from many sources:

Our society overvalues youth and beauty and sets them as a standard for measuring women's value. This is layered on top of a sexist view that women are valuable only for looks and reproductive capacity, so that a woman is regarded either as youthfully beautiful or no longer beautiful. In addition to sexism compounded with ageism, many women also face discrimination based on race, disability status, and sexual orientation. When we are viewed in these stereotyped ways, we must struggle for participation in work and community as well as to have our contributions taken seriously.[8]

Ageism can present real barriers to older women in their ability to find and retain employment as well as to maintain a sense of connection with others. Society judges women mostly on their physical appearance and devalues them as they age. Even the women's movement has, until recently, failed to address the needs of older women.

Within the population of older Americans, women are the majority. This is especially so for elderly women of color. Sex ratios (males per 100 females) among the elderly are estimated to be at levels such as 62 black men for every 100 black women and 82 Asian men for every 100 Asian women.[9] The growing number of older women suggests an increasing number of elderly women in trouble with alcohol and other drugs.

Aging often is closely linked with poverty and loss of economic and social status for women. Although poverty in the overall elderly population has been reduced to nearly the average for the population as a whole, it continues to be higher for older women. Older women are more likely to be alone and poor. Because women outlive men by an average of 7 years, many married women experience widowhood for some parts of their later lives. About three out of four women will be widowed, and opportunities for remarriage are low.[10] Widowed women often lose significant financial support from their husbands.[11]

Older women of color continue to have the most serious problems of all. Due to their disadvantaged status, their lifetimes of poor health care, poor nutrition, and limited resources cause earlier, chronic, and serious health conditions.[12] Single older women, especially women of color, need strong community ties and substantial family support to maintain an adequate standard of living.

The issue of family, community support, and partners is more complex for older lesbians. Older women who are alcoholic often are unable to develop and maintain adequate support systems because of the impact of their drinking on themselves and others. Older women share the need for connections and relationships as much as, if not more than, do other women.

Supportive relationships can make the difference between life and death for an elderly woman who has been estranged from adult children and friends. Children and grandchildren often are the main emotional connection for older women. The emotional and social isolation of alcoholism is compounded by the aging process. Older alcoholic women often are surrounded by bewildered children who have difficulty in recognizing the symptoms of alcoholism in their older parents. Adult children might attribute the problems of alcoholism and drug abuse to aging.

When an elderly parent is alcoholic, the attitude of family members tends to be negative and unsupportive. The opposite also might be true if family member are overprotective, enabling the older person to continue drinking by sheltering her. An older woman, often alone because of the loss of a spouse, might get a strong sense of connection from friendships, either old or new, with same-age peers. Alcoholism often makes the ability to maintain old friendships and to develop new ones next to impossible.

The moral and social beliefs of most of today's older women were shaped prior to 1950, when alcoholism became publicly recognized as a disease. *Alcoholics* and *alcoholism* are words associated with humiliation, disgrace, and moral weakness for many older women. To be called an alcoholic is considered a social disgrace. Women who have grown up during the temperance movement and prohibition of the 1920s and 1930s might bring to their drinking particularly entrenched attitudes about the sinfulness of women who drink, increasing the secrecy, denial, and shame about their drinking. These women, now in their 70s and 80s, often see themselves as "fallen women" and feel unworthy, and they might isolate themselves from their family and friends. They might be surrounded by others who share similar attitudes toward older women's drinking and, therefore, could be further isolated from developing same-age relationships.

Elderly women and men can face a range of losses as they get older. These include illnesses and deaths of family, friends, and partners, which means the losses of lifetimes of support and companionship. There also is the loss that comes with geographic separation from family. For example, many grandparents do not live near their grandchildren. Loss of money through earned income has not only economic but also symbolic meaning. Money represents power, status, value, and independence. Lack of money can affect vital areas of self-esteem. Retirement brings a range of losses that can include status, gratification, identity, and privacy as living circumstances have to change. There also are changes of bodily functions and a perceived loss of attractiveness. There are societal pressures on women not to express their sexual natures as they age. With aging, there can be changes in sensation as the senses become less acute. The most powerful of these changes can occur in one's capacity for memory and thinking acuity. This often happens gradually. The result of all these changes is that self-respect, integrity, dignity, and self-esteem might be threatened.[13]

As life expectancy increases, women are more vulnerable to the natural course of disease and to biological stress. Problems such as hypertension, cancer, arthritis, and diabetes, as well as difficulties with vision, hearing, and mobility loss, become increasingly common. In fact, women over 65 years old are likely to suffer from at least two chronic health conditions, putting limitations on an independent lifestyle.[14]

Elderly Women and Prescription Drugs

The media today deliver a strong message that pain and discomfort need not be tolerated, and a vast array of remedies is available over the counter or by prescription to treat a wide variety of ills. As people age, the ready availability of these drugs provides compelling inducement to individuals experiencing the negative effects that may be associated with the aging process. The average person over 65 years old takes two to seven prescription medications daily.[15] Drug problems in older women are almost exclusively related to the use of legal (prescription or over-the-counter) drugs. Overprescription by physicians might be motivated by a sincere desire to improve the quality of life of elderly patients. Older women might not fully realize the risks associated with combining certain prescribed and over-the-counter compounds or their contraindication with alcohol consumption. Mislabeled bottles, outdated medications, self-prescriptions, and medications shared with others without a physician's orders pose frequent and potentially serious hazards.

Unfortunately, the health problems of the elderly can be aggravated by the medical profession's insensitivity to the psychological and physiological changes of elderly women. All too often, drugs are prescribed when clinicians take inadequate drinking histories or do not take into account the dramatically altered way in which elderly women metabolize medications. Thought rarely is given to an older woman's ability to afford the medication or to comply with directions, especially if she is drinking alcoholically.

As women age, they metabolize drugs more slowly; thus, drugs remain in the body for a longer period of time. Older drinkers consume less alcohol by quantity than do younger drinkers, but tolerance to both alcohol and drugs diminishes with the metabolic changes that accompany the aging process. Women may truthfully report consuming a lower quantity of alcohol, although the negative consequences are just as great. For example, studies have shown that aging can cause an increased sensitivity to the effects of alcohol. Elderly people, therefore, can experience an onset of alcohol problems, such as a decreased tolerance to alcohol as well as less coherence and coordination at lower doses, even though their drinking patterns have not changed.[16]

Excessive use of alcohol can bring on or aggravate many physical ills and can lead to mental deterioration. Drinking can harm the body of an older woman through direct organ involvement and the effects of inadequate nutrition. The effects of alcohol in an elderly woman also can mask valuable warning signals of other physical disorders such as cardiac pain. In addition, older problem drinkers have higher rates of suicide attempts than do aged nonproblem drinkers.

The diagnosis of alcoholism frequently is missed or denied by counselors working with older women. Part of the reason for this is the pattern of an older woman's drinking, which tends to be more hidden. Most older women do not seek treatment voluntarily for their drinking because of the stigma attached. Often, a passive and more reclusive lifestyle and living on a modest fixed income contribute to a pattern of solitary drinking that can go undetected. Medical practitioners might not ask, or might be uncomfortable asking, older women about their drinking or drug use. If they do, then they might find the older women claiming to be nondrinkers or moderate-drinking persons. Counselors might mistakenly ascribe changes in behavior and personality to aging instead of to alcohol. There is a tendency for counselors to view elderly women as untreatable, harmless, and hurting only themselves. These negative attitudes toward aging, alcoholism, and women can converge in a treatment system that allows alcoholic women to continue to drink undetected and overlooked. It has been found that older adults with substance abuse or psychiatric problems often are given less specialized treatment than are younger patients. They are more likely to be directed to medical management of the problem rather than to rehabilitative treatment.[17] Women most frequently are seen in medical and social service settings by staff who might have little or no training in identifying and diagnosing alcoholism in older women. Elderly alcoholic women have received little systematic attention in agencies that serve the elderly and in alcoholism agencies.

There are definite patterns and signs of alcoholism to look for in working with older women. Identifying alcoholism in an elderly woman often requires a comprehensive assessment of the physical, psychological, and social spheres of her life. An alcoholic woman might have experienced a drinking problem for many years. It might have begun when the woman was much younger, and somehow she managed to live to an old age. An alcoholic woman might not have developed a drinking problem until late in life, possibly in response to one or more late-life crises such as retirement and the death of a spouse or child. This woman might have been a moderate social drinker or abstainer until recently. An older woman might maintain an alcohol dependence on small amounts of alcohol. This is especially true if the person is taking medications or has other physical illnesses that affect the body's functioning. Denial, guilt, and shame are part of an older woman's feelings about her drinking. She also might view alcohol medicinally, that is, as a coping mechanism. There are common clues that counselors and others can look for as signs that alcoholism is present in an older woman's life. When a configuration of these symptoms is present, it is important to explore a woman's use of alcohol and medications.

The first step toward successful alcoholism intervention with the older woman is exploring our personal attitudes on aging, women, and alcoholism. Approaching an older woman about her drinking often is best done in the safety and security of her own home or at the facilities of medical providers with whom she is familiar. Privacy, respect for her personal history, and an understanding of the stigma that the words *alcoholism* and *alcoholic* might hold for her are imperatives. The words *drinking* and *drinking problem* can be substituted. It often is helpful to introduce the issue of her drinking repeatedly over time in the context of a supportive relationship. A genuine expression of concern that is consistently shared is needed to confront the well-established denial and defenses of the older woman drinker. Explain what help is available and the nature of that help. For example, describing to the older woman what her stay in a detoxification program or treatment center might be like can be helpful in addressing her fears.

Potential Signs of Alcoholism and Drug Abuse in Older Women

- Neglected appearance and hygiene
- Frequent car accidents
- Neglect of or overattention to home, bills, and pets
- Malnutrition and anemia
- Isolation from family and friends
- Mood swings or erratic behavior
- Repeated falls
- Leg bruises
- Cigarette burns
- Confusion
- Empty cupboards
- Combining alcohol and medications
- Withdrawal from social activities
- Attempts or concerns with suicide
- Depression
- Health complaints
- Memory impairment

An older alcoholic woman often arrives in an acute medical setting as a result of illness complicated by alcohol and/or medications. It is imperative to intervene at this time, stressing the positive impact that getting sober will have on her physical health and on many other aspects of her life. Being specific and direct about the problems that the older woman is experiencing as a result of her drinking is essential. Inform her of the help that is available, and give her information about how and where to get that help. Letting her know that there is hope for a better life in recovery is important. Developing a number of supports for a woman such as family, friends, physician, and other counselors can help an older woman to regain a sense of worth and a life important enough for her to get sober.

Several researchers stress the importance of a well-coordinated approach to treatment, one that includes an interdisciplinary treatment team with the inclusion of the family or significant others and a comprehensive plan of individualized support services. Social supports and the development of new relationships are seen as key variables in the successful treatment of the elderly problem drinker. It has been suggested that treatment of elderly women and men can be effective when delivered through facilities serving senior citizens, such as senior centers, outpatient geriatric medical or psychiatric programs, nursing homes, and home care programs, or through peer outreach and in-home intervention or treatment.

Alcoholics Anonymous (AA) can be an especially important treatment resource for an older woman, as can existing alcoholism services. She will meet many older peers at AA meetings. Some alcoholism programs and elder services are developing support groups for older alcoholics. Family members of older women also can benefit from attending education and support groups. As one older woman described her decision to stop drinking, "I want to live my life fully and face my death with dignity."

Concepts of aging are changing as women are living longer and with improved health. The belief that alcoholism among elderly women is immoral and untreatable is false. Older alcoholic women who stop drinking frequently can participate in a full and rich life. Intellectual growth and social participation return to a sober woman if she participates in support groups for her sobriety, elder services, and family activities. Even very ill or frail women can continue to learn and be socially involved. At any age, an older alcoholic woman who is involved in recovery can reap the rewards of better health, a sense of well-being, and a restoration of dignity and community.

References

1. Thanks go to Anita Shipman for her initial contributions to this chapter.

2. National Center on Addiction and Substance Abuse, *Under the Rug: Substance Abuse and the Mature Woman,* foreword and accompanying statement by Joseph A. Califano, Jr., chairman and president of the National Center on Addiction and Substance Abuse (New York: Columbia University, CASA, 1997). Available: http://www.casacolumbia.org/pubs/jun98/foreword.htm

3. Wihelmina A. Leigh and Malinda A. Lindquist, *Women of Color Health Data Book: Adolescents to Seniors* (Bethesda, MD: National Institutes of Health, 1998). Available: http://www.4woman.gov/x/owh/pub/woc/references1.htm

4. National Center on Addiction and Substance Abuse, *Under the Rug.*

5. E. Gomberg, "Women's Drinking Practices and Problems from a Lifespan Perspective," in National Institute on Alcohol Abuse and Alcoholism, *Women and Alcohol: Issues for Prevention*

Research, NIH Publication No. 96-3817 (Washington, DC: Government Printing Office, 1996), 194.

6. Ibid.

7. L. Rubin, *Women of a Certain Age: The Midlife Search for Self* (New York: Harper & Row, 1979), 13-41.

8. Boston Women's Health Book Collective, *Our Bodies, Ourselves: For the New Century* (New York: Simon & Schuster, 1998), 548.

9. Leigh and Lindquist, *Women of Color.*

10. Boston Women's Health Book Collective, *Our Bodies, Ourselves,* 553.

11. Leigh and Lindquist, *Women of Color.*

12. Ibid.

13. Jean Kinney and Gwen Leaton, *Loosening the Grip* (St. Louis, MO: Times Mirror/Mosby, 1987), 298-310.

14. Boston Women's Health Book Collective, *Our Bodies, Ourselves,* 570.

15. National Institute on Alcohol Abuse and Alcoholism, *Alcohol and Aging,* Alcohol Alert No. 40 (Washington, DC: Government Printing Office, 1998). Available: http://www.niaaa.nih.gov

16. Ibid.

17. U.S. Department of Health and Human Services, *Ninth Special Report to the U.S. Congress on Alcohol and Health,* NIH Publication No. 97-4017 (Washington, DC: Government Printing Office, 1997), 383.

■ Staff Training Activities

Activity 1: Images of an Older Alcoholic Woman
Activity 2: Case Studies
Activity 3: Creative Treatment Planning With Older Alcoholic Women

Activity 1:   Images of an Older Alcoholic Woman

Ask the group members to share words and thoughts that come to mind when they think of an alcoholic woman over 60 years of age.

Examples:

Lonely	Homebound	Helpless
Isolated	Hidden drinker	Abandoned
Sad	Despair	Dementia
Homeless	Other drugs	Confused
Humiliated	Health problems	Denial
Hopeless	Fearful	Indifferent

Discussion:

■ If you remove the word *alcoholic,* then how do these words relate to the stereotypes of aging? Similarities? Differences?

■ What are the stigmas that an older alcoholic woman faces in reaching out for help?

Activity 2:   Case Studies

Break the group into small groups of four or five people. Ask these small groups to read case studies and to respond to the questions at the bottom of each sheet.

Case Study 1

Ms. R is an 84-year-old, white single woman living alone in a private, subsidized elderly housing building. She worked for the same company as an office worker for many years and retired at 65 years of age. Her older brother and sister are dead, as are several of her close friends. She has lived in her present apartment for the past 10 years and says that she goes to the building activities but has no close friends now like she once did because "I don't like to get close with just anyone."

Ms. R says that she drank occasionally with friends during her life but that she started drinking more frequently after she retired. During the past 10 years, while living in this building, she drank more. She emphasizes that she is a "periodic drinker," not a "habitual drinker." She usually drinks alone in her apartment about every 2 or 3 weeks for 3 or 4 days using 1 pint of liquor. She has fallen down several times over the past 2 years. She now thinks that she should stop drinking because it might be making her eyesight worse. She has agreed to counseling after a referral was made by her building manager and social worker, but she wants to meet the counselor only every 2 or 3 weeks because "I want to see how I do on my own."

1. What are the signs that Ms. R is having a problem with alcohol?

2. What else about her drinking would you ask Ms. R?

3. What would be the treatment plan you would recommend to Ms. R if you were her counselor?

Case Study 2

Mrs. K is a 65-year-old woman living alone in an apartment in a mixed-income housing project. For the past month, she has been followed by a visiting nurse since her discharge from the hospital, where she had stayed for a week with the diagnosis of anemia. The nurse has noted the smell of alcohol during several visits, but Mrs. K never seems to be noticeably intoxicated. Mrs. K is taking Folate for anemia and Darvocet for arthritic pain, and she had been started on an antidepressant while in the hospital. She has had appointments at a neighborhood health center for medical follow-up but has not kept most of the appointments including those with a social worker. When asked about her drinking, she says, "I drink four to five highballs a day. I really don't drink much. It just seems like it because I'm so tired all the time." She complains about difficulty in sleeping at night. She has a housekeeper twice a week and one woman friend who visits her nearly every day. Other than the hospital stay, Mrs. K has not been out of her apartment for several months.

Mrs. K's husband of 34 years died 2 years ago from alcoholic liver disease. She concedes that she has drunk more since his death. She also says that her only past experience with treatment for alcohol problems was a 2-day stay ("That's all I needed") at a private alcoholism treatment hospital, being brought there by her husband's sister the day after his funeral. She has two children by a previous marriage whom she has not seen for more than 40 years. She has one brother, a physician who lives 100 miles away and sees her occasionally.

The visiting nurse wanted to make a referral for outreach/evaluation to an alcoholism counselor. Mrs. K agreed to a home visit, but only reluctantly.

1. What makes you question how long Mrs. K has had a problem with alcohol?

2. What are examples of her denial, and how would you respond to them?

3. What is the best treatment plan at this point in time?

Activity 3:   Creative Treatment Planning With Older Alcoholic Women

With older women, it is important to start with physical and emotional safety. "You have to pull someone out of the water before you can dry them off." Outline the following planning strategies:

1. It might be necessary to intervene to initiate treatment.

   Referral to a 2- to 6-week treatment program might be necessary for a woman to get sober.

2.   Monitor a woman's home situation.

What are the supports and hazards in relation to her health or sobriety?

3.   Develop a crisis plan.

Check out the plan with client, family, and others, especially if the woman has a relapse.

4.   Explore community resources.

Nutrition sites, Meals on Wheels, Alcoholics Anonymous, and elderly services address treatment needs as well as issues of isolation.

5.   Use a systems approach.

Develop a network of people to help a woman maintain her independence or to move her into treatment. It might be necessary to educate other counselors about alcoholism.

6.   Learn communication skills with older women.

Respect age differences. Be aware of the language that you use. Get to know the woman first. Begin with problems from her perspective and then ask about her drinking. Respect confidentiality. Validate her life experiences.

Client Training Activities

Activity 1

An important part of your work with the older alcoholic woman involves listening for and paying attention to the moralistic attitudes she holds and has internalized in regard to alcoholism. Such attitudes can be barriers to treatment. Counselors should take an active role in educating women about the progressive nature of the disease and its symptoms and stages. Clients might not be aware that anyone can be affected by a drinking problem, from famous people such as Betty Ford, to respected priests and clergy, to any man or woman. Perhaps the client is aware of someone in her family who had a drinking problem. How was this person regarded?

Older women might have very different standards by which they judge women who drink as opposed to men who drink. If women who drink in public are "immoral" and your client only drinks at home, then she might use this to deny that she has a problem. She might have an inordinate fear of "what people would think" if they knew that she had a drinking problem that keeps her from seeking help or from admitting that she is in trouble.

1.   While educating the client about alcoholism and being mindful of moralistic attitudes, it also is important to stay focused on the drinking behavior and its consequences.

The following questions can help in your assessment. Notice the use of *drinking problem* instead of *alcoholism*. Again, initially using the euphemism could be helpful because the word *alcoholic* might be too frightening or challenging.

- Have you ever had a drinking problem or taken more pills than prescribed?

- Have you had family members whose drinking concerned you?

- Do family members ever bring up your drinking to you?

2. Make the connection between the symptoms of alcoholism and the problems your client may present:

Fatigue	Memory loss (blackouts)
Insomnia	Mood swings
Falls	Heartburn after drinking
Anxiety	Friends and family pulling away

3. Be aware of the importance of social and spiritual supports, especially Alcoholics Anonymous, in providing assistance to help your client work through losses associated with alcoholism and changes due to aging. These supports also can help the woman to recognize her strengths and to maintain a sense of hope as she recovers.

Activity 2

Know who is in your client's life. This includes family members, friends, health care providers, housekeepers, legal services, social service agencies, clergy, and neighbors. Help her to take an inventory of who these important supports are. At the same time, you can begin to visualize this picture of your client's world. Even antagonists are important if the client seems bonded in negative relationships.

NAME/ADDRESS/ PHONE NUMBER	NATURE OF RELATIONSHIP	FREQUENCY OF CONTACT
a. Jane Smith 3 Maple Street Boston, MA 267-1234	Neighbor; known for 39 years	Helps daily with shopping
b. Peter Brown Visiting nurse association 776-1000	Visiting nurse since December 1988	Once a week
c. Joan Doe 3 Elm Street Somerville, MA 628-1234	Sister; not very close	Once a month

1. Assure the client that you always will consult her, and in fact that you need her permission, before contacting agencies or people in her support network. Obtain signed releases well in advance to formalize the contact. Protect your client and respect her rights.

2. You now are a member of the client's support network. Working with an older client might require more involvement than usual in the referral and treatment process as both an advocate and a support person.

3. Familiarize yourself with the network of support services for elders. The advantage of working with an older population is that there is an established group of services available to elders that is not always available to middle-aged or younger people. These include home care services, visiting nurse associations, Meals on Wheels, senior drop-in centers, and adult day care centers.

4. Use case conferencing with all service providers and immediate family members to develop a clear image of the client and how her alcoholism and resulting behaviors are affecting the woman and her system. Have in place an appropriate treatment plan to be used in a crisis as well as a strategy and an approach shared consistently by all members of the system. It probably will be necessary to provide alcohol and drug education as well as referrals to Al-Anon. You might be the only member of this treatment team who is clear that alcoholism or drug abuse is the primary issue, and you must be prepared to advocate your position. Systems and counselors, unfortunately, are prone to becoming a parallel to the alcoholic family system, with their own symptoms of codependency.

Activity 3

Discharging or closing the case on an elderly alcoholic client should be given careful consideration. If discharge seems appropriate, then a thoughtful discharge plan must be considered, especially if the client is not abstinent. This might be an appropriate time to communicate with other counselors in the client's system about monitoring the client and developing a follow-up plan if her condition were to change. Leave the door open for the client to return for further services.

1. Consider doing a home visit with a client. Respect the fact that she is giving you permission to enter her home, and thank her for allowing you to see her in her home.

2. Have available pamphlets, lists of resources, and any written directions a client might need to find Alcoholics Anonymous meetings or other support services. Include larger print materials in your handouts. Alcoholics Anonymous publishes a large-print pamphlet titled *Time to Start Living* that is specifically for older alcoholics.

Resources

Cambridge Council on Aging
Address: 806 Massachusetts Avenue, Cambridge, MA 02139
Phone: (617) 349-6220
and
Address: 167 Holland Street, Somerville, MA 02144
Phone: (617) 625-6600

(This agency provides information, referral, and housing services to the general elderly population including substance abuse services for women age 60 years or over residing in Cambridge or Somerville.)

Older Women's League
Address: 666 Eleventh Street, N.W., Suite 700, Washington, DC 20001-4512
Phone: (202) 783-6686, (800) 825-3695

(This is a local and national membership organization that advocates for older women.)

15

Substance-Abusing Women in the Workplace

Dramatic demographic changes have occurred in the U.S. workforce during the past few decades. More jobs are open to women, and more women—out of choice or out of necessity—are in the workforce than ever before. Many are the sole support of their families, juggling enormous financial, social, and emotional responsibilities. Many working women, especially single parents, are struggling to survive at or below the poverty level. More than half of the women in the United States are employed outside their homes. The percentage of women in professional and managerial positions has increased 170% since the 1950s.[1] The number of households with two working spouses; single mothers with children; or single, separated, widowed, or never-married women is increasing dramatically.

Alcoholism and substance abuse are major problems for women at all levels of the employment world. Women traditionally have been socialized to handle multiple roles and to service the needs of others. For some women, the opportunities and challenges of work situations are gratifying. For others, especially single working mothers who lack social and financial support, stress and work/home demands can become overwhelming, putting them at risk for alcohol and drug abuse. Employee assistance programs (EAPs) and occupational alcoholism programs (OAPs) have been effective forms of early intervention for many male employees in the workforce, but they have been far less successful in reaching women.

Miller suggests in her work on the psychology of women that women are taught to undervalue their work and to overvalue their relationships. Thus, women who work either by choice or by necessity can experience anxieties and difficulties related to a conflict between their sense of self at work and their sense of self in their personal lives. Moreover, women's sense of empathy and need to be related to others sometimes has been misunderstood in work situations as helplessness and dependency. Both women and men tend to assign higher status to positions when they are filled by men.

The effects of employment status on women's drinking are quite complex, and research during the past 10 years has produced some varied findings. Early studies reported that housewives were half as likely to report drinking problems as were employed or unemployed women, debunking the stereotype of the "hidden alcoholic housewife." However, it has since been found that although women who are employed tend to drink more frequently and are less likely to abstain compared to homemakers, there is no difference between the two groups in the rates of *heavy* drinking and of problems due to drinking.[2] In another study, it was found that "women in particular age groups (e.g., were unmarried or without a full-time work role) or who had lost social roles (e.g., through separation, divorce, or children's departure from home) had higher rates of problem drinking than did women with multiple social roles."[3] Unemployment puts women at risk for alcohol abuse, in part, because of the economic deprivation that results as well as the feelings of failure and defeat it can produce.

Certain populations of working women have suffered inordinately from external and internal stress due to sexism, discrimination, and problems associated with the workplace. Single mothers, women in professional and middle management positions, older women, women of color, and lesbians all face a range of pressures that put them at risk for physical problems, emotional stress, and alcohol and drug abuse.

"More than half of the black workforce (52[%]) is female, with many of these workers earning poverty-level wages. Although nearly 8 million black women (out of the total of 17 million black women) worked in 1995, one sixth (nearly 17[%]) of them earned incomes at or below the federal poverty level. More than a fourth of all young black female workers ages 18-24 [years] earned incomes at or below the poverty level."[4]

Despite women's gains in management and professional jobs, the majority of working women still are too frequently the victims of occupational segregation and suffer from low earnings and limited opportunities for advancement. Female job holders are significantly poorer than their male counterparts. Government statistics report that women earn only 75% of what men earn, although women and men are, on average, equal in years of education completed. Of all employed women, 48% are concentrated in low-paying, virtually sex-segregated jobs (e.g., clerical, service, health care, teaching), which sometimes are referred to as "pink-collar" jobs.[5] Many women are trapped in a female job ghetto where they face not only sex discrimination but also discrimination based on race, sexual orientation, and disability.

Women are disadvantaged in the labor market in more than just a differential in earnings. Women workers have higher unemployment and discouraged worker rates,[6] more involuntary part-time and seasonal work, and few wage increases over their lifetimes. Lucrative overtime work often is denied women through both discrimination and the conflicting demands of home or family.

One of the most dramatic changes in labor force participation rates in the United States since the mid-1950s has been the rapid entry of mothers into the workforce. This is true of mothers of both older and younger children, but the most rapid increase has been among mothers with preschool children. Few working mothers have the luxury of ending their workdays at 5 p.m. When they arrive home from their jobs, most still are expected to make dinner, do housework, and attend to the needs of husbands and children. Most working mothers clearly have dual responsibilities for both their homes and jobs, often resulting in immense physical and emotional burdens on them. Many husbands share domestic chores with their wives grudgingly and only when asked and reminded. The average employed woman puts at least 26 hours per week into household duties in addition to her job, amounting to a 66-hour workweek plus travel time. Physical exhaustion and lack of leisure time are two common results.[7]

The economic and social stresses that women, particularly alcoholic women, face in life often are much more difficult than those faced by men. Poverty still is primarily a woman's condition. To quote Susan B. Anthony, "Women are the poorest of the poor, and the alcoholic woman is even poorer." A majority of the poor are women, particularly women of color. Many women are single heads of households, earning much less than men working at the same jobs and often having little or no work experience. A 1995 survey found that in the United States, 47% of female-headed Hispanic families and 48% of female-headed black families live below the poverty level.[8] The profile of the American family is changing, and more and more women are the single parents and sole support of school-age children.

Single Mothers

Single mothers of young children are a special group within a special population. Nearly all studies show them at the highest risk for mental health problems, and their numbers are increasing dramatically. At the present time, divorced or unmarried mothers of young children are a growing percentage of the American female population. It is clear that work for most of these mothers is an economic necessity. Single mothers, who often are young themselves and are raising small children alone, experience high levels of stress and low levels of well-being due, in part, to the hardships that they must endure.

Research has shown that single-parent mothers experience a level of stress significantly higher than that experienced by other groups. Within the single-parent mother population, those who never have been married experience even greater strains. Their children, often the result of out-of-wedlock teenage pregnancies, are born into the most precarious mother-child units in our society.

A single mother faces a multitude of economic and social barriers including inadequate child care, escalating housing costs, and lack of support, all of which can be overwhelming. The ongoing stress experienced by single mothers puts them at high risk for physical and emotional illnesses and might encourage them to use alcohol and drugs as a way in which to cope or escape.

Professional and Middle Management Women

As more women have moved into management positions, women's drinking and drug abuse has become more visible. For women who carry a risk for substance abuse, on-the-job stress and heightened peer pressure to drink can contribute to the development of alcohol and drug problems. Women in less traditionally female jobs can face discrimination and a work environment subtly or overtly hostile to their participation, causing them to work twice as hard as men to "prove" their competence. Drinking in the business world still is, for many, an accepted norm. For some women, it appears to them that drinking is a necessity of corporate life. Job-related situations, including business functions, conferences, and after-work meetings, promote drinking. Although this in itself does not lead to alcohol abuse, it puts women who are at risk in an extremely vulnerable situation in which it is difficult to refuse drinks for fear of being further ostracized from the male peer group. Women who are working to be accepted in the business and corporate world often are under pressure to adopt the administrative and social styles of their male colleagues. Alcohol can both be part of and contribute to stresses to perform and belong.

Employee Assistance and the Alcohol or Drug-Abusing Woman

Some of the early intervention programs most successful in reaching and treating alcoholic and drug-abusing men have been EAPs and OAPs. Most large corporations have programs to pressure male problem drinkers into treatment under the threat of being fired. The supervisors who are able to recognize and deal with the symptoms of alcoholism and drug abuse in men often are unable to do the same for women.

A number of factors contribute to the low rate of identification and referral of women workers with alcohol and drug problems, many of them related to attitudes toward women in the workplace and the stigma surrounding women's drinking and drug abuse. Male-to-female ratios on referral to company programs range from 5-1 to 15-1, with men far exceeding women. According to one study, women often work in jobs much below their capacity, so that many of them are able to function effectively even when suffering from alcohol and drug abuse without coming to the attention of supervisors.[9]

Women often are the "first fired" because they are considered more expendable to the organization than are male employees. The stigma around alcoholism and drug abuse in women can create an aura of protectiveness, so that absences and poor performance are ignored or hidden. Male supervisors, in particular, find it difficult to discuss alcoholism and other drug problems with female employees.

The lack of treatment opportunities offered to women is related to their generally lower job status. There is less financial stake in a woman with low pay who has little opportunity for advancement in the organization.

Despite the low identification and referral rate of women to treatment through employment, those women who are referred to treatment show an improvement rate similar to that of men. In a study of women's use of occupational programs, it was found that supervisory training and the organization of women's occupational groups were important components in increasing services to women. Supervisory training improved attitudes toward women and increased confrontation as an approach to employees of either sex.[10]

Substance-abusing women in the workplace often face a no-win situation if the only treatment options are 28-day inpatient programs that require them to leave their homes and families or lose their jobs. Many women who work are balancing the responsibilities of work and children by themselves and are unwilling or cannot find the supports to take care of children while they go to treatment. Many EAPs are developing outpatient day programs, as well as on-the-job consultant and counseling services, that are far more practical and realistic alternatives for working mothers. As in every aspect of women's treatment, it is critical to take into consideration the special circumstances of a woman's situation. She does not have a "wife" to take care of the home and family while she confronts an alcohol or drug problem. She also needs recognition and help in dealing with the multiple roles and stresses in her life as she faces the challenge of getting sober.

References

1. U.S. Department of Health and Human Services, *HHS Issues First Comprehensive Survey of Working Women's Health,* PHS Publication No. 98-1415 (Washington, DC: Government Printing Office, 1998). Available: http ://www.cdc.gov/niosh/wwh2.html

2. National Institute on Alcohol Abuse and Alcoholism, *Women and Alcohol: Issues for Prevention Research,* NIH Publication No. 96-3817 (Washington, DC: Government Printing Office, 1996), 28.

3. Ibid., 29.

4. Wihelmina A. Leigh and Malinda A. Lindquist, *Women of Color Health Data Book: Adolescents to Seniors* (Bethesda, MD: National Institutes of Health, 1998). Available: http://www.4woman.gov/x/owh/pub/woc/references1.htm

5. Boston Women's Health Book Collective, *Our Bodies, Ourselves: For the New Century* (New York: Simon & Schuster, 1998), 144.

6. A *discouraged worker* is a person who has given up looking for work.

7. Alan Pifer, "Women Working: Toward a New Society," in Karen Wolk-Feinstein, ed., *Working Women and Families* (Beverly Hills, CA: Sage, 1970), 19-35.

8. Leigh and Lindquist, *Women of Color.*

9. M. Edith Heinemann, *Treatment Considerations: A Response,* NIAAA Research Monograph, No. 16, Women and Alcohol: Health-Related Issues (Washington, DC: U.S. Department of Health and Human Services, 1984), 154-60.

10. Ibid., 157.

Staff Training Activities

Activity 1: What You Already Know
Activity 2: Stresses That Women Face in the Workplace
Activity 3: Elements of Employee Assistance Programs

Activity 1:   What You Already Know

As a warm-up activity, review the "Questionnaire on Alcoholism and Drug Abuse in the Workplace." Ask each person to answer the questions based on her or his opinion. Discuss each question as a group and see what people already know about alcoholic and drug-abusing women in the workplace.

Questionnaire on Alcoholism and Drug Abuse in the Workplace

	Agree	Disagree
1. There are fewer woman alcoholics than men alcoholics and drug abusers in the workforce.	___	___
2. Women employees have fewer stress problems than men employees.	___	___
3. Loss of employment is less important to a woman than to a man.	___	___
4. Recovering substance abusers returning to work should be handled the same as any other sick employees.	___	___
5. A man's drinking and drug abuse is more disruptive on the job than a woman's.	___	___
6. It is easy to identify a woman alcoholic.	___	___
7. An alcoholic woman's recovery is not the company's problem.	___	___
8. A company can be an effective tool for motivating an employee into treatment.	___	___
9. A recovering substance abuser is not a good employee.	___	___
10. It is cost-effective for a company to have an employee assistance program that includes treatment for alcohol and drug abuse.	___	___

Activity 2:   Stresses That Women Face in the Workplace

Women in general, but especially women with children, women of color, and older women, face discrimination as well as economic and social barriers in the workplace. Ask group members to brainstorm what comes to mind when they think of women in the workplace.

Examples:

Low pay	Overlooked by employee programs
Job instability	Poor
Lack of child care	"Drink like the boys" to be accepted
Single parents	No support at home
"First fired"	"Pink-collar jobs"
Overworked and tired	Depressed

Activity 3:   Elements of Employee Assistance Programs

Go over the elements of an employee assistance program.

1.   Facts and experience suggest that the occupational environment might be one of the most efficient and economical means of providing an opportunity for early identification and treatment of alcoholism as well as alcohol- and drug-related problems.

2.   Chances for recovery are increased by reaching the substance abuser at an earlier stage for the following reasons:

- Physical health has not deteriorated significantly.

- Financial resources are not as depleted.

- Emotional supports still exist in the family and community.

- Threat of job loss is present as a motivator.

3.   Employee assistance programs are organized in a variety of ways, from an in-house counselor to contracts with outside groups for these services. Programs also may be structured as "broad brush" (i.e., dealing with any of the many problems that may affect employees' performance) or more narrowly restricted to alcohol and drugs only.

4.   Whatever the program structure, the following are among the common signs and symptoms used to identify the problem drinker or substance abuser:

- Chronic absenteeism

- Change in behavior

- Physical problems

- Spasmodic workplace

- Lower quantity and quality of work

- Partial absences

- Lying

- Avoiding supervisors and coworkers

- On-the-job drinking

- On-the-job accidents and lost time from off-the-job accidents

Client Training Activities

Activity 1

Help the client to look at how her alcoholism or drug abuse has affected her life in the areas of work and career. As she achieves and maintains her sobriety, she may identify and deal with a number of recovery issues related to work including the following:

- Guilt feelings over past job performance, lack of motivation, absenteeism, and interpersonal conflicts related to substance abuse

- Finding balance in work, setting realistic work goals, and asking for supervisory support

- Help in developing assertiveness skills, in part, to negotiate for her needs on the job and to increase personal effectiveness and self-esteem

- Realizing that she might be overqualified for, or no longer interested in, the job she has due to her potential and capabilities having been hindered by active substance abuse (the client might be at point where she needs help exploring options for retraining, education, or furthering her career)

In this last category, the client might need a referral to a career counselor. Perhaps there is an agency in your area that specializes in work and career issues for recovering alcoholics and drug abusers.

Activity 2

Go over "Strategies for Dealing With Stress" outline.

Strategies for Dealing With Stress: Coping, Cooperation, and Change

A. How to cope: We use our strengths to deal with stress.
1. *Nutrition:* I eat regularly and choose foods that are good for me such as more fruits and vegetables and less fried and sugary foods. I drink enough water each day.
2. *Exercise:* I make sure that I get out and stretch my body a little each day. Even a half-hour walk every day will make me feel better about myself.
3. *Self-awareness:* I know who I am and what particular things can stress me out and get me down. I know what my limits are. For example, I know when I am going to run out of patience.

4. *"Letting go" techniques:* When I get stressed, I can take some time to let go for a while. I can use relaxation techniques, meditation, a mini-vacation—all to get a little time and space away from the situation so that I can calm down.

5. *Sleep and rest:* I get enough sleep at night and will take a nap during the day if I need to. I can take brief relaxation breaks during the day so that I can cool off before another stressful situation comes up.

6. *Mental rehearsal:* If I think that an upcoming event will be stressful, then I can imagine what might happen and prepare for how to deal with it in the most positive way that I can.

7. *Personal planning:* I manage my time wisely by planning in advance. I make sure to schedule enough time for each day's activity, set priorities for getting the most important things done first, and not cram too many things into one day.

8. *Detached concern:* I try to keep a particular situation in perspective. If it becomes something beyond my control, then I can detach from it and not get too stressed. I can choose to come back to the problem at another time when I am in a calmer mood.

9. *Modify expectations:* When I become stressed out because things are not going my way or I cannot control a situation, I can de-stress by realizing that I cannot expect everything to be perfect. Instead, I can focus on the little steps and smaller goals that have been achieved, even though the bigger goal or problem is not yet fixed.

10. *Assertiveness training:* I can learn how to be assertive and stand up for myself. I am learning to say no when I mean no, and I am standing by my decisions.

11. *Humor:* When a situation gets too stressful, I do not always have to look at the serious part of things. I can see the funny part of the problem and even make a joke about it. I can learn to laugh at myself and lighten my own mood.

12. *Delegate:* If I have too much to do, then I realize that I do not have to do it all by myself all the time. I can ask for help (whether it is a coworker, a friend, or my children).

B. Cooperation: We create and use support systems whenever we need them.
1. *Seek professional help:* Counselors, church leaders, doctors, advisers, and other professionals in your community can give you valuable advice, information, and help. You can obtain medical, legal, financial, and spiritual help at low or no cost. Your counselor can help refer you to someone who can help you solve your problem.

2. *Self-help organizations:* Places such as Alcoholics Anonymous and Weight Watchers are places to meet with others in similar situations. Sharing your story with others who understand makes your stress more manageable.

3. *Other sources of support* in building your sober network can come from your coworkers, family, friends, clubs and recreational groups, and social action and social change organizations.

C. *Change:* We can change our own behavior to help reduce our stress. Here is a list of some of the ways in which we can change. Change itself will produce a certain amount of energy and stress, but in the long run it is worth it.
1. Job change
2. Personal life
3. Change of attitude
4. Educational level
5. Changing stressful policies or procedures
6. Changing ways of communicating
7. Changing relationships with children
8. Institutional or political change

Resources

Center for Substance Abuse Prevention (CSAP)
Address: 5600 Fishers Lane, Rockwall II Building, 9th floor, Rockville, MD 20857
Phone: (301) 443-0365
Web: http://www.samhsa.gov/csap

(CSAP, a part of the Substance Abuse and Mental Health Services Administration [SAMHSA] of the Public Health Service, U.S. Department of Health and Human Services, oversees and coordinates national drug prevention efforts, funds demonstration grant programs, coordinates a national training system for prevention, and manages an information clearinghouse.)

CSAP Workplace Helpline
Phone: (800) 843-4971

(Operated by CSAP, the helpline is staffed Monday through Friday, 9 a.m. to 8 p.m.)

Employee Assistance Professionals Association (EAPA)
Address: 2101 Wilson Boulevard, Suite 500, Arlington, VA 22201
Phone: (703) 522-6272
E-mail: eapamain@aol.com, eapprescen@aol.com
Web: http://www.eap-association.com

(EAPA publishes an extensive selection of brochures, books, and research publications on prevention, treatment, and education. The Resource Center responds to professional information requests without charge.)

Mainstream Inc.
Address: 1030 15th Street, N.W., Suite 1010, Washington, DC 20005
Phone: (202) 898-1400 (voice/TDD)

(This nonprofit organization works with employers and service providers to increase employment opportunities for persons with disabilities.)

Women Work: The National Network for Women's Employment
Address: 1625 K Street, N.W., Suite 300, Washington, DC 20006
Phone: (202) 467-6346, (800) 235-2732

(This agency helps women of all backgrounds to achieve economic self-sufficiency through education, training, and employment.)

Conclusion

16

Wellness for Women in Recovery

Wellness is a critical concept for recovering women. Making ongoing self-care a priority enhances the client's quality of life in sobriety and helps to prevent relapse. Wellness is comprised of a combination of factors that encompass the whole of a woman's physical, emotional, and spiritual health and being. There is growing appreciation that this "holistic" approach is extremely helpful when applied to recovery. In this concluding chapter, we look at the body, mind, and spirit connection for ways in which to enhance the lives of women in recovery.

Physical health is influenced by factors such as nutrition, rest, and exercise. Emotional health, which also has been shown to correlate with and influence physical health, involves developing and integrating positive realistic attitudes and the ability to cope with a variety of stressors. If the client has a strong ongoing support system through Alcoholics Anonymous (AA), Narcotics Anonymous (NA), friendships, or family relationships, then it will add to his or her emotional well-being and help to prevent relapse. Spiritual health is more of an individual matter and implies a return to values, conscience, and sense that one is part of a larger whole. Spiritual practices can range from involvement in organized religion, to meditation, to introspective assessment of one's values. Active addiction and alcoholism damage the client's spirit, self-worth, and sense of belonging in the world, although at first some women experience drugs and alcohol as enhancing these qualities.

The client might be unaware of the importance of nutrition, exercise, and rest during her recovery from alcoholism or drug abuse. Alcohol or other drugs seriously deplete the user's system of nutrients essential to health. In active addiction, there is neither time nor money to pursue healthy practices. Diets are insufficient and based on what is cheapest or easily available. Consequently, there is much nutritional damage that needs to be repaired. Research has shown that most alcoholics suffer from some degree of malnourishment and unstable blood sugar chemistry.[1]

Nutrition

Poor nutrition has been shown to actually exacerbate postacute withdrawal symptoms (or to reactivate them, even in long-term sobriety), increasing the levels of physical discomfort. As an ongoing piece of advice, the adage to "eat something sweet" in times of craving alcohol or drugs can backfire. Eating sugar can produce an instant lift, but in alcoholics whose blood sugar-producing capabilities are more erratic, this lift is quick, intense, and followed by a sharp crash that can feel like depression or contribute to anxiety and lack of concentration. Eating sugar also can increase appetite and lead to further "unconscious eating," which can turn into problems with compulsive overeating and use of food to deal with feelings. Concentrated sweets actually can produce a stress reaction within the body, as does caffeine, a stimulant drug.

When working with women on nutrition, counselors first need to ascertain the presence of any eating disorders. Once these have been ruled out, they need to gain information on clients' eating habits over a 1- or 2-week period. Changes in diet can be introduced slowly so that women do not feel overwhelmed.

Smoking

Another substance that affects the lives of many alcoholic and drug abusing women is nicotine. Research indicates that women have a harder time quitting smoking than do men, and it might have less to do with just the actual physical addiction of nicotine. For women, things such as the social ritual of pulling a cigarette from the pack, smoking with others in a social group, and the sight and smell of tobacco smoke can cause conditioned responses that are difficult to break.[2] Stopping drinking, drug use, and cigarette smoking concurrently might be too overwhelming for a woman. Although early sobriety usually is not the best time to consider stopping smoking, hopefully the counselor can address smoking as a health and addiction issue as recovery progresses. When recovering women do quit, they express feeling "newly sober" as they struggle with mood swings and other discomfort as part of nicotine withdrawal. Women might resume smoking out of fear of relapsing into alcohol or drug use, reinforcing their sense of hopelessness about being able to stop smoking. Support, structure, smoke-free spaces, nutrition, exercise, assertiveness skills, and new ways in which to cope with feelings all are necessary to help a woman stay off cigarettes.

Exercise

The importance of exercise as a function of self-care in sobriety is demonstrated by research linking regular exercise with significant psychological and physical benefits:

> The body responds to physical activity in ways that have important positive effects on musculoskeletal, cardiovascular, respiratory, and endocrine systems. These changes are consistent with a number of health benefits including a reduced risk of premature mortality and reduced risks of coronary heart disease, hypertension, colon cancer, and diabetes mellitus. Regular participation in physical activity also appears to reduce

depression and anxiety, improve mood, and enhance ability to perform daily tasks throughout the life span.[3]

Qualities such as the relief of depression and improved mood can reinforce the positive gains of beginning an exercise program. The counselor should encourage exercise as a positive addition to the client's life and to help her set reasonable goals when beginning a program. Some women might be able to look back at sports activities that they enjoyed as children or before their addictions "took over" and find that swimming, running, bicycling, or walking appeals to them. The chances for maintaining an ongoing program are best when the activity chosen is enjoyable, is accessible, and can be done on a regular basis. Warm-up exercises, as well as a stretching and cool-down periods after exertion, should be included to prevent injuries. Prior to having the client begin an exercise program, the counselor should recommend a physical examination with a health care practitioner to assess general health and to see whether there are any lingering effects from alcohol or drugs.

Stress

Stress is a natural reaction to life events. All of us have been programmed with the "fight or flight" response, an adaptation to perceived danger in the environment. Anxiety elevates blood pressure, and stress activates physiological responses. Stress causes the instantaneous release of many hormones, two (adrenalin and cortisol) of which also are strong inhibitors of the immune system, which is present to keep us disease free. Chronic stress reactions have a powerful impact on the body, causing stress-related illnesses such as ulcers, skin rashes, and migraines.

The reality is that stress cannot be avoided and is a part of everyone's life. Immunological studies "reveal that the inability to feel in control of stress, rather than the stressful event itself, is the most damaging to immunity."[4] Stress management actually involves learning to live with stress. Developing positive coping strategies is one of the essential tasks in remaining sober and drug free, and newly recovering women will need time and guidance to realize this task. Women actually might cause themselves more stress than is necessary in tackling what can feel like new or accumulated responsibilities in early sobriety. Help can be elicited from sponsors, other friends in recovery, counselors, and support groups: "The effects of stress are buffered by effective coping and also by the love and support of other people. . . . It's only through relations with others that we develop the outlook of hardiness and come to believe in our own capabilities and inner goodness."[5] It is vital for the counselor to communicate to the client that having stress in her life does not mean that she is necessarily "doing something wrong."

Relaxation Techniques

Specific techniques can be helpful in managing stress. Many substance abuse treatment programs have added new components to teach clients relaxation and meditation skills. Techniques can be as simple and accessible as deep breathing exercises or can involve using guided visualization exercises on prepared audiotapes. Relaxation requires that the client slow down and participate in activity that allows her to set aside her routine or worries. Many recovering women never have experienced a state of physical relaxation that was not drug induced, and others do not know how to "play," have fun, or slow down.

Meditation can foster an inward focus that can help the client to achieve a sense of control and balance. The counselor should have the client get into a relaxed state and practice some visualization exercises. The counselor should help the client to imagine herself in a safe place or as accomplishing a desired goal. Relaxation techniques such as those we have described have been shown to reduce negative and anxious states of being. In this light, their usefulness to alcoholics and drug abusers in recovery is invaluable given that negativity can lead to relapse. In conjunction with body work such as acupuncture, acupressure, and massage, the effects of relaxation and visualization are increased. Although often termed "New Age," all the practices described so far are age old. They involve looking at the whole woman by examining health, attitudes, values, the way in which feelings are experienced and expressed, self-esteem, and the ability to be in relationship with others.

Spirituality

The spiritual aspects of recovery are the hardest to define because they vary from person to person in how they are incorporated and addressed in a recovering client's life. The twelfth step of AA refers to "having had a spiritual awakening" as a result of following the Twelve Steps and emphasizes the importance of AA members coming to believe in a "power greater than ourselves" as a way out of the hopelessness, self-centeredness, and fear that alcoholism engenders. "Spiritual awakening" is further defined as "the personality change sufficient to bring about recovery from alcoholism."[6]

Recovering women who develop qualities such as honesty, hope, self-care, self-esteem, and responsibility toward self and others indicate profound changes in both their personality styles and their outlooks on life. The message of AA, backed by research on relapse prevention, is that continual work is required to maintain sobriety and that growth must continue: "Recovery from addiction is like walking up a down escalator. It is impossible to stand still. When you stop moving forward, you find yourself moving backward."[7]

Recovery from alcoholism or drug abuse is an ever-unfolding journey. The developmental tasks of later recovery are many, and they must be founded on a sobriety-centered lifestyle. Women will begin to reveal and repair past traumas; explore healthy intimacy in a variety of styles of relationships as mothers, daughters, and partners; and continue to struggle with and grow in self-esteem. If the counselor can provide a solid recovery program that also emphasizes proper nutrition, regular exercise, positive emotional supports, and strategies for living with stress, then he or she can foster wellness. The counselor should encourage the client's own sense of spirituality. Whether she reads; meditates; prays; or participates in healing groups, spiritual communities, or AA/NA, she will feel a sense of belonging and connection that is markedly different from the isolation she lived with as a consequence of drinking or taking drugs.

References

1. Katherine Ketcham and L. Ann Mueller, *Eating Right to Live Sober* (New York: New American Library, 1986), 22.

2. Neil Swan, "Women's Dependence on Smoking Affected by Something in Addition to Nicotine," *NIDA Notes* 12, no. 3 (May/June 1997). Available: http://www.nida.nih.gov/nida_notes/nnvol12N3/womens.html

3. Centers for Disease Control and Prevention, *1996 Surgeon General's Report on Physical Activity and Health,* No. S/N 017-023-00196-5 (Atlanta, GA: CDC, 1996). Available: http://www.cdc.gov/nccdphp/sgr/summ1.htm

4. Joan Borysenko, *Minding the Body, Mending the Mind* (New York: Bantam Books, 1988), 21.

5. Ibid., 25.

6. Anonymous, *Alcoholics Anonymous* (New York: Alcoholics Anonymous World Service, 1955), 569.

7. Terence Gorski and Merlene Miller, *Staying Sober: A Guide for Relapse Prevention* (Independence, MO: Independence Press, 1986), 129.

■ Staff Training Activities

Activity 1: Definitions of Terms
Activity 2: Body, Mind, and Spirit
Activity 3: Nutrition for Recovering Women
Activity 4: Guided Visualization Exercise

Activity 1:   Definitions of Terms

Have the group work together to define the following terms to establish common points of reference on the concepts being introduced. Use a blackboard or flip chart and write so that all can see. Suggested definitions are included in the following to help guide the exercise:

Wellness: A combination of physical fitness and sound emotional health; achieved by proper nutrition, regular exercise, and efficient stress management

Holistic health: Based on the idea that the body, mind, and spirit form an integrated whole and that health is best when all three levels exist in a balanced state; also, people's interactions with family, community, and the world as they shape their health

Stress: Physiological response to any demand placed on the human mind and body; reaction to all experiences that are evidenced by changes in body chemistry; feeling of being under pressure

Recovery: Moving from disease to health; a long-term process that requires physical, behavioral, social, and spiritual change; includes abstinence and moves beyond cravings; seeing oneself and one's values, actions, and relationships in a larger perspective

Spirituality: Belief in a power or an energy greater than oneself including the belief in some meaning or order in the universe that is experienced as a source of healing, acceptance, or belonging; a direct experience with this power; an examination of values and a movement toward wholeness

This exercise is useful in opening up discussion on more personal levels because some of the definitions might arise from the group members' own experiences.

Activity 2:   Body, Mind, and Spirit

Break into three groups and have each group compose a list of activities and associations that relate to enhancing wellness in each of the categories. Assign one group to do "body," one to do "mind," and one to do "spirit."

Examples:

Body (physical)	Mind (emotions/mental health)	Spirit (belief/faith/soul)
Exercise (name forms)	Listen to music to relax	Pray
Nutrition	Develop a positive attitude	Help others
Stop smoking	Learn new skills/work on communication	Be close to nature
Get plenty of rest	Talk with friends	Look beyond oneself

1. Share lists. Try to list 8 to 10 items for each category. Members from other groups might want to add suggestions to the lists. Do any activities or organizations combine all three?

2. What activities do the participants use? Do people tend to focus more on one aspect than others? What do they wish they could incorporate into their lives? Think about the effects of active alcoholism and drug abuse on these pursuits. Where might a newly sober woman begin to enhance the quality of her life?

Activity 3:   Nutrition for Recovering Women

Following is a list of suggestions to help recovering women use good nutrition as a part of their recovery. You also might want to remind your staff that newly recovering women sometimes need help in planning nutritious meals. They might need to learn how to shop for and use unprocessed and fresh foods in their diets. They also might need to learn how to plan meals in advance as they begin to care for themselves.

General guidelines for healthy nutrition:

■ Increase fiber and complex carbohydrates, emphasizing fresh fruits and vegetables, legumes, whole grain, and unprocessed products.

■ Decrease the amount of fat consumed by using low-fat dairy products and reducing fatty meats, adding fish and poultry instead.

Particular recommendations for recovering women:

■ Avoid sweets and caffeine.

■ Cut down on refined processed foods and foods with added salt and sugar such as canned foods.

■ Nutritious, between-meal snacks can be added where appropriate to even out blood sugar levels and to help reduce mood swings and irritability.

Possible interventions to help a client change her eating patterns:

■ Introduce changes slowly.

■ Look at her current eating patterns by keeping a log of her eating over a 1- to 2-week period.

■ Increase the whole foods in her diet.

■ Teach how to read labels on product packaging to gain awareness of added salt, fat, and sugar.

■ Join with other sober women determined to eat more healthfully, and support one another in the process.

Activity 4:   Guided Visualization Exercise

Lead your staff in a guided visualization exercise by reading them the following script. When you read, make sure to pause; three dots (. . .) indicates a short pause of 10 to 15 seconds, and a dash (—) indicates a minute-long pause.

Sit comfortably in your chairs. If necessary, loosen belts or buttons to be comfortable. You might wish to sit or lay on the floor. . . . Close your eyes now, and begin to become aware of your breathing. . . . Breathe into your belly, feeling it expand as you inhale, and contract as you exhale. . . . Inhale, exhale. . . . Take time to allow the breath in, feel the expansion . . . and then slowly exhale. — Continue this. . . . Allow anxiety and tension to slip from you. Let your thoughts and worries leave you with each exhale. . . . If thoughts arise, then notice them and let them go, almost like bubbles rising to the surface and then floating away, gently bringing yourself back to concentrating on your breath. . . . Continue to breathe. . . . Let tension dissolve. . . . Feel the softness in your belly as you inhale and release. —

Now, I want you to imagine that you are in a place where you feel peaceful and at ease. It might be somewhere you have traveled or walked to. It might be a special place where you felt safe as a child, or a place you dream of visiting, perhaps a sunny meadow or a room with a favorite chair. — Visualize your place. . . . Be aware of the sounds, the temperature, the colors. — See yourself there . . . how you are dressed. . . . Feel how comfortable and safe you feel, how at ease you are. . . . This is your place; rest here. See yourself, and feel the peace and ease in your body. — If other thoughts intrude, bring yourself back to this place of relaxation by focusing on your breathing, your belly expanding, releasing, the rising and falling. — Feel peaceful. — — — [Let participants stay here in silence for 3 or 4 minutes.]

Remember that this is a safe place that you can return to at anytime, that all you have to do is breathe deeply and remember. . . . Look around at your place, and begin to say good-bye. You might choose to bring the feelings of safety and peace back with you. . . . Come back slowly now, noticing the way your body feels against the chair or cushion. . . . Become aware of this room and the energy it holds. . . . Still feeling at peace, slowly open your eyes and return.

Once participants have returned, open for discussion on what this experience was like. Would this be a helpful exercise to use with clients?

■ Client Training Activities

Activity 1

Teach your client about a holistic approach to health and disease. Help her to begin to understand the relationship between wellness and ongoing recovery from substance abuse by focusing on the many aspects of the person she is. Seeing that self-care and self-empowerment are connected to nutrition, exercise, stress management, and spirituality might be new to her. Help her to work on her own goals toward greater wellness. Help her to assess her current strengths and problem areas as well as to lay out possible goals. Help her to come up with manageable and achievable steps toward reaching these goals.

After completing an outline of goals, discuss ways in which your client might sabotage herself and possible obstacles that might get in her way. For example, what interferes with an exercise program? Perhaps economics? Family commitments? Boredom? Old myths or stereotypes about women who "work out"? Explore these obstacles. Perhaps she needs support to complete a goal. Who can help her? Self-esteem issues and fear of failure might surface as she contemplates making changes. Together, you can devise a plan to help intervene with self-sabotage and instead help her to support herself.

Activity 2

Relaxation techniques are tools that can provide many beneficial results for recovering women:

■ *Progressive muscle relaxation:* This exercise involves tensing and relaxing all the muscle groups. It can be done while sitting in a chair or while lying down. The client takes a deep breath and also tenses or clenches her toes and feet as hard as she can, holds tightly for a few seconds, and then releases as she exhales. She then repeats this, inhaling, tensing, holding, and exhaling and releasing, moving up the body. She tenses the legs, buttocks, stomach, arms, hands, and particularly facial muscles. At the conclusion, after the client tenses and releases her entire body twice, have her breathe in deeply, hold, and exhale. Have her notice how her body feels at this point, that is, whether she feels tense or more relaxed. This exercise can be done at any time such as before bed, prior to doing deeper meditation, or when she is experiencing tension.

■ *Simple breathing exercise:* Many people breathe slowly due to stress, exertion, or habit. In this exercise, you will move the woman's awareness to her breath and teach her to breathe so as to take in more oxygen. The action of focusing on the breath also serves to physically break the cycle of worry and tension. The directions can be read as written to the client or group. Directions: "Sit comfortably in a straight-backed chair. Place your hand on your abdominal area, and without trying to change your breathing, notice whether your belly expands or flattens as you inhale. Try this now, noticing the next several breaths. If your hand moves as you inhale, then you are breathing from your diaphragm. If your belly does not move or goes flat as you inhale, then you are breathing from your chest. To shift to abdominal breathing, exhale and make a sigh of relief as you exhale. Let go. The next breath will automatically fill the abdomen. [Pause and allow the client to experience this.] Continue to breathe in this manner, inhaling deeply to fill your belly, exhaling slowly and fully to empty it." At this point, continue on with the Guided Visualization Exercise in the Staff Training Activities of this chapter.

Activity 3

Spiritual questions and concerns will arise for many recovering women as they begin to learn about the spiritual concepts of Alcoholics Anonymous and/or Narcotics Anonymous as expressed through the Twelve Steps. A variety of feelings will surface as women address spirituality. Counselors can be safe people with whom to explore these feelings. Here are several ways in which to initiate discussing spirituality with a recovering woman:

1. Have the client share her own story about what spirituality has meant in her life, in her family of origin, and in her present family. What spiritual ties and values have been important?

2. Ask her to reflect on her own personal definition(s) of spirituality. Encourage her to find her own meanings, to discover for herself what feels spiritual, whether that is being by the ocean, partici- pating in organized religion, or meditating. She might wish to keep a journal to record some of this self-exploration.

3. Ask her about any sense of loss in spiritual areas, especially losses incurred due to drinking or drugging.

4. Spiritual questions and concerns might predominate in later recovery. Clients who ask "Is this all there is?" might be beginning spiritual questioning, needing to look within to consider their places and directions in life. Involvement in a deeper study of the Twelve Steps might be important at this time. Referral to various religious or spiritual advisers and support groups also is a possibility. Addressing these issues might unearth feelings of sadness, anger, or guilt. Remind your client that spiritual growth and understanding is a journey, that is, a slowly unfolding process that takes time.

Activity 4

The "Ongoing Goals and Plans in Recovery" worksheet is appropriate at any stage of recovery, although it is best begun after 3 months of sobriety have been attained. Have your client fill out a sheet similar to the following one. Encourage her to do the following:

■ Use extra paper if necessary.

■ Add other areas of concern such as physical health, legal problems, spirituality, and relationship with a higher power.

■ Develop incremental goals that are clear and manageable.

■ Think carefully about the resources in the "Resources/Supports: Who Can Help" box. (Clients usually experience difficulty with this section. Working closely with your client on this part might help to uncover any problems she has in asking others for help. Asking for and accepting help is a necessary ingredient of a solid recovery program.)

Ongoing Goals and Plans in Recovery

AREA OF CONCERN	WHERE I AM NOW	CHANGES I WOULD LIKE TO MAKE	STEPS TO TAKE TOWARD MAKING CHANGES AND REACHING GOALS	RESOURCES/SUPPORTS: WHO CAN HELP
Sobriety including Alcoholics Anonymous involvement, sponsor, Twelve Steps				
Further treatment, counseling, etc.				
Family and significant others				
Support system				
Employment				
Further training or education				

Index

About the Author

Monique Cohen, LICSW, MHP, currently serves as Program Director of the CASPAR Outpatient Clinic, located in Cambridge, MA. The clinic provides comprehensive substance abuse treatment to individuals and families struggling with either one or multiple addictions. Given her interests in both clinical work in the field of addiction as well as public policy and training, Cohen decided to write this manual to share her experience with other providers working with primarily women clients. In addition, Cohen provides training through her affiliation with CASPAR, Inc., to local community agencies, students, universities, and hospitals in various issues related to addiction, women's treatment, and dual diagnosis. She has served on various local task forces in Massachusetts in an attempt to influence local and state substance abuse policy-related decisions.